The New York Times
60-Minute Gourmet

LARGE-TYPE EDITION

The New York Times
60-Minute Gourmet

LARGE-TYPE EDITION

Pierre Franey

WITH AN INTRODUCTION BY

Craig Claiborne

WEATHERVANE BOOKS
New York

This 1988 edition is published by Weathervane Books, distributed by
Crown Publishers, Inc., 225 Park Avenue South, New York, New York 10003,
by arrangement with Times Books, a division of Random House, Inc.

Printed and Bound in the United States of America

Library of Congress Cataloging-in-Publication Data

Franey, Pierre.
The New York times 60-minute gourmet / Pierre Franey : with an
introduction by Craig Claiborne.—Large-type ed.
Includes index.
ISBN 0-517-66988-9 (lg. print)
1. Cookery.   2. Large type books.   I. Title.   II. Title: New York
times sixty-minute gourmet.   III. Title: 60-minute gourmet.
[TX652.F67 1988]
641.5'55—dc19   88-17145
CIP
ISBN 0-517-66988-9
h g f e d c b a

This book
is dedicated to
Barbara Gelb

Editor's Note

Over the years, we have received many requests for a large-type edition of *The New York Times 60-Minute Gourmet*, one of Pierre Franey's most popular cookbooks. We are, therefore, pleased to present *The New York Times 60-Minute Gourmet Large-Type Edition*. Because the type size has been significantly increased, there are fewer recipes in this edition than in the original one. However, the more than 200 recipes that do appear in this book are just the same as they were in the original *The New York Times 60-Minute Gourmet*.

Contents

Introduction

I FIRST MET PIERRE FRANEY AS PART OF A RE-portorial fluke.

Suffice it to say that, although I was restaurant critic of *The New York Times* for more than a decade, I was not ushered from the cradle into the luxury restaurants in this world with an inbred knowledge of the world's great cuisines. Far from it. I was raised in a small town in Mississippi, and my knowledge of the world's gastronomy was limited to that of traditional Southern culture.

I had, in a sense, found myself and my identity when I was thirty-three years old. At that advanced age my credits included a degree in journalism from the University of Missouri, an avid if amateur interest in cooking, and a job in Chicago where I eked out (but barely) a living in public relations for a broadcasting company. I was bored to death. And desperate.

Through some miracle too intricate to outline here, I applied for and was accepted by the Hotel School of the Professional Hotel Keepers' Association in Lausanne, Switzerland. It was then, and to my mind still is, the pre-eminent school for hotel management in the world. It was there, within a thirteen-month period, I discovered that horizons in food were unlimited. I discovered white wine sauces and the thousands of things one can do with mayonnaise and hollandaise and puff pastries; I learned about omelets, soufflés and fish dishes based on something called meunière. I also learned the fine points of table service and menu planning and banquets. Prior to that training I knew painfully little about wines, but at that school I learned the intimate details about how to pour it.

When I came back to America, I arrived in New York and unpacked my bags. And, by scrimping here and there, I saved enough money to visit some of the best restaurants in the city. What I found was appalling. Sauces with the consistency of mucilage, the most unimaginative, stereotyped menus, incompetent waiters with soiled uniforms and soiled fingernails.

Not many months after my arrival I joined *The New York Times* as food editor and, in that capacity, I could afford to dine, and often, in the best restaurants the city had to offer. I found the same dreadful sameness from the Brooklyn Bridge to the Battery. I must say that the restaurant scene today bears little resemblance to what it did then. There are now dozens of fine, elegant, and imaginative French restaurants in town. They have style or class or name it what you will. Not then.

There was in those days only one restaurant whose kitchen and table service seemed to approximate in quality what I had been taught at that hotel school. That was the then flourishing Le Pavillon, in its heyday at the time. It was considered by most connoisseurs to be—and there was no doubt in my mind that it was—the finest French restaurant in America. The late Ludwig Bemelmans, a man of unswerving taste, once stated that it was to his mind the best French restaurant in the world. Under the direction of Henri Soulé, uncompromising in his standards, it made the rest of the city's watering places—even the best known—look like bistros.

Thus that kid (no longer a kid) from the sticks decided to take on all the French restaurants in town. I decided to write an article, for which I subsequently won a publisher's award, about the terrible state of French restaurants in Gotham. It appeared on a

Sunday with the headline, "The Decline of Elegance in New York's Restaurants."

In the article I stated quite flatly that Le Pavillon was the only restaurant in town with the style and quality of a first-rate establishment. And that included the now defunct but well-known Colony and the Chambord, which had fallen into incompetent hands.

To accompany the article an illustration was necessary, and I telephoned Soulé to ask if I might photograph his chef in the Pavillon kitchen. I was scared to death of him, but he responded with kindness and I was invited into those hallowed premises beneath the dining room.

When I arrived with my photographer I was introduced to the chef. A man of modest height and somewhat athletic build, wearing a toque blanche and an immaculately starched white uniform with apron, his name was Pierre Franey.

He was photographed standing before a silver platter containing a whole baked striped bass with a champagne sauce. It was simply but spectacularly garnished with puff pastry crescents and sculptured, turban-shaped mushrooms.

After the photography session we sat down to dine and we founded a friendly rapport which has continued for nearly twenty years. During the course of those years we have cooked and worked together, discussing and preparing thousands of dishes, in the beginning mostly on weekends and his days off.

A few years ago *The New York Times* decided to greatly expand its food coverage and introduced a section called "Living." As part of this expansion (Le Pavillon had been closed for several years), Pierre Franey was engaged as a member of the food staff. Somewhat hesitatingly, a member of the upper hierarchy of the editorial staff proposed that he write a column on fine dishes that could be prepared in an hour or less. A column for those who might be pressed for time—after work, spur-of-the-moment occasions, sudden guests, and so on. It had been felt that with his background, he might find it a mission impossible or demeaning.

Pierre found the idea interesting, and justly so. On reflection he realized that a good many of the dishes he has cooked since his childhood require less than an hour, start to finish, to prepare. Some dishes, as he points out here, must be cooked as hastily as possible to be perfect. In that category one could number a hundred fish dishes, dishes made with eggs, and so on.

This book contains the complete range of cooking times. There are omelets that can be made in seconds as well as lamb chops which demand almost the outer limit of 60 minutes. There are broiled fish dishes that require about 15 minutes, sautéed chicken dishes that demand about half an hour, and so on.

It should be added that this book is not only for those who would cook in haste. It is a serious book that is based on Pierre's solid background in French cooking. Many of the recipes could be reproduced in books on the classic French tradition dating back to Escoffier and before.

Craig Claiborne

East Hampton, New York

The New York Times
60-Minute Gourmet

LARGE-TYPE EDITION

The Gourmet in the Kitchen

There are seemingly numerous fantasies in the public mind about the daily grind in the kitchens of what are called the grand luxe restaurants of the world. Paramount among these is the notion that all great chefs, particularly the French, are men of violence and emotion, more temperamental than opera stars. Most of the first-rate chefs I've known in my career are gentle and often-times meek. They like to ski and dance and make love, and one or two that I know may even enjoy, when they spend a quiet evening at home, a martini or two before dinner.

There is a second prevailing notion that, with the exception of dishes like salade nicoise and céleri rémoulade, all the dishes that go from stove burner to table top are intricately involved, endlessly complicated dishes, any of which requires the better part of a day and night to bring to the proper state of perfection.

It simply isn't true. There are many dishes, to be sure, that require numberless hours of simmering and skimming and stirring and putting through sieves to yield an ultimate result. These involve bases like fonds bruns or brown sauces for fish and poultry; things like glazes and half glazes to enrich and ennoble sauces for fish, meat, and whatever; quenelles of fish and veal and so on.

But there are, to balance this, countless thousands of dishes that can be—indeed, must be—made in seconds to bring them to their state of absolute perfection. This would embrace a volume of recipes that includes fish and seafood—fillets of sole, clams, mussels, and so on—and egg dishes such as omelets or such a simple masterpiece as scrambled eggs with tarragon. Reckoning in minutes rather than seconds, there are the grilled and broiled foods, among the most popular on luxury menus. And the sautéed dishes. To choose but one example of the latter, there is the excellent sauté of chicken beauséjour with its thyme, garlic, and bay leaf, a dish that requires less than 45 minutes to prepare, start to finish. The ingredients are to be found in any supermarket and any conscientious home cook can prepare it with ease and expertise. You don't have to be a budding Escoffier to master it. This book, then, is dedicated to the proposition that the home cook can prepare dishes of elegance and excellence, with the exigencies of time considered.

If you wish to cook in a hurry and without frustration, there are certain factors to be considered. Certain hints and admonitions to ease the burden—if you think of it like that—and increase the pleasure of cooking when time is telescoped.

If I had to name the two most important considerations for cooking in haste and in pleasure, they would be these. First off, outfit your kitchen with the best equipment, the cost of which will fit your purse or pocketbook and budget. That is not to say that you need indulge in a costly professional range, although if your bank account can accommodate it, I would certainly recommend it; a good range is forever. It is also not to say that you must outfit your pot racks with the grandest, most costly tin-lined copper pots and saucepans from Europe. Not at all.

What I do recommend is that you buy the finest cookware that you can afford, adding to your collection as the budget allows. In saucepans and skillets you should look for those with heavy bottoms and, to the greatest degree possible, easy to clean. A

[4]

heavy black iron skillet is dandy, but it does rust unless you take scrupulous care of it. If you can't afford heavy copper, heavy aluminum skillets and heavy enamel-coated cast-iron skillets are generally excellent and so are the utensils in heavy metal called Calphalon. The word "heavy" is accented here because if the metal used, particularly in skillets, is thin, foods are very apt to burn unless they are watched constantly.

You needn't have a "battery" of equipment to cook well. You should have one large and one small appropriate skillet; a large saucepan or small kettle for boiling things in quantity and for cooking pasta, such as spaghetti; a medium-size saucepan and a small saucepan.

Among your most important utensils, you should count at least one large and one small first-class knife. The large knife should have a heavy stainless blade and in this you should not stint. The knives should be of first-quality stainless. Stainless is stressed here because certain "acid" vegetables, such as onions and shallots, will be discolored if chopped with a non-stainless steel blade. The knives will also rust if allowed to sit in the sink. By all means buy a food processor, even if it is one of the least expensive models. And a coffee maker. And a corkscrew.

You will also need a flat, sturdy chopping board or surface, which brings up another point. Most amateurs in the kitchen believe that if they have a counter made of wood, such as maple block, then that is to chop on. That's not the way professionals do it. You need a portable chopping board or surface—one that lies flat and stays in place as you work. I frankly prefer the relatively new, white polyethylene chopping surfaces. They are portable, they are easily cleaned, and they can be placed in the dishwasher for thorough cleaning. One of these "boards" that measures about 10 by 17 inches is suitable for most purposes, although I prefer a larger size, one that measures 16 by 20 inches. That is a personal idiosyncrasy, however, and for ordinary home use I recommend the smaller size. It is easier to store and to clean. Wood surfaces, in time, become nicked and breed bacteria.

At the end of this chapter there is a lengthier discussion of utensils and gadgets that would be of value in a very well equipped kitchen.

To name the second most important asset for hasty cooking with comfort and ease, I would state without qualification that it is organization. This "organization" should commence before you buy a single ingredient or take a saucepan down from the rack. You should take into thorough consideration, making a list as necessary, of the ingredients and utensils you will need to prepare the dishes you have in mind. Don't take anything for granted, be it a pound of butter you "thought" you had in the refrigerator or the carton of cream you were "sure" was sitting next to the milk.

Once you are ready to attack a dish, I strongly recommend that you assemble all the ingredients necessary for the preparation of the dish in one area. To choose one simple and obvious dish, consider the preparation of fish chowder. Bring to your work surface the following: onions, celery, potatoes, the fish, milk, butter, and whatever else the recipe requires. Gather these into a neat grouping. Get out the proper saucepan or small kettle and put it on the stove.

You will save yourself a good deal of time and bother if you lay out a length of wax paper on the work surface and start peeling and trimming the onions, celery ends, and so on. When the peeling and trimming are done, simply gather the sheet of paper together and discard it.

Now proceed to the cubing of the potatoes (which must be dropped into cold water to prevent discoloring), the chopping of the onions and celery, adding them to glass measuring cups as they are prepared. Keep the ingredients neatly grouped and always keep your working surface wiped and clean between the cubing, chopping, and so on. Always keep in mind that clutter is distracting, a hindrance, and an enemy of time.

And incidentally, have a place for everything—the salt container, the pepper, the milk, and so on. Don't shift things about from day to day. Have a spot for the butter, the milk, and the cream in the refrigerator so that your hand projects automatically to the right place. It's a great time saver.

You can save yourself time and money if you will exercise forethought a day or an evening ahead. For example, if a dish you have planned for tomorrow's dinner calls for cooked shrimp, lobster, or chicken you will greatly simplify matters if you cook the shrimp, lobster, or whatever the night before. Remember that pre-cooked seafood, to choose one example, costs more than the raw product.

And there are many vegetables and seasonings that can be chopped or minced or otherwise prepared the evening before. Garlic can be finely minced and stored compactly in a small container and covered with plastic wrap so that air does not circulate around it. (It can also be covered with a little oil to keep air out.) Onions can be chopped, put in a bowl, and covered with plastic wrap and kept for many hours without damage to taste. So can shallots and fresh parsley.

Lettuce leaves can be rinsed clean in cold water and patted or spun dry before storing in plastic wrap or bags for use the next day. Potatoes can be peeled and cubed and kept in a basin of cold water in the refrigerator for a day or so. You can scrape carrots the day before, core green peppers or cabbage, and so on.

Think twice before throwing things out, half an onion, say. If you only use one half for a meal, cover the other half closely in plastic wrap and refrigerate. It will be in good condition for at least one more day.

If circumstances permit (and there are rare exceptions in my mind when they would not), you might consider extending your night-before programming to the dinner table. If you know you will be pressed for time when you come home to prepare a meal, it would seem the most logical thing in the world if your preparations included setting the table as completely as possible to receive guests. Place mats or tablecloths could be installed on the table, the places set with silver, napery, wineglasses, and the like. If you're going to be all-out fancy with flowers, an arrangement of blossoms will also keep very neatly in the refrigerator.

If you are a really conscientious host or hostess and are pressed for time, as this book presumes you to be, you will probably want to serve coffee at the end of the meal. Therefore, as long as you are organizing to the last degree, you might make all preparations the night before for coffee brewing and serving. Make ready the coffee cups and spoons, have the cream in a pitcher in the refrigerator (if the cream is fresh it won't spoil) and the sugar spooned into a proper server. If you plan to serve cordials or after-dinner liqueurs, bring those glasses out, too.

You will probably serve a beverage of some sort, probably wine or beer (if there is sauerkraut). You can deposit a bottle of white wine in the refrigerator the night before. As a matter of fact, you can uncork it the night before if you recork it immediately and refrigerate it. The red wine can be placed in a cool place, but don't refrigerate it the night before. I hasten to add that, to my taste, some red wines benefit from a little chilling, a Beaujolais or an Italian wine, say, half an hour before they are served. The red wines can and should be opened about an hour before you are ready to serve them. You might open the red wines before you start preparing the meal.

If you have a fine hand at cooking, if you cook at all properly, you will need access to a decent number of herbs and spices. In season, I use fresh herbs to the greatest extent possible. My herb garden is fairly modest, but throughout the summer I have a constant supply of such herbs as tarragon, rosemary, thyme, parsley, sorrel, and basil. I have a fresh bay bush for bay leaves, but that is a rarity. I buy other herbs in season at a greengrocer—fresh coriander, dill, and so on.

In winter, however, like everyone else I am largely dependent on dried herbs and spices. These, with the exception of bay leaf and thyme, are kept in a cool, dark place in the pantry to preserve their color and flavor. I have my bay leaf and thyme in a cool place next to the stove, and the reason for this is that I use both in considerable quantity while testing recipes. Otherwise I would leave these, too, in a cool, dark place. Remember that a bright color, even for dried herbs and spices, is an indication of freshness in flavor.

There follows an alphabetical list of dried herbs and spices that I would consider essential for a spice rack. The most important of these are italicized, with bay leaf and thyme the most important of them all.

Allspice, whole or ground
Basil
Bay leaves
Caraway seeds
Cayenne pepper or hot ground red pepper
Chili powder
Cinnamon, ground and/or in stick form
Cloves, whole and/or ground
Coriander, seeds or ground
Cumin, seeds or ground
Curry powder
Marjoram
Mustard powder
Nutmeg, whole and/or ground
Oregano
Paprika
Black peppercorns and ground black pepper

White peppercorns and ground white pepper
Hot red pepper flakes and/or whole dried hot red pepper
pods
Rosemary
Saffron, in stem form or powdered
Tarragon
Thyme
Vanilla extract

For a "complete" spice shelf, you might consider the following:
Anise seeds
Cardamom seeds and/or ground
Celery seeds and/or salt
Fennel seeds
Ginger, ground
Juniper berries
Mace, ground
Mint leaves
Pickling spices
Poppy seeds
Savory, summer
Sesame seeds
Turmeric
Vanilla beans

And the following non-spices:
Monosodium glutamate
Saltpeter
Cream of tartar

I am one of those people—as many of my friends are—who
believe that some foods are equally if not more delicious when
used as leftovers rather than when freshly cooked. Like many
another, I prefer cold turkey sandwiches with fresh mayonnaise

to the original roast bird. Cold leftover poached fish makes one of the best cold salads. Cold leftover duck is delicious, although it must not be kept too long. And turkey soup made with the carcass and other bits of leftovers is superb.

If you dine and/or entertain often at home, and time is a factor (which is almost assuredly the case if you are reading this), there are many delectables—standbys, if you will—that you might consider always keeping in stock either in the refrigerator or on the pantry shelf, such as the case may be. Some of the finest meals I can recall were those that required no more effort than slicing and arranging foods in an appetizing fashion on platters. You might keep on hand well-flavored salamis and smoked meats, headcheese and pâtés (the keeping time of these goods varies, of course, and some must be eaten within a reasonably short time after purchase). Have on hand for a platter of such charcuterie (or cold meats or cold cuts, as it is called in America) a jar or two of fine imported mustards (kept in the refrigerator) and imported cornichons (small, sour French pickles) to use as garnish. Plus a crusty French or Italian loaf. Stocks of such breads, tightly wrapped, keep well in the freezer and can be reheated before serving.

I also almost always have in my home refrigerator a wheel or two of Brie or Camembert or other cheeses that could be served on the spur of the moment. When tightly wrapped in plastic wrap or foil and refrigerated, the shelf life of most cheese is far greater than most people suspect. And, for cooking purposes, I always have—closely wrapped—a supply of Swiss or Gruyère cheese for "gratinéed" dishes, plus Parmesan (whole chunks; Parmesan is always best if freshly grated the moment before it is used) for gratinéed dishes or to sprinkle on pasta.

In addition to this, on my pantry shelves I keep a constantly replenished supply of canned fish products—sardines, tuna, and salmon mostly—for hasty meals. For such meals—whether of sliced meats or sardines—I would generally serve a cold salad

[11]

and there will almost always be in my refrigerator fresh cucumber, tomatoes, and eggs for hard-cooking and/or turning into fresh mayonnaise.

Which reminds me that many new cooks over the years have asked about how best to maintain salad oils, such as olive oil, if they are to be maintained over a long period of time. Refrigeration is the answer, although I must confess that in my own home, oils, whether olive or corn oil, are used in such quantities that rancidity through nonuse is almost out of the question.

A few words might be added here about expediting the cooking of certain foods. If you have a dish that is to be baked—let us say a chicken that is to be cut into serving pieces and baked with a liquid poured around it—it will hasten the cooking time a great deal if you use a metal baking dish, one that can be heated on top of the stove. Place the dish on the stove and get the liquid to the boil before placing the dish in the oven.

I am also often asked if I make everything from scratch, especially such staple and often called for ingredients as chicken stock or beef broth, and the answer is no. It is certainly true that I prefer to use fresh chicken or beef broth, but like everyone else, I am frequently caught in the web of needing either chicken or beef broth on the spur of the moment. Thus I keep in my larder for such emergencies an ample supply of canned broths. Plus bottles of clam juice, which can—in an emergency—be substituted for fish stock. I also almost always have a case or so of canned tomatoes on my shelves, and tomato paste. I would no more use a can of tomato sauce (the flavor is terrible) than dehydrated onion or garlic, or instant rice (an abomination and insult to a cook's intelligence) because a sauce made with canned tomatoes is infinitely preferable and easy to make. And when fresh tomatoes are out of season, canned tomatoes are far superior for other uses as well.

I would also point out that the freezer is a great boon for home cooks. The use of a TV dinner is, to my mind, unthinkable. But there are many foods that can be frozen to advantage—including tomato sauces, meat casseroles, and so on.

A word of caution about reheating foods that have been frozen. Freezing tends to dilute the strength of various spices in any dish. Therefore, it is best to always taste the defrosted product and add more seasonings according to taste. And speaking of seasonings, always use salt sparingly when cooking. Remember that it can always be added at the end of cooking time. It can't be taken away, no matter what people say about adding raw potatoes to the dish to extract the salt.

At times there have been two "quarrels" with the column known as "60-Minute Gourmet" and by way of expiation I would like to point out the following:

It has been said that there might seem to be an excessive number of recipes for rice, noodles, and potatoes. The answer is that these foods have been considered, in the finest kitchens in the world, the basic and ideal accompaniments for main courses. Certain stews and ragouts, for example, simply go with noodles in one form or another. Rice is the best and most logical accompaniment for many dishes, be they meat, poultry, or fish. The same is true of potatoes. For subtle, psychological reasons, these "starches" are not always interchangeable where taste is concerned. I have done my utmost in the menu planning here to choose the ideal accompaniment (noodles, rice, or potatoes) and to vary the preparation to the greatest degree possible.

It has further been said that there is no emphasis on dessert. To my mind, desserts that might be labeled "gourmet" are for the most part too intricate to be included in the planning of a meal to be executed in less than an hour. The preparation time for a first-rate dessert is simply too elaborate. In the long run, fruit with cheese is probably the greatest of all ways to end a meal. And the home cook has at his or her disposal a number of foods that may be purchased at the grocery and supermarket. Ice cream (with a variety of liqueur toppings added at home) is excellent and takes seconds to prepare and serve. To tell you the truth, the one dessert most often served in my home when I am pressed for time is the following, the fruits and berries of which change with the season:

Macédoine des Fruits
(A mixed fruit dessert)

1½ cups seedless grapes

1½ cups seedless or seeded orange sections

3 cups fresh fruit, such as peaches and plums, seeded and cut into wedges

1½ cups fresh berries, such as strawberries or blueberries or a mixture of berries

5 tablespoons confectioners' sugar

3 tablespoons Cognac

3 tablespoons Kirsch

3 tablespoons Grand Marnier

1. Combine all the fruits in a mixing bowl and sprinkle with sugar. Blend well. Chill until ready to serve.

2. When ready to serve, add the Cognac, Kirsch, and Grand Marnier. Stir to blend and serve immediately.

Yield: About six servings.

Earlier on, at the beginning of this chapter, I stated that a more elaborate discussion of kitchen equipment would be appended. In addition to the appliances and gadgets mentioned earlier, you can make your cooking more comfortable and pleasurable if you have the following:

A wire whisk of respectable weight and size; a large, plain metal spoon; a large, slotted or perforated metal spoon; a kitchen timer; a large two-pronged fork; a pancake turner; a swivel-bladed vegetable scraper; a colander or sieve of suitable size; a set of graduated glass measuring cups (from 1 to 4 cups); a standard set of metal measuring spoons; a nest of mixing bowls; a can opener; a beer can opener; a flour sifter; a grater with assorted grating surfaces; a heavy pair of kitchen scissors; a salad basket (preferably a spin-dry utensil); rubber or plastic spatulas.

Other utensils or gadgets that would be valuable if not essential include a pair of kitchen tongs; a large spatula; a lemon squeezer; a larger wooden spoon for stirring; a rolling pin; a pastry blender; a dish-draining rack; a spice rack; an ice pick; a dispenser for paper towels, plastic wrap, wax paper, and aluminum foil; an electric juice extractor; and a pastry brush. You may wish to add an electric toaster, although I prefer toast made in the oven.

Poultry

WHEN I HAVE BEEN ASKED OVER THE YEARS the most basic thing an aspiring cook could be taught, the answer is almost invariable. If you learn a few basic techniques of cookery, the rest of it is only applied logic. There are astonishingly few ground rules for the various forms of cookery. If you can make a basic mayonnaise, for example, you can make a sauce rémoulade or a sauce tartare with the simple additions of a few ingredients, such as chopped anchovy, capers, pickles, and so on.

Similarly, if you can make a basic hollandaise, the technique of making variations on it—béarnaise, sauce Choron, and so forth—are easy to come by. A basic white sauce becomes a mornay with the addition of cheese, and a brown sauce becomes a sauce madère with the addition of Madeira wine.

One of the most basic foods to be learned, if hasty cooking is your goal, is a basic method of sautéing chicken. If you know the few easily learned steps involved, your range in flavors is almost limitless. You simply start with the base and add flavors according to your taste and imagination.

To illustrate what I mean, a basic sauté is outlined here. It is as simple as this: You brown cut-up pieces of chicken in butter. When cooked on both sides, the pieces are removed for a brief period. You pour off the fat (most of it) from the skillet and add chopped shallots, then wine. The wine is reduced briefly and chicken broth is added. You swirl in a touch of butter and return the chicken pieces to the sauce. That's all there is to it.

The second recipe is a basic variation. This is the addition of a single herb, rosemary. It could be tarragon. Or you might use any of a dozen other herbs or spices. For the wine, you might substitute red for white. Or use tomatoes in lieu of the chicken broth. And you might add heavy cream, to mention but one more of a hundred—perhaps a thousand—possibilities.

Serve the dish, if you will, with buttered noodles.

Poulet Sauté
(A basic sauté of chicken)

1 2½-pound chicken, cut into serving pieces
Salt and freshly ground pepper to taste
3 tablespoons butter

1 tablespoon finely chopped shallots
2 tablespoons dry white wine
½ cup chicken broth

1. Sprinkle the chicken pieces with salt and pepper.

2. Melt 2 tablespoons of the butter in a heavy skillet and, when it is melted, add the chicken pieces skin side down. Cook about 10 to 15 minutes or until golden brown on one side.

3. Turn the pieces and cook 10 to 15 minutes longer, turning the pieces occasionally.

4. Remove the chicken pieces and arrange them neatly on a serving dish, piling them up as necessary. Keep warm.

5. Pour off the fat from the skillet and add 1 tablespoon finely chopped shallots. Cook, stirring briefly, and add the wine. Cook until reduced by half.

6. Add the chicken broth and simmer, stirring, about 1 minute, or until the sauce is reduced to about ½ cup. Add salt and pepper to taste. Swirl in the remaining tablespoon of butter. Pour the sauce over the chicken and serve.

Yield: Four servings.

Poulet Sauté au Romarin
(Chicken sauté with rosemary)

1 2½-pound chicken, cut into
serving pieces
Salt and freshly ground
pepper to taste
3 tablespoons butter

1 teaspoon finely chopped
fresh rosemary leaves
1 tablespoon finely chopped
shallots
2 tablespoons dry white wine
½ cup chicken broth

1. Sprinkle the chicken pieces with salt and pepper.

2. Melt 2 tablespoons of the butter in one or two heavy skillets and, when it is hot, add the chicken pieces skin side down. Cook 15 minutes, or until they are golden brown on one side.

3. Turn the pieces and add the chopped rosemary. Cook 10 to 15 minutes longer, turning the pieces occasionally.

4. Remove the chicken pieces and arrange them neatly on a serving dish, piling them up as necessary. Keep warm.

5. Pour off the fat from the skillet and add the shallots. Cook, stirring briefly, and add the wine. Cook until reduced by half.

6. Add the chicken broth and simmer, stirring to blend well, about 1 minute. Continue to cook and when the sauce is reduced to about ½ cup, swirl in the remaining tablespoon of butter. Pour the sauce over the chicken and serve immediately.

Yield: Four servings.

IN THE SCHEME OF THINGS, IT DOESN'T SEEM IN the least surprising that of the various categories in this book—veal, beef, fish, and so on—there are more than twice as many chicken recipes as in any other category.

To my mind as a chef (and part-time home cook), chicken is probably the most versatile of all foods. It also is, as has been pointed out elsewhere, historically the least expensive of basic foods. Long before Henry the Fourth declared that every peasant should have a chicken in every pot (and long before they named the poule au pot after him), chicken was known as the food of both the poor and nobility alike. Chickens are simply one of the easiest of all edible creatures to feed and propagate—with the possible exception of fish, however, but the coastlines and waters of this world are too far apart for a universal catch.

One of my favorite chicken preparations is completed with a basic assembly of ingredients that are known in their blend as a persillade (there is also a beef salad with a good deal of chopped parsley that is known simply as a persillade). These traditional ingredients are fresh bread crumbs, garlic and/or shallots, and a handful of chopped parsley. The name, incidentally, derives from the French word for parsley, persil.

Once the ingredients for the persillade are blended, the other preparation and cooking of the dish is a child's game. Pieces of seasoned, cut-up chicken are turned in butter and broiled. The pieces are turned once and broiled again. The chicken is sprinkled with the parsley and bread crumb mixture and baked without much further ado until done. As a final step, you may run the dish under the broiler for a split second to give a browner and more desirable texture.

A buttered vegetable, such as broccoli or cauliflower, is complementary with this dish. The vegetable should be cooked until crisp-tender and a lemon butter poured over. The recipe given here is for broccoli with lemon butter.

[19]

Poulet en Persillade

(Chicken with parsley sauce)

1 2½-pound chicken, cut into serving pieces
Salt and freshly ground pepper to taste
4 tablespoons butter
¼ cup bread crumbs

2 tablespoons finely chopped shallots
1 small clove garlic, finely minced
2 tablespoons finely chopped parsley

1. Preheat the broiler.
2. Sprinkle the chicken pieces with salt and pepper.
3. Melt the butter in a heatproof baking dish large enough to hold the chicken pieces in one layer. Turn the pieces in the butter. Arrange the pieces skin side down in the baking dish and place under the broiler about 6 inches from the source of heat.
4. When the chicken has broiled about 5 minutes, remove from the oven and turn the pieces skin side up. Return to the oven and continue broiling about 5 minutes longer.
5. Blend the bread crumbs, shallots, garlic, and parsley. Blend well. Sprinkle this over the chicken and baste to coat well with the butter.
6. Set the oven heat at 400 degrees and add the chicken. Bake 10 minutes.
7. Just before serving, reheat the broiler. Run the chicken briefly under the broiler to brown quickly.

Yield: Four servings.

Brocoli au Citron
(Broccoli with lemon butter)

1 small bunch broccoli
  Salt to taste
2 tablespoons butter

Juice of ½ lemon
Freshly ground pepper to
taste

1. Cut and trim the broccoli into flowerets. The pieces should be bite-size but not too small.

2. Bring enough water to the boil to cover the broccoli when added. Add salt to taste and add the broccoli pieces. Cook briefly, about 3 to 4 minutes or until crisp-tender. Drain well.

3. Melt the butter in a saucepan and add the lemon juice. Pour this over the broccoli. Sprinkle with salt and pepper and serve.

Yield: Four servings.

THERE IS A HASTILY MADE CHICKEN DISH REPresented here that has an interesting legend behind it. In its original form it was called chicken Marengo and was served to Napoleon on the day he defeated the Austrians on the battlefield near the village of Marengo in the northwest of Italy in mid-June 1800. Culinary history states that Napoleon's chef was a man named Dunand.

With victory at hand, the chef sent scouts into the countryside to find provisions for a meal. They returned with crayfish from a nearby stream or river, chicken, eggs, tomatoes, garlic, and oil from a nearby farm, and a skillet.

Dunand cooked the chicken in oil, then added tomatoes, a little water, and garlic. The dish was served with the steamed crayfish over the chicken and fried eggs as a garnish. Napoleon is said to have told his chef that it was one of the finest meals he'd ever eaten. The legend continues that on his return to France, the General asked the chef to repeat the dish. He did. But he omitted the crayfish, which he considered out of place with chicken. He used wine in lieu of water and added fresh mushrooms—champignons de Paris—to the ingredients. The commander complained vehemently and the crayfish garnish was restored; crayfish are now always used with a true Marengo.

What Dunand, back in France, had created was a chicken à la provençale, which is the dish outlined here. It is a true regional specialty, incorporating in its ingredients chopped anchovies and green onions in the style of Provence. It is, indeed, simply made. Chicken parts are seasoned and cooked in oil. The pieces are then cooked in a mixture of wine and tomato with mushrooms, plus the inevitable provençale seasonings—garlic, bay leaf, and thyme. The total cooking time for the dish is approximately half an hour. And while it simmers there is plenty of time to prepare the rice dish which, for reasons unknown to me, is called riz egyptienne or Egyptian rice. This is a simply made fluffy rice dish containing among its elements one chicken liver (taken from the chicken cooked à la provençale) and small cubes of cooked ham. The chicken dish goes well with a dry white wine, a rosé from Provence, or a somewhat robust dry red wine.

Poulet Sauté Provençale
(Sautéed chicken with tomatoes)

---

1 2½- to 3-pound chicken, cut into serving pieces
Salt and freshly ground pepper to taste
3 tablespoons olive oil
½ pound mushrooms, left whole if small; otherwise halved or quartered, depending on size
1 bay leaf
¼ teaspoon dried thyme

¾ cup finely chopped onion
1½ teaspoons finely chopped garlic
2 tablespoons flour
½ cup dry white wine
1 cup crushed tomatoes
¾ cup chicken broth
6 flat anchovy fillets, chopped
24 bottled, small, pitted, green olives, drained

1. Sprinkle the chicken pieces with salt and pepper. If desired, set the chicken liver aside to prepare rice with liver as a side dish for the chicken.

2. Heat the oil in a skillet and add the chicken pieces skin side down. Cook over moderately high heat 3 to 5 minutes or until golden brown. Turn the pieces and continue cooking about 3 minutes or until golden brown on the second side.

3. Add the mushrooms and continue cooking. Add the bay leaf, thyme, onion, and garlic. Cook, shaking the skillet and stirring the chicken pieces so that the other ingredients are evenly distributed around and between the pieces.

4. When the chicken has cooked about 10 or 12 minutes (total cooking time, start to finish), remove the pieces to a serving dish.

5. Sprinkle the ingredients in the skillet with flour, stirring to blend evenly.

6. Add the wine, tomatoes, and broth. Stir and bring to the boil.

7. Return the chicken pieces to the skillet. Add the juice that may have accumulated around them. Add the anchovies and salt and pepper to taste. Cover closely and simmer 5 minutes.

8. Add the olives and continue to cook 5 minutes.

Yield: Four servings.

Riz Egyptienne
(Rice with chicken livers)

---

1 **chicken liver**	1 **cup rice**
1 **tablespoon plus 2 teaspoons butter**	1½ **cups chicken broth**
¼ **cup finely chopped onion**	⅔ **cup cooked ham, cut into ¼-inch dice**
⅔ **cup fresh mushrooms, cut into ½-inch dice**	

1. Cut the liver in ¼-inch pieces. Set aside.

2. Melt 1 tablespoon of the butter and add the onion and mushrooms. Cook, stirring occasionally, until wilted. Add the rice and cook, stirring, until the rice is coated. Add the broth and bring to the boil. Cover closely and cook 17 minutes.

3. Meanwhile, heat the remaining butter in a skillet and add the liver and ham. Cook, shaking the skillet and stirring, until the liver is cooked and the ham is heated through.

4. Add the liver and ham to the rice and toss gently with a two-pronged fork to blend the ingredients.

Yield: Four servings.

IN FRENCH KITCHENS, CHEFS AND COOKS OFTEN communicate in the form of a code that has been used for generations. You say, "Add a bouquet garni," instead of, "Make a bundle of herbs and spices including parsley, sprigs, thyme, and bay leaf." You say, "Give me a duxelles," instead of, "Make a hash of chopped mushrooms cooked in butter with a touch of shallots." And you say, "Use a soubise," instead of, "Make a purée of onions simmered down until thickened."

Similarly, in menu writing a catalogue of names serves as a code. Dishes made with carrots are called crécy, a place name; dishes made with cauliflower are listed for some mysterious reason as du barry; and dishes relating to asparagus are called argenteuil, another place name. Perhaps the best known of these menu names in America is florentine, which appears on thousands of menus all over this country and abroad. It indicates the presence of spinach in any given dish; historians are imprecise as to the exact relation between spinach and the city on the banks of the River Arno.

Chicken breasts florentine are an excellent entrée, and I must say that one of the choicest items in many supermarkets in America is boneless chicken breasts. If they are not in your supermarket, your local butcher (if he is accommodating enough) will quickly bone chicken breasts for you.

To make the dish, you could use breasts that are not only boneless but skinless, but if you have a choice it is best to leave the skin on. The breasts, when cooked, retain their shape better.

To prepare chicken breasts florentine, the breasts must be cooked in a blend of wine and broth. The cooking liquid is used to prepare a sauce. As the chicken poaches, there is ample time to cook the spinach, press it, and reheat it in butter. The sauce requires a very few minutes to make, and that's the sum of it. Chicken breasts florentine, a salad, and, perhaps, cheese could make an excellent meal any season of the year.

[25]

Suprêmes de Volaille à la Florentine
(Chicken breasts with spinach)

4 whole, unsplit, boneless chicken breasts with or without the skin, about 2½ pounds
Salt and freshly ground pepper to taste
2 tablespoons plus 2 teaspoons butter
1 tablespoon finely chopped shallots
½ cup dry white wine

½ cup chicken broth
2 sprigs parsley
2 10-ounce packages fresh spinach cooked as for épinards en branche (see recipe)
2 tablespoons flour
1 cup heavy cream
1 egg yolk, lightly beaten
1 or 2 tablespoons grated Gruyère or Parmesan cheese

1. Place the chicken breasts opened up on a flat surface skin side down. Sprinkle with salt and pepper. Fold the chicken breasts, reshaping them skin side out. Smooth the skin over.

2. Butter the bottom of a skillet with 2 teaspoons of the butter and sprinkle with the shallots. Add the reshaped breasts seam side down. Add the wine, chicken broth, and salt and pepper to taste. Add the parsley and bring to the boil. Cover and simmer about 15 to 20 minutes, or until the breasts are just cooked through. Remove from the heat.

3. As the chicken cooks, prepare the spinach according to the recipe.

4. Drain and reserve all the liquid from the chicken breasts. There should be about 1½ cups. Keep the chicken breasts covered.

5. Melt the remaining 2 tablespoons of butter in a saucepan and add the flour, stirring with a wire whisk until blended. Add the reserved cooking liquid to the butter-flour mixture, stirring with the whisk. When thickened and smooth, simmer about 5 minutes. Add the heavy cream and cook about 2 minutes.

[26]

6. Remove from the heat and add the egg yolk, stirring briskly.

7. Preheat the broiler.

8. Spoon the spinach into the center of a heatproof serving dish. Arrange the chicken breasts seam side down over the spinach. Spoon the sauce over the chicken and spinach. Sprinkle the cheese on top of the breasts and run under the broiler until bubbling on top.

Yield: Four servings.

Épinards en Branche
(Spinach with butter)

---

2 10-ounce packages fresh spinach
2 cups water
Salt and freshly ground pepper to taste

⅛ teaspoon freshly grated nutmeg
1 tablespoon butter

1. Pull away and discard any tough stems and blemished leaves from the spinach. Rinse and drain the spinach.

2. Pour the water into a kettle and bring to the boil. Add salt to taste and the spinach. Stir down to wilt.

3. Bring to the boil, stirring occasionally, and cook about 5 minutes. Empty the spinach into a colander and drain. Press with the back of a wooden spoon to extract most of the liquid. Squeeze between the hands to extract additional moisture.

4. Put the spinach on a flat surface and chop it coarsely.

5. Add salt, pepper, and nutmeg.

6. Put the butter in a skillet and, when it starts to brown, add the spinach. Cook, tossing and stirring, just to heat through.

Yield: Four servings.

[27]

OVER A PERIOD OF TIME I HAVE HEARD NUMER-
ous readers lament: "But some of your recipes are so
l-o-n-g." The fact is that, with certain exceptions, the
length of a recipe isn't necessarily related to the cooking time.
The recipe for the following dish is a case in point. It consists of
nine "steps." If you read carefully, however, you will note that
the first four steps are nothing more than telling you to trim and
cut carrots and asparagus in a certain way and to cook them
quickly in boiling water. Nothing complicated there.

The reason for the steps is primarily to improve the presentation of the dish once it is finished and ready to be served.
The dish itself is an easily made, very simple sauté of chicken
breasts, using the most basic "classic" technique. In that the
breasts are skinless and boneless, the cooking time is shortened
considerably. And the technique is this:

The breasts are seasoned and coated lightly with flour. The
flour will aid in the quick-browning process. The breasts are
cooked on two sides in butter, about 10 minutes in all, and then
removed from the skillet.

Shallots, an almost indispensable ingredient in fine French
cookery, are added, then a dry white wine. The wine (it will dissolve the skillet's brown particles, which add flavor) is cooked
down and a bit of tomato paste is added. The tomato paste will
give a smattering of flavor, but it is primarily for color. A little
chicken broth will "extend" the sauce, and heavy cream—only
2 tablespoons—which enrich and smooth it.

The accompaniment? Buttered noodles simply cooked and
served with chopped fresh tomatoes quickly sautéed in butter.

Suprêmes de Volaille Printanier

(Chicken breasts with asparagus and carrots)

4 cups water
Salt to taste
8 fresh large asparagus spears
1 carrot
2 skinless, boneless chicken breasts split in half, about 1½ pounds, ready-to-cook weight
Freshly ground pepper to taste

1 to 2 tablespoons flour
3 tablespoons butter
1 tablespoon finely chopped shallots
½ cup dry white wine
1 tablespoon tomato paste
¼ cup chicken broth
2 tablespoons heavy cream

1. Bring 4 cups of water to the boil with salt to taste.

2. Scrape the sides of the asparagus spears, leaving the tips (about 2 inches from the top) unscraped. Cut off and discard the tough base of the spears. Set aside.

3. Scrape the carrot and trim off the end. Cut the carrot crosswise into 2-inch lengths. Cut each length into ¼-inch slices. Stack the slices and cut them into ¼-inch strips (like small french fries). Set aside.

4. Drop the vegetables into the boiling water and cook about 4 minutes or until crisp-tender. Do not overcook. Drain well and set aside.

5. Sprinkle the chicken pieces with salt and pepper to taste. Dredge lightly in flour and shake off any excess.

6. Melt 2 tablespoons of the butter in a skillet. When quite hot but not brown, add the chicken pieces. Cook on one side over moderately high heat about 4 minutes. Turn and cook on the other side until golden brown, about 2 to 4 minutes. Cover and cook about 4 to 5 minutes, or until tender.

7. Transfer the pieces to a warm platter, arranging them neatly. Add the shallots to the skillet. Stir and cook briefly. Add

the wine and cook until reduced by half. Add the tomato paste, stir, and add the chicken broth. Stir in the cream.

8. Melt the remaining tablespoon of butter in a skillet. Add the asparagus and carrots and salt and pepper to taste. Cook just to heat through and coat with butter.

9. Arrange equal portions of asparagus and carrots between the chicken breast pieces. Spoon the sauce over the chicken and serve.

Yield: Four servings.

Nouilles à la Tomate
(Noodles with fresh tomato)

½ pound thin noodles
Salt to taste
1 large ripe tomato, about ¾ pound

2 tablespoons butter
Freshly ground pepper to taste

1. Bring enough water to the boil to cover the noodles when added. Add salt to taste.

2. Core and peel the tomato and cut it into ½-inch cubes.

3. Drop the noodles into the boiling water and cook until tender.

4. Meanwhile, melt 1 tablespoon of the butter in a saucepan and add the tomato and salt and pepper to taste. Cook about 1 minute, stirring occasionally.

5. Drain the noodles and return them to the kettle. Add the remaining tablespoon of butter and salt and pepper to taste.

6. Serve the noodles with the tomatoes spooned over.

Yield: Four servings.

TO JUDGE FROM THE QUESTIONS PUT TO ME over a period of years, the occasional cook seems little aware that the techniques for cooking are in most cases both staple and repetitive. A good case in point are the various breaded dishes that, if you are properly organized, are a snap to prepare. Particularly, meats such as veal scallopine or breast of chicken require a minimum of cooking time in the skillet.

With rare exceptions, the procedure for breading foods follows a standard outline. The foods, depending on their thickness and basic tender nature, may be pounded lightly with a flat mallet, the side of a heavy knife, or the bottom of a small, clean heavy skillet. The "flattening" should be gentle but firm. It also helps if the food is placed between pieces of clear plastic wrap, or, as a second choice, wax paper.

Use three flat utensils for the breading process. In one add flour seasoned with a little salt and pepper. In the second add a beaten egg or two (depending on the amount of meat to be coated), blended with a small spoonful or so of water. To the third add a supply of fresh bread crumbs, ample enough to coat the meat. Dip the pieces of meat first in flour, patting to coat and shake off any excess. Add the pieces of meat one at a time to the egg, patting with the fingers to coat well. Immediately add the meat pieces one at a time to the crumbs and pat to coat. At this point the meat may be transferred to a pastry rack and allowed to stand until ready to cook. It can be cooked immediately.

That's all there is to it other than cooking the foods either in butter or a combination of butter and oil. If all butter is used, the foods may brown too quickly and burn. With the oil the burning point is considerably lowered and they may cook for a longer period.

Breaded foods are called à l'anglaise in French, which is to say English-style. One of the most easily made of such dishes are chicken breasts, flattened, breaded, and cooked until golden

[31]

all over. They are served with lemon wedges. An excellent accompaniment for the dish are zucchini and carrots with chopped fresh mint. Recipes for those—to be cooked start to finish in less than an hour—are given here.

Suprêmes de Volaille Panés à l'Anglaise
(Breaded chicken breasts)

2 whole skinless, boneless chicken breasts, about 1 pound total weight
¼ cup flour
Salt and freshly ground pepper to taste
1 egg

2 tablespoons water
1 cup or more bread crumbs
¼ cup peanut, vegetable, or corn oil
1 tablespoon butter
Seeded lemon slices for garnish

1. Cut the chicken breasts in half. Trim off the thin cartilage and other extraneous matter.

2. Place the breasts, one at a time, between two sheets of plastic wrap and pound lightly with a flat mallet or the bottom of a heavy skillet.

3. Dredge the breasts on all sides in flour seasoned with salt and pepper.

4. Beat the egg with the water in a flat dish. Dip the meat on all sides in egg, patting with the fingers.

5. Dip the breasts in bread crumbs to coat on all sides. Tap the sides lightly with the flat part of a heavy knife to help the crumbs adhere.

6. Heat the oil and butter in one or two skillets and add the chicken pieces. Cook until golden brown on one side, about 3 to 5 minutes. Turn and cook about 3 to 5 minutes on the other side. Remove and serve hot garnished with lemon slices.

Yield: Four servings.

Courgettes et Carottes à la Menthe

(Zucchini and carrots with fresh mint)

3 carrots, about ½ pound, trimmed and scraped

2 zucchini, about ¾ pound, ends trimmed

2 tablespoons butter

Salt and freshly ground pepper to taste

2 teaspoons finely chopped mint or parsley

1. Cut the carrots into ¼-inch rounds and set aside.

2. Cut the zucchini into ¼-inch rounds and set aside.

3. Melt the butter in a heavy skillet and add the carrots and salt and pepper. Cover and cook about 3 to 5 minutes, or until half cooked.

4. Add the zucchini and cover. Shake the skillet occasionally. Cook 4 to 5 minutes, or until all the vegetables are crisp-tender. Sprinkle with salt, pepper, and mint.

Yield: Four servings.

MANY FACTORS ARE INVOLVED IN THE TIME required to prepare any dish, be it a simple dinner or an elaborate dish, such as a coulibiac, which may require as many as six different preparations combined in one single presentation. It helps enormously, of course, if you know how to cut and slice and chop efficiently. But the proper tools or equipment are a great aid in any form of hasty cooking. A dull knife can hinder a cook as much as a cluttered work surface, which is the bane of a professional. As you work, you should clean and rid your immediate work area of unnecessary ingredients and any other nonessentials. You should also plan ahead, determine the ingredients to be used, and decide the order in which they should logically be cleaned and otherwise made ready for cooking.

There are certain "tricks," too, that will expedite the preparation of food. I am often asked why my recipes call for starting a dish on top of the stove before it is placed in the oven, and the answer is basic: It hastens the baking time. The heat that is rapidly generated on top of the stove may save as much as 5 or 10 minutes baking.

That pertains to the 60-minute dish here, parsleyed chicken with vegetables. There is another "trick" outlined in the recipe. Cooks are instructed to make a slit at the bend where each chicken thigh and leg meet without severing the two pieces. This is frequently a good idea whenever thighs and legs of chickens are cooked together without splitting the pieces apart. That joint requires more cooking time than the rest of the chicken and with a partial cut, the cooking is hastened.

Poulet Persillé aux Légumes

(Parsleyed chicken with vegetables)

1 3- to 4-pound chicken, cut into quarters
Salt and freshly ground pepper to taste
3 tablespoons butter
½ cup bread crumbs
3 tablespoons finely chopped shallots

1 teaspoon finely chopped garlic
3 tablespoons finely chopped parsley
Assorted vegetables (see recipe for marmite des légumes)

1. Preheat the oven to 425 degrees.

2. Using a sharp knife, such as a boning knife, make a slit at the bend between each leg and thigh without severing the pieces.

3. Sprinkle the chicken pieces, including the liver, gizzard, and neck, if they are used, with salt and pepper.

4. Grease a shallow heatproof baking pan large enough to hold the chicken in one layer with 1 tablespoon of the butter. Arrange the quartered chicken pieces over it. Dot the chicken with the remaining 2 tablespoons of butter. Add the liver, neck, and gizzard between the pieces.

5. Place the baking pan on top of the stove and heat to sizzling. Place the dish in the oven and bake 30 minutes, basting occasionally.

6. Meanwhile, blend the crumbs with the shallots, garlic, and parsley.

7. After the half hour of baking, remove the pan from the oven. Baste the chicken liberally and sprinkle with the crumb mixture. Return the chicken to the oven for 10 minutes, or until the crumbs are golden brown.

8. Scatter the vegetables over the chicken, if desired, or serve them separately.

Yield: Four servings.

[35]

Marmite des Légumes
(Assorted vegetables)

8 small baby carrots, or 2 large carrots, about ¼ pound

1 white turnip, about ¼ pound, peeled

1 Idaho potato, about ¼ pound, peeled

¼ pound string beans, trimmed and cut into 2-inch lengths

12 small white onions, peeled

2 tablespoons butter

Freshly ground pepper to taste

1. Scrape the carrots and leave them whole if they are small. Otherwise, cut the larger carrots in half crosswise. Cut each half in two to make 8 pieces. Set aside.

2. Peel the turnip and potato. Cut them in half. Cut each half into 8 segments.

3. Add the string beans and carrots to a saucepan and add water to cover and salt to taste. Bring to the boil and simmer 8 minutes.

4. Add the potatoes, turnips, and onions and cook about 3 minutes. Drain well.

5. Melt the butter in a skillet and add the vegetables and salt and pepper to taste. Cook about 5 minutes, stirring and shaking the skillet so that the vegetables cook evenly.

Yield: Four servings.

WE WERE REMINISCING—FOR THE THOUSANDTH time, of course—on the elaborate changes that have been made in American taste and food habits within recent memory. My memory stretches back to that World's Fair of 1939 when I first came here to work in the restaurant of the fair's French pavilion.

Many of the dishes created in the pavilion kitchen were not overly daring, and yet they were at the time a novelty to the thousands of fairgoers and were consumed with obvious relish. Chicken in red wine sauce—particularly coq au vin—and boeuf bourguignon were among the dishes in which the public indulged with uncommon enthusiasm.

Both those dishes have become so familiar by now that they seem almost as American as they were French. In a way, it seems a shame that both dishes have lost some of their original éclat, for they have an honest and inherent goodness. And one of them, chicken in red wine sauce, is a snap to make. The most basic such dish is a simple sauce with mushrooms, chopped shallots, and red wine, with herbs and spices. The cooking time for browning the chicken in butter is about 12 minutes. After that you simply add the wine and seasonings, cover, and cook until the chicken is done and the sauce is ready to be strained.

I have deliberately avoided calling it coq au vin, for that dish in its classic incarnation is a bit more complicated and time-consuming, calling as it does for rendered pieces of salt pork (lardons), glazed small white onions, and, finally, croutons.

Thus, the recipe here is called au brouilly. The day the dish was recently made I used a glass of Brouilly, an excellent Beaujolais that happened to be handy. Any good dry red wine, preferably a Burgundy, would suffice. The chicken and a hastily prepared gratin made with noodles and cheese are a fine combination. That plus a salad would suffice.

Poulet Sauté au Brouilly
(Chicken in red wine sauce)

1 2½- to 3-pound chicken, cut into serving pieces and including back, neck, gizzard, and liver
Salt and freshly ground pepper to taste
2 tablespoons butter
¼ pound mushrooms, left whole if very small; otherwise halved, quartered, or sliced
¼ cup chopped shallots
1 teaspoon finely chopped garlic
2 tablespoons flour
1½ cups dry red wine, preferably a Brouilly
½ cup plus 2 tablespoons chicken broth
1 bay leaf
1 sprig fresh parsley
2 sprigs fresh thyme or less, or ¼ teaspoon dried thyme

1. Sprinkle the chicken pieces with salt and pepper.

2. Melt the butter in a skillet large enough to hold the chicken parts in one layer without crowding. Add the chicken pieces skin side down.

3. Cook the chicken over moderately high heat until golden brown, about 6 or 7 minutes. Turn the pieces and cook about 5 minutes longer.

4. Add the mushrooms, shallots, and garlic and stir to blend. Cook about 1 minute and sprinkle the flour evenly over all.

5. Add the wine and half a cup of broth and bring to the boil.

6. Add the bay leaf, parsley sprig, and thyme. Add salt and pepper to taste and cover. Cook 15 to 20 minutes.

7. Using a slotted spoon, transfer the meaty parts of the chicken to a heatproof casserole. Add the mushrooms to the casserole, but leave the back, gizzard, and so on in the skillet.

8. Strain the sauce over the chicken, pressing with the back of a wooden spoon to extract the juices from the solids. Add the remaining 2 tablespoons of broth and swirl it around to thin the

sauce remaining in the skillet. Strain this over the chicken. Reheat thoroughly.

Yield: Four servings.

Nouilles au Fromage
(Noodles with cheese)

¾ pound medium or fine egg
noodles
Salt
2 tablespoons butter
Freshly ground pepper to
taste

⅛ teaspoon freshly grated
nutmeg
1 cup heavy cream
¼ pound grated Gruyère or
Swiss cheese, about 1¼ cups
loosely packed

1. Preheat the broiler.
2. Cook the noodles in boiling salted water until tender. Drain. Return the noodles to the kettle and add half the butter, salt, pepper, and nutmeg. Toss to blend.
3. Spoon the noodles into a hot serving dish. Heat the cream and pour it over the noodles.
4. Sprinkle the cheese over the noodles and dot with the remaining butter. Run under the broiler until the cheese melts.

Yield: Four servings.

FROM ITALIAN FRIENDS I HAVE LEARNED THAT the name of the dish, chicken scarpariello, means chicken shoemaker-style. It is an interesting name because the lowest compliment you can pay a French chef is to say, "He cooks like a shoemaker."

In any event, a friend and colleague, Luigi Nanni, chef-patron of two of New York's best Italian restaurants—Nanni's and Il Valleto—was contacted by telephone, and he explained briefly that the dish is a sauté of chicken cooked until golden brown in olive oil and quickly finished with a bit of garlic, white wine, and lemon juice. It is a dish from the south of Italy.

On the day I decided to cook this dish, one of the first shipments of broccoli di râpé appeared in the vegetable section of one of the largest supermarkets in Southampton.

My knowledge of this somewhat bitter but excellent vegetable also came to me through a good friend and excellent cook, Ed Giobbi, the artist and cookbook author of Katonah, New York. Broccoli di râpé is easily prepared. It is necessary to simply trim away any tough bottom stalks. All the rest of the vegetable is edible—the leaves, stems, and "buds" or flowers. When these are washed and drained briefly, the vegetable is cooked in olive oil with a bit of garlic and crushed hot red pepper. It cooks quickly.

Some may complain that it is bad planning to link two dishes containing olive oil and garlic in the same menu. To my taste the two dishes complement each other and a bit of flexibility would seem in order where menu-planning is concerned.

The logical way to prepare this menu is to begin with the chicken. As it cooks, the broccoli di râpé can be trimmed and washed and put on to cook shortly before the chicken is ready.

The important thing to keep in mind in preparing this menu is to use your judgment in cooking the chicken. It should be browned over high or moderately high heat. The heat must be reduced somewhat so that the chicken will be cooked throughout at the end of the cooking time. The total cooking time for a 3½-pound chicken to serve four is from about 20 to 25 minutes.

It is recommended that this menu include the usual salad with cheese as a second course and, if desired, a final course of fresh fruit or a purchased or previously made dessert.

Poulet Scarpariello
(Chicken in white wine)

---

1 3½-pound chicken, cut into serving pieces
Flour for dredging
Salt and freshly ground pepper to taste
¼ cup olive oil
2 tablespoons butter

2 teaspoons finely minced garlic
½ cup dry white wine
Juice of 1 lemon
3 tablespoons finely chopped parsley

1. Dredge the chicken all over in flour seasoned with salt and pepper.

2. Heat the oil in a heavy skillet large enough to hold the chicken pieces in one layer. Add the chicken pieces skin side down and cook until golden brown, 8 to 10 minutes. Do not cover.

3. Turn the chicken pieces and cook 10 to 12 minutes longer. Do not cover. At the end of this time the chicken should be cooked through to the bone. Adjust the heat and cooking time accordingly.

4. Carefully pour all the fat from the skillet, leaving the chicken in the skillet. Add the butter to the skillet and when it is hot, add the garlic. Pour the wine around the chicken and bring to the boil. Squeeze the lemon juice over the chicken and sprinkle with parsley. Cover closely and cook 3 minutes longer.

Yield: Four servings.

[41]

Brocoli di râpé à la vapeur
(Steamed broccoli di râpé)

1 pound tender, bright green, unblemished broccoli di râpé (see note)

¼ cup olive oil

1 tablespoon finely minced garlic

1 hot dried red pepper, crushed with seeds, or ½ teaspoon hot red pepper flakes

Salt and freshly ground pepper to taste

1. Using a small paring knife, cut off and discard the bottom stalks. The tender leaves and stems plus the buds of the vegetable should be left intact. Rinse the vegetable well and place it in a colander. Drain but allow the water that clings to the leaves to remain.

2. Heat the oil in a heavy skillet or casserole with a tight-fitting lid. Add garlic and red pepper. Immediately add the prepared broccoli di râpé and stir, using a two-pronged fork, turning the vegetable in the oil until the leaves start to wilt. Sprinkle with salt and pepper and cover closely. Cook about 3 to 5 minutes, turning the vegetable occasionally so that it cooks evenly.

Yield: Four servings.

Note: Broccoli di râpé is available in some supermarkets and stores that specialize in Italian foods.

I HAD NEVER COOKED BEFORE I WAS PACKED OFF on a train to go to Paris to become apprenticed as a chef shortly after my fourteenth birthday. At that time I lived in the small village of St. Vinnemer in Burgundy, and the total population was said to be exactly 396 people. The town is not listed in most atlases. Legend had it that when anyone moved, someone else arrived; when someone died, another child was born, and so on.

My father served the town proudly in two capacities. He was both mayor and chief fireman. He also took pleasure in the thought that I had chosen cooking as a profession.

The time of my first visit home one year later coincided with St. Barbe's Day and St. Barbe just happened to be the patron saint of firemen.

It was a time of considerable revelry, and my father volunteered that I would cook the meal for all the volunteer firemen in town and their families, a total of about thirty people.

I hadn't the courage to tell him that in the first year of apprenticeship in any kitchen of France back in those days, your time was spent peeling potatoes and onions, sweeping floors and cleaning pots and pans. Serious cookery would come later.

In any event, I couldn't disappoint him, so after brooding over the problem I decided there was one dish I could concoct without fear or trembling. It was one of the most basic dishes of the entire French repertory, a simply boiled chicken with a sauce suprême or cream sauce with chicken broth as its foundation. It was a huge success, and that dish to this day remains a favorite of mine.

The chicken requires 30 minutes to simmer. The broth in which it is cooked may be used in cooking the rice to accompany the dish and the sauce to spoon over it. If on the other hand you have a spare quantity of broth in the refrigerator or freezer, you might use this for the rice and sauce and the total cooking time would be reduced to slightly more than half an hour.

It is recommended that this menu include the usual salad with cheese as a second course and, if desired, a final course of fresh fruit or a purchased or previously made dessert.

Poulet Poché Sauce Suprême
(Poached chicken in cream sauce)

---

1 2½-pound chicken, trussed
5 cups water or chicken broth
1 bay leaf
1 small onion stuck with 2
   whole cloves
2 allspice
1 large carrot, cut in half
   widthwise
3 large ribs celery, each about
   6 inches long
   Salt to taste
6 peppercorns
2 sprigs fresh thyme, or ½
   teaspoon dried thyme

1 cup rice
3 cups chicken broth (broth in
   which the chicken is cooked
   here may be used)
2 tablespoons butter
2 tablespoons flour
1 cup heavy cream
   Juice of ½ lemon
   Freshly ground pepper to
   taste
⅛ teaspoon freshly grated
   nutmeg
   Pinch of cayenne pepper

1. Place the chicken in a small kettle or large saucepan and add the water, bay leaf, onion with cloves, allspice, carrot, celery, salt, peppercorns, and thyme. Bring to the boil and partly cover. Simmer 30 minutes.

2. Place the rice in a saucepan and add 2 cups of the chicken broth (the rice may be cooked before or after the chicken is finished). Bring to the boil and cook 20 minutes.

3. Meanwhile, melt the butter in a saucepan and add the flour, using a wire whisk. When blended, add the remaining 1 cup of chicken broth, stirring rapidly with the whisk. Cook

about 5 minutes and add the cream. Simmer about 10 minutes. Add salt to taste and the remaining ingredients.

4. To serve, untruss the chicken. Remove the skin from the chicken (except the wing skin).

5. Arrange the hot rice on a dish. Cut the carrots and celery into 2-inch lengths. Place the chicken on the rice, along with the carrots and celery. Spoon the sauce over the chicken and serve.

Yield: Four servings.

COOKING WELL, LIKE ALMOST ANY PROFESSION or hobby, is to a great degree psychological. It has to do with "aptitude," which implies a feeling of security in what you are about. Many people are terrified of cooking because they have a mistaken notion that it is an impossibly exact science. They're afraid, so to speak, of fitting a round hole with a square peg.

One of the best chicken dishes in the French repertoire is called poulet Vallée d'Auge, chicken in cream sauce, a celebrated dish of Normandy made with cut-up chicken and vegetables and flavored with Calvados, the famed applejack of the region.

Since the chicken and vegetables are first cooked separately and then combined so that they finish cooking together, the first "fear" to come into an amateur cook's mind is probably that either the chicken or the vegetables will be undercooked or overcooked. That they won't "finish the race together."

The thing to remember is that in most cases there is a lot more latitude in cookery than most amateur cooks believe. Of course, you wouldn't want to serve undercooked chicken. Or mushy, overcooked vegetables. But cooking times have a way of compensating for themselves. If the vegetables cook 4 or 5 minutes longer than the "ideal" time you would allot them, they are still going to be highly edible. Perhaps a trifle less "toothy" than you would have them, but don't say a word and your guests won't suspect a thing.

In preparing the dish you will note that the chicken is sautéed in butter for the first few minutes of cooking. The vegetables are prepared for cooking and what one calls "blanched" or "parboiled" before the final steps. To go about this, it is preferable to prepare all the ingredients for cooking before you start. Salt and pepper the chicken pieces, then proceed to scraping, peeling, and cutting the vegetables. Then begin.

As the chicken is put on to cook, add the vegetables to a kettle and bring to the boil. Relax. Everything is going to be all right.

Poulet Vallée d'Auge
(Chicken with applejack sauce)

---

1 2½- to 3-pound chicken, cut up for frying
Salt and freshly ground pepper to taste
1 large or 2 medium-size potatoes, about 1 pound, peeled
2 carrots, about ⅓ pound
¼ pound string beans
8 small white onions, or 4 small- to medium-size onions, about ½ pound, peeled
1 zucchini, about ¼ pound
6 tablespoons butter
¼ cup Calvados, Cognac, or bourbon
1 cup heavy cream

1. Sprinkle the chicken pieces with salt and pepper.

2. If one large potato is used, cut it into 8 pieces (''cubes'') after peeling. If two potatoes are used, cut into quarters after peeling. Cover with cold water to prevent discoloration.

3. Trim and scrape the carrots. Cut each carrot in half. Cut each half into thirds.

4. Trim off the ends of the beans. Cut the beans into 1½-inch lengths.

5. If the onions are small, cut them in half. If larger, cut into quarters.

6. Trim the end of the zucchini. Cut in half lengthwise, then cut each half into quarters.

7. Melt 4 tablespoons of the butter in a large heavy skillet and add the chicken skin side down. Cook about 10 minutes.

8. As the chicken cooks, place the potato, carrots, beans, and onions in a saucepan and add cold water to cover. Add salt to taste and bring to the boil. Cook 1 minute at the boil and drain.

9. When the chicken is browned on one side, turn it. Cook 5 minutes.

10. Melt the remaining 2 tablespoons of butter in another skillet and add the drained vegetables and zucchini. Sprinkle with salt and pepper and shake the skillet or stir gently occasionally to redistribute the vegetables. Cook about 5 minutes. The vegetables at this point should not be cooked until tender. They will be cooked again with the chicken.

11. Add the Calvados or other spirit to the chicken and cover the chicken. Cook 10 minutes and uncover. Add the cream and vegetables and bring to the boil. Season with salt and pepper and cover. Cook 10 minutes and serve.

Yield: Four servings.

DURING MY TENURE AS CHEF AT LE PAVILLON Restaurant, it almost goes without saying that the clientele that passed through those doors was both international and celebrated. It also goes without saying that the owner, Henri Soulé, held some of his customers in higher esteem than others. The gentleman was inclined—a natural inclination—to pamper those of whom he was particularly fond, whether it was a matter of seating or a complimentary bottle of champagne. His solicitude and care were never more apparent than when those whom he particularly liked and/or admired were hospitalized.

He was known by that small segment of his clientele for the Pavillon's poule au pot, or chicken in the pot. He hated hospital food himself, and whenever he ascertained that a favored guest, temporarily indisposed, was well enough to eat, he would dispatch his movable feast to the patient's bedside and not without ceremony.

The kitchen would be charged with adding a whole, small chicken to an earthenware crock and over it was ladled a piping hot, rich, and nourishing broth containing carrots, celery, turnips, leeks, and rice. It was not so much the healing powers of the dish that spurred him on. Poule au pot also happened to be one of the dishes on which he personally preferred to dine.

In any event, the chicken and broth in the crock would be covered closely with the lid and a tablespoon tied on top of it. A personal note would be added, addressed to such people as John F. Kennedy, Margaret Truman, Cole Porter, the Duchess of Windsor, and so on. For clients of this caliber he would send Martin Decre, Soulé's second and right-hand man in the dining room, to see to the small but important details of carving the chicken and serving the broth while it was still steaming.

At its best, a poule au pot is an excellent dish and certainly one of the easiest to prepare, simply a matter of cutting up a few vegetables and cooking them as timing demands. It is, of course, a meal in itself and the success of the dish depends in large part on how rich, fresh, and strongly flavored the chicken broth is when it is added to the chicken and vegetables.

This dish, plus fruit and cheese, would be an ample meal for a late spring or summer evening.

Poule au Pot d'Henri Soulé
(Henri Soulé's chicken in the pot)

---

1 3-pound chicken
3 carrots, scraped, quartered lengthwise, and cut into 1½-inch lengths
3 ribs celery, trimmed, split lengthwise, and cut into 1½-inch lengths
2 or 3 turnips, about ½ pound, trimmed and cut into pieces about the same shape as the celery and carrots

1 cup leeks, quartered lengthwise and cut into 1½-inch lengths
1 zucchini, trimmed, quartered, and cut into 1½-inch lengths
6 cups chicken broth
¼ cup rice
Salt and freshly ground pepper to taste

1. Truss the chicken and place it in a kettle. It should fit snugly or else too much water must be added and the subsequent soup will be weak and watery. Cover with water and add the carrots, celery, turnips, leeks, and zucchini. Bring to a full boil and drain well.

2. Return the chicken to the kettle and add the chicken broth. Add all the vegetables except the zucchini. Simmer 20 minutes. Add the zucchini and simmer 5 minutes longer.

3. Add the rice and salt and pepper to taste, and cook until the rice is tender, about 10 minutes.

4. Untruss the chicken. Cut it into serving pieces and serve in four hot soup bowls with equal amounts of vegetables and rice in each bowl.

Yield: Four servings.

THERE SEEMS TO BE A COMMON ASSUMPTION among the restaurant-going public that all the dishes that emerge from a professional kitchen are, of necessity, intricate and complex in their preparation. There are, of course, some dishes that require various stocks and bases which may require a day or more to simmer and reduce to a proper or desired consistency. And there are various creations that do require a highly specialized if not to say arcane knowledge to produce successful results.

I thought of this recently while cooking a quickly made sautéed chicken dish, a dish known as chicken beauséjour. During my years as chef of Le Pavillon in New York, this was a great favorite of the clientele, Europeans and Americans alike. And yet it is as easy to make as any dish that is sort of elegant in its simplicity. It consists of chicken cut into pieces as for frying, and sautéed in butter with a few herbs, namely bay leaf and thyme. White wine is added and cooked down, and the dish is served traditionally with fine buttered noodles or rice. I prefer noodles.

The cooking time for chicken beauséjour is less than half an hour; preparation time is negligible. The noodles should be cooked, of course, shortly before the chicken is ready to be served.

Serve the dish with a salad and a choice of cheese and a simple purchased dessert.

Poulet Sauté Beauséjour
(Sautéed chicken with wine and herbs)

1 1¾- to 2-pound chicken, cut
into serving pieces
Salt and freshly ground
pepper to taste
3 tablespoons butter
2 whole cloves garlic, unpeeled
1 large bay leaf

2 sprigs fresh thyme, or ½
teaspoon dried thyme
⅓ cup dry white wine
⅓ cup water
Buttered thin noodles,
optional

1. Sprinkle the chicken pieces with salt and pepper to taste. To facilitate cooking, make a gash in the underside (opposite the skin side) of each chicken leg.

2. Melt 2 tablespoons of the butter in a heavy skillet and add all the chicken pieces skin side down. Do not add the liver. Cook 5 to 7 minutes, or until golden brown, and turn the pieces. Add the garlic, bay leaf, and thyme.

3. Add the liver and reduce the heat. Cook over moderate heat, turning the pieces so that they cook evenly. The total cooking time at this point should be from 17 to 20 minutes.

4. Remove the chicken pieces to a hot serving platter and add the wine to the skillet. Cook over high heat, stirring to dissolve the brown particles that cling to the bottom and sides of the pan. Cook until the wine is reduced by half. Add the water and boil briskly about 30 seconds.

5. Swirl in the remaining butter and salt and pepper to taste.

6. Spoon the sauce over the chicken and serve with buttered thin noodles (see recipe).

Yield: Four servings.

Nouilles Fines au Beurre
(Buttered fine noodles)

½ pound thin noodles
Salt
2 tablespoons butter at room
temperature

Freshly ground pepper to
taste

1. Drop the noodles into a large quantity of boiling salted water. Cook about 2 or 3 minutes, or until tender. Do not overcook.

2. Drain the noodles and return them to the kettle. Toss them with the butter and add salt and pepper to taste. Serve hot.

Yield: Four servings.

ONE OF THE ULTIMATE GOALS OF WHAT MIGHT be called "fast stove" cookery could be a main course in which the principal components are cooked simultaneously. One of the prime examples of this—and a dish that is, by the way, excellent for special occasions—is what is known in French kitchens as poulet grillé à l'américaine, or grilled chicken American-style.

Just why this dish is called American is not immediately apparent. To the French mind, however, it simply seems like a dish that might have been put together by an American chef. In spirit, at least, it is closely related to the English mixed grill (with mutton chop, kidneys, and so on).

Before you begin this recipe, there is a point to remember: The foods—chicken, bacon, sausages, tomatoes, and mushroom caps—are first broiled and some of the ingredients are "finished" in a hot oven.

Although grilled chicken American-style requires no great ingenuity in its preparation, it is a dish that requires some concentration because of the varied cooking times of the various foods.

One of the most interesting of the meal's components is the chicken, which is prepared à la diable. That is to say, it is "deviled," or made more tangy, by brushing with mustard thinned with a little dry white wine before breading at the very end.

There is one thing for certain. Although this dish could be said to have class or style, it is, nonetheless, copious. Therefore, vegetable accompaniments other than the grilled tomato are nonessential. A well-made green salad with the dish or as a separate course with one or more cheeses and a crusty loaf of bread would be ample. A proper wine for this dish would be a dry red California or French wine. Something not too costly or elegant.

Poulet Grillé à l'Américaine
(Chicken with mixed grill)

1 3-pound chicken, split for broiling
Salt and freshly ground pepper to taste
Peanut, vegetable, or corn oil for brushing
4 slices bacon

4 links sausages
2 ripe tomatoes
4 large mushroom caps
1 tablespoon Dijon mustard
1 tablespoon dry white wine
4 to 8 tablespoons bread crumbs

1. Preheat the broiler to high. You will use both the broiler and the oven, preheated to 450 degrees, to cook the dish.

2. Sprinkle the chicken, including the liver, with salt and pepper. Brush all over with oil.

3. Arrange the chicken halves skin side down in a baking dish. Cover each half with 2 slices of bacon.

4. Arrange the liver separately on the baking dish. Arrange the sausages in the same dish.

5. Split the tomatoes in half. Slice off the stems of the mushrooms. Arrange the tomatoes cut side up and the mushrooms stem side up in a separate dish. Sprinkle the tops with salt and pepper and brush the tops with oil.

6. Place the dish with the chicken under the broiler about 4 to 5 inches from the source of heat. Broil about 2 to 3 minutes, or until the bacon is crisp. If necessary, turn the sausages and liver to prevent burning. Use your judgment. Broil the tomatoes and mushrooms about 2 to 3 minutes. Turn the mushrooms and continue broiling 2 to 3 minutes. Remove and keep warm.

7. When the bacon is crisp, remove it. Turn the chicken and other pieces. Broil the chicken skin side up until it is nicely browned, about 2 to 3 minutes.

8. Leave the chicken skin side up and place in the oven. Turn the sausages and liver as necessary.

[55]

9. When the chicken, sausages, and liver have baked 15 minutes, remove the sausages and liver. Transfer them to the dish with the tomatoes and mushrooms.

10. Continue baking the chicken. When the chicken has baked 5 minutes longer, turn each half skin side down. Blend the mustard and wine. Brush the top side with the mustard mixture. Sprinkle each half with 1 or 2 tablespoons of bread crumbs. Continue baking 10 minutes.

11. Turn the chicken halves skin side up. Brush with the mustard mixture and sprinkle each half with 1 or 2 tablespoons of bread crumbs. Return to the oven and bake 5 minutes, at the end of which time return the dish of tomatoes, mushrooms, sausages, and liver to the oven to reheat.

12. Bake 5 minutes longer and serve.

Yield: Four servings.

THERE ARE MANY INESCAPABLE ASSOCIATIONS in the world of food, and if you ask any Frenchman to associate words with foods, the name chicken would inevitably bring to mind the quotation of my fellow countryman, Henri the Fourth:

"Je veux qu'il n'y ait si pauvre paysan en mon royaume qu'il n'ait tous les dimanches sa poule au pot." (I want there to be no peasant in my kingdom to be so poor that he cannot have a chicken in his pot every Sunday.)

Chicken may not be the most aristocratic of foods, but it is certainly the most versatile, whether it is simply cooked as a poule au pot or turned into a fine ragout with a rich Burgundy sauce.

If, in this book, there seems to be a preponderance of chicken dishes, it is for a very good and logical reason. Chicken is quite simply—in the long run—the most available of foods, season in and season out. And, in addition to its incredible number of uses, it may well be the food least likely to have pitfalls in the ways in which it is cooked.

If there is one danger in cooking chicken, it is probably that it may be undercooked, although as many tourists have discovered in my homeland, there are those who prefer chicken—when spit-turned, for example—a bit underdone, but that's a question of taste.

The fact is that there is a good deal of latitude in the cooking conditions of chicken. If the cooking time is, to choose a random example, 30 minutes and the time is extended 5 or 10 minutes, chances are the dish will still be admirable. To put it another way, the cooking time for most chicken dishes—as opposed to those made with fish, for example—is about as flexible as any meat or seafood dish that comes to mind.

In the recipe outlined here, the chicken is first placed under the broiler, turned to broil on the second side, then baked until done. The broiling, actually, is to give texture to the skin of the fowl before finishing the dish with oven heat. This dish is an all-in-one affair in which, for the last few minutes, the chicken is baked with pre-cooked vegetables. Actually the preparation of the vegetables demands a little more time and effort than does the chicken. Therefore, it is best to prepare the vegetables and get them ready to cook before proceeding to the chicken.

Poulet Grillé à la Moutarde
(Chicken grilled with mustard)

---

1 4-pound chicken, split for broiling
Salt and freshly ground pepper to taste
2 tablespoons imported mustard, such as Dijon or Düsseldorf

2 tablespoons peanut oil
Sautéed vegetables (see recipe)
1 tablespoon red wine vinegar
2 tablespoons finely chopped parsley

1. Preheat the broiler.
2. Sprinkle the chicken halves with salt and pepper. Arrange the halves in one layer in a baking dish and brush on all sides with mustard.
3. Arrange the chicken skin side down in the dish and sprinkle the top with oil.
4. Place under the broiler and cook 10 minutes. Turn the halves and broil 10 minutes longer.
5. Pour off all the fat from the baking dish. Turn the chicken pieces.
6. Reduce the oven heat to 400 degrees.
7. Scatter the sautéed vegetables around the chicken and place the chicken in the oven. Bake 10 minutes.
8. Place the chicken in the baking dish on the stove. Add the

vinegar to the pan liquid, cooking a few seconds over high heat. Sprinkle with parsley.

Yield: Four servings.

Légumes Sautés
(Sautéed vegetables)

¾ pound very small potatoes, peeled

1 large carrot, about ¼ pound, trimmed and scraped

4 small white onions, peeled

Salt to taste

2 tablespoons butter

12 mushrooms, about ⅓ pound
Freshly ground pepper to taste

1. If the potatoes are not very small, cut them in half. Put them in a skillet with water to cover.

2. Cut the carrots into 2-inch lengths. Cut each length into quarters. Cut the onions in half.

3. Add the carrots and onions to the potatoes. Add salt to taste and bring to the boil. Boil 10 minutes and drain.

4. Add the butter to a skillet and, when quite hot but not brown, add the vegetables. Cook over relatively high heat, shaking the skillet and stirring the vegetables. Add the mushrooms and sprinkle with salt and pepper. Continue cooking, shaking the skillet and stirring, about 7 or 8 minutes.

Yield: Four servings.

ALTHOUGH I HAVE BEEN IN THE UNITED STATES for more than thirty years, one thing that is a constant source of wonder is the number of people who tell me that they had never known the flavor of tarragon during their childhood. In most home gardens in France, it is as common as parsley and chives. As a child I grew up eating omelets aux fines herbes, which always contained tarragon, and also enjoyed tarragon-flavored roasts and a variety of mayonnaise dressings with tarragon. One of the best-known (and one of the best) tarragon-flavored dishes is chicken with tarragon, which comes in many versions.

Actually it is a quickly and simply made dish that contains only six major ingredients, one of which is white wine used to "deglaze" the pan once the chicken is cooked. And a bit of water to dilute the concentrated pan juices destined to be served as a sauce.

Rice is a natural accompaniment for this dish and that could be cooked according to package directions (although it is preferable to cut down on the water recommended by most packagers).

Another excellent seasonal accompaniment for chicken with tarragon is a simply made dish of zucchini cooked with olive oil and lemon. The important thing about this dish is the haste with which it is cooked. You must avoid cooking the zucchini until it becomes soft; it must retain a slightly crunchy "bite" to keep its character.

Poulet à l'Estragon
(Chicken with tarragon)

1 2- to 2½-pound chicken,
  split in half as for broiling
  Salt and freshly ground
  pepper to taste
2 tablespoons butter
2 tablespoons finely chopped
  shallots

2 teaspoons finely chopped
  fresh tarragon, or 1
  teaspoon dried tarragon
½ cup dry white wine
¼ cup water

1. If the backbone is still attached to one of the chicken halves, hack it away or have this done by the butcher at the time of purchase. This will hasten the cooking. Reserve the backbone. Also, it is best to sever the joint that connects the thigh bones with the legs. Do not cut through. Leave the thighs and legs otherwise attached.

2. Sprinkle the chicken with salt and pepper.

3. Melt the butter in a heavy skillet large enough to hold the whole chicken. Add the chicken skin side down. Surround it with the gizzard, liver, heart, neck, and backbone.

4. Cook about 10 minutes, or until golden brown on the skin side, and turn. Cook about 5 minutes. Remove the chicken briefly.

5. Add the shallots to the skillet and cook briefly. Add the tarragon and wine. Cook, stirring to dissolve the brown particles that cling to the bottom of the skillet. Stir in the water.

6. Return the chicken to the skillet skin side up and cover. Cook about 15 minutes. Continue cooking, basting often, about 5 minutes longer, or until the chicken is thoroughly tender and nicely glazed.

Yield: Four servings.

[61]

Courgettes au Citron
(Zucchini with oil and lemon)

2 or 3 zucchini, about 1¼
  pounds
3 tablespoons olive oil

Salt and freshly ground
  pepper to taste
Juice of ½ lemon

1. Trim off the ends of the zucchini. If large, quarter them and cut each quarter into 2-inch lengths. If smaller, cut them in half and cut each half into 2-inch lengths.

2. Heat the olive oil in a skillet and add the zucchini and salt and pepper. Cook, shaking the skillet and stirring the vegetable around, until it starts to take on color.

3. Add the lemon juice and cover. Cook about 3 minutes. When ready, the vegetable should be crisp.

Yield: Four servings.

THERE IS A COMMON BELIEF THAT MOST OF THE traditional and classic dishes of French cooking require hours and days of preparation to bring about their ultimate goodness, but this is, in hundreds of cases, totally fallacious. One of the great and best-known dishes in French culture (actually it is more a specialty of the Anjou region than any other) is a fricassée of chicken or veal.

Basically a fricassée consists of cooking chicken or veal in butter while browning it very lightly, if at all. A touch of onions and mushrooms is cooked with the chicken before the addition of cream. When the dish was recently prepared in my kitchen, a few sprigs of fresh tarragon were added to give it a different turn of flavor and it is an excellent combination. A touch of dried tarragon could be effectively substituted for the fresh herb.

The word *fricasser* has a few interesting uses, incidentally, in the French language. You can *fricasser* a fortune, which is to say, squander it. Copious kissing is sometimes referred to as a "fricassée de museaux" or a fricassée of cheeks. And a scandalous, poorly written article or pot-boiler is called a fricassée.

In the kitchen, the total cooking time for a well-made fricassée of chicken for a party of four is less than half an hour. And the use of the word party is deliberate. This is the sort of dish you could serve with pleasure to a special and friendly gathering.

A simple dish of rice and a salad would serve well with this meal. If, however, you wanted to serve a platter of rice with a bit of difference, you might offer your guests a rice that is both flavored and colored with a small spoonful of turmeric.

To plan such a menu, it would be best to start the preparation with the cooking of the chicken. When it is put on for its final simmering, you should start the rice. Incidentally, if the fricassée is not served the moment it is ready, little will be lost if it is set aside briefly and reheated.

Fricassée de Poulet à l'Estragon
(Fricassée of chicken with tarragon)

1 3½-pound chicken, cut into serving pieces
Salt and freshly ground pepper to taste
3 tablespoons butter
2 tablespoons flour
⅓ cup finely chopped onion
1 small clove garlic, finely minced
5 sprigs fresh tarragon with leaves and stems, or 1 tablespoon dried tarragon
1 carrot, scraped, quartered, and cut into 1-inch lengths
¼ pound mushrooms, rinsed and drained
1½ cups water
1 cup heavy cream
1 tablespoon finely chopped fresh tarragon, or 1 teaspoon dried tarragon

1. Sprinkle the chicken with salt and pepper.

2. Melt the butter in a heavy skillet large enough to hold the chicken in one layer. Cook the chicken pieces, turning occasionally, without browning them. After about 5 minutes, add the chopped onion, garlic, and tarragon sprigs.

3. Sprinkle with flour, stirring to distribute the flour evenly. Add the carrot, mushrooms, and water. Cover and cook about 15 to 20 minutes.

4. Remove the chicken pieces to a serving dish and keep them warm. Remove the tarragon sprigs if they are used. Let the sauce cook down, stirring often, about 5 minutes.

5. Add the cream and salt and pepper to taste. Simmer about 3 minutes. Stir in the chopped tarragon and pour the sauce over the chicken. Serve with rice.

Yield: Four servings.

Riz au Tumerique
(Turmeric rice)

2 tablespoons butter
2 tablespoons finely minced
  onion
1 small clove garlic, finely
  minced

1 cup rice
1 tablespoon powdered
  turmeric
1½ cups chicken broth
1 bay leaf

1. Melt half the butter in a saucepan and add the onion and garlic. Cook until wilted and add the rice and turmeric. Stir to coat the rice.

2. Add the broth and bay leaf. Cover and bring to the boil. Cook exactly 17 minutes. Uncover and stir in the remaining tablespoon of butter.

Yield: Four servings.

ONE OF THE CLUES TO FIRST-CLASS QUICK OR 60-minute cooking—or any other successful cookery for that matter—is logic and organization. A case in point is the main dish outlined below: Cornish game hen bonne femme, an American bird cooked in a traditional French manner. It has, by the way, all the components necessary for a main course—chicken, potatoes, and mushrooms.

As far as organization is concerned, if you read through the recipe—and you should read through recipes before you start to cook—you will discover that the cooking of the dish is divided into two parts. The Cornish hens are baked for twenty minutes. During this period potatoes and mushrooms are cooked in a bit of butter. These two operations could and should occur simultaneously to diminish the total cooking time.

Incidentally, this dish brings up another interesting point: Can one say with authenticity exactly how many a particular dish will serve? The answer is, not really. Who are the guests and what is the nature of their appetites? When this recipe was tested, three people at the table were content to dine on half a bird each. A fourth devoured a whole bird. To arrive at the number of servings in this case you have to estimate the appetites of those you are feeding. Thus, the following recipe may serve as many as eight light eaters, or suffice for only four very hungry guests.

Cornish game hens bonne femme (the name means "good wife" and implies that the dish is bourgeois in concept) would go very well with nothing more than a tossed green salad and purchased first-quality ice cream or fresh fruit with cheese.

Cornish Game Hens Bonne Femme
(Roast game hens with potatoes and mushrooms)

4 Cornish game hens, about 1
pound each
Salt and freshly ground
pepper to taste
4 tablespoons butter
1 onion, cut into quarters, or
8 very small peeled white
onions

¾ pound potatoes
¼ pound mushrooms, about 8
¼ cup water
½ teaspoon chopped rosemary,
fresh or dried

1. Preheat the oven to 425 degrees.

2. Rub the game hens inside and out with salt and pepper. Truss them, if desired. (It helps them to hold their shape.) Place them breast side down in a buttered heatproof baking dish and dot with 2 tablespoons of the butter. Scatter the gizzards and necks around the hens. Reserve the livers. Add the quartered onion or onions and place the dish over a low flame on top of the stove. This is done only to expedite the cooking time in the oven, and to get the baking dish hot. Place in oven and bake 20 minutes.

3. Meanwhile, peel the potatoes and cut them into ½-inch cubes. Drop them into cold water in a saucepan. Bring to the boil.

4. As the potatoes come to the boil, rinse the mushrooms and pat them dry. Cut them into quarters and set aside.

5. When the potatoes reach the boil, drain them. Melt the remaining 2 tablespoons of butter in a skillet and add the potatoes. Cook, shaking the skillet and tossing the potatoes so that they brown evenly, about 5 minutes. When lightly brown, add the mushrooms and salt and pepper to taste. Cook about 10 minutes, tossing and shaking the skillet.

[67]

6. At this point the hens should have completed their first 20 minutes of cooking. Turn the hens on their backs. Sprinkle the livers with salt and pepper and add them to the baking dish. Continue baking about 10 minutes.

7. Scatter the potatoes and mushrooms around the hens and continue cooking about 15 minutes, basting often. Remove the hens. Lift them up and let the cavities drain before they are removed. Add the water and rosemary to the vegetables in the pan. Bring to the boil on top of the stove, stirring. The hens may be served whole or cut in half. Serve the mushrooms and potatoes and the pan sauce with the hens.

Yield: Four to eight servings.

FOR ANYONE WHO CARES ABOUT NEW EXPERI-
ences in eating, one of the more obvious pleasures of
travel is the sampling of dishes not altogether common
in one's own kitchen or milieu. On a trip to Italy, particularly in
Tuscany, we dined several times on various birds stuffed with a
blend of prosciutto and rosemary, a most agreeable combination
of flavors and certainly not common in the French repertory.

We had a picnic in the company of friends who contributed
their share of home-cooked dishes. One of the best was cold
roast quail with rosemary and prosciutto. Cooked ham of the do-
mestic sort could certainly be substituted, but the filling would
lose part of its full, assertive taste.

Sometimes the stuffings are made with pieces of prosciutto
rolled around sprigs of rosemary; sometimes the two are chopped
together. The combination makes a fine filling for Cornish game
hens. The results are pleasant to say the least.

One of the best accompaniments for the dish is a simply made
rice baked with the livers of the game hens and chopped mushrooms.

For accounting purposes, let it be said that game hens stuffed
with prosciutto and rosemary is one of those deadline dishes
when you play the game of 60-minute gourmet. It is, indeed,
possible to prepare and cook the dish in an hour, but you won't
have many seconds to spare when the roast birds and the rice are
cooked and ready to serve.

The birds require about 45 minutes cooking time, the rice
about 20 minutes or less. Therefore, you should start the chickens and get them into the oven before you turn to cook the rice.

Cornish Game Hens with Prosciutto

4 Cornish game hens, about 1 pound each

¼ pound prosciutto or other ham

2 teaspoons dried rosemary leaves

Salt and freshly ground pepper to taste

4 tablespoons butter

4 thin slices fatback

¼ cup chicken broth

1. Preheat the oven to 425 degrees.

2. Set aside the hens' gizzards, necks, hearts, and livers. The livers will be used for a rice dish to accompany the birds.

3. Chop the prosciutto and rosemary. The mixture should be coarsely chopped. Add pepper and blend. Stuff the cavity of each bird with equal portions of the mixture. Truss the hens with string. Sprinkle the birds with salt and pepper to taste.

4. Rub a metal baking dish with 1 tablespoon of the butter. Arrange the birds on their backs in the baking dish. Dot each with the remaining butter. Place one slice of fatback over each bird to cover. Scatter the necks, gizzards, and hearts around the birds. Place the dish on top of the stove and heat until the butter is sizzling.

5. Place the dish in the oven and bake 15 minutes.

6. Remove the pieces of fatback, but set them aside, and turn the chickens on their sides. Bake 15 minutes, basting occasionally.

7. Turn the chickens to their other sides and cook, basting occasionally, 10 minutes longer.

8. Turn the birds on their backs and put the slices of fatback over the birds again and bake 5 minutes longer, basting often.

9. Remove the baking dish from the oven and tilt it. Skim off and discard most of the surface fat from the pan liquid. Add the chicken broth and bring to the boil, basting all the while.

10. Untruss the hens and serve, if desired, each bird with one piece of fatback and the pan gravy. Serve with rice.

Yield: Four servings.

Foies de Volaille et Champignons au Riz
(Rice with liver and mushrooms)

2 tablespoons butter
¼ cup finely chopped onion
¼ pound fresh mushrooms, cut into small cubes, about 1½ cups
Salt and freshly ground pepper to taste

1 cup raw rice
4 livers from the Cornish game hens, chopped, about ¼ cup
1⅓ cups chicken broth

1. Preheat the oven to 425 degrees.
2. Melt half the butter in a saucepan and add the onion. Cook, stirring occasionally, until wilted. Add the mushrooms and cook, stirring, about 3 minutes. Add salt and pepper to taste. Add the rice and stir.
3. Add the broth and bring to the boil. Cover closely and place the saucepan in the oven. Bake 17 minutes.
4. Remove and fluff the rice and mushrooms. Melt the remaining tablespoon of butter in a skillet and when quite hot, add the chopped livers and salt and pepper to taste. Cook about 45 seconds. Scrape the liver and butter into the rice and toss to blend.

Yield: Four servings.

THE FAME OF LUXURY RESTAURANTS RESTS SEcurely on sauces and bases made with costly ingredients. And while these may have required hours, even days, of simmering, sieving, and subsequent preparation, there are scores of exceptions.

One exception, a dish that is easily made, is molded rice pilaf stuffed with sautéed chicken livers and served with a tomato and mushroom sauce. Start with the rice. As it cooks, the sauce should be put on to cook. The livers should be cooked quickly at the last minute. A commendable second course is a salad of broccoli and avocado.

Pilaf Foies de Volaille
(Chicken liver pilaf with tomato and mushroom sauce)

---

3 tablespoons butter
2 tablespoons finely chopped onion
1 cup Carolina rice
1½ cups chicken broth
Salt and freshly ground pepper to taste
½ bay leaf

1 sprig thyme or ½ teaspoon dried thyme
1 sprig parsley
2 dashes Tabasco sauce
1 pound chicken livers
½ cup vegetable, peanut, or corn oil
2½ cups tomato and mushroom sauce (see recipe)

1. Preheat the oven to 450 degrees.
2. Melt 1 tablespoon of the butter in a small casserole and add the onion. Cook, stirring, until wilted. Add the rice and stir briefly. Add the broth, salt, pepper, bay leaf, thyme, parsley, and Tabasco and bring to the boil.
3. Cover and place the dish in the oven. Bake exactly 17 min-

utes and remove from the oven. Remove the bay leaf, parsley, and thyme and stir in a tablespoon of butter. Set aside, covered.

4. As the rice cooks, prepare the chicken livers. Trim off any tough veins. Quarter the chicken livers and set them aside.

5. Heat half the oil in a skillet, and, when it is hot and almost smoking, add half the chicken livers. Sprinkle with salt and pepper. Cook quickly, tossing and shaking the skillet and turning the livers so they cook evenly. Take care not to overcook the livers. Drain quickly in a sieve.

6. Heat the remaining oil, and, when it is very hot, add the remaining livers and salt and pepper. Cook quickly, as before, and drain.

7. Wipe out the skillet and add the remaining tablespoon of butter. Add all the livers and toss quickly, about 30 seconds or so. Set aside.

8. Butter a 3-cup mold and add about one third of the rice. Using a metal spoon, press the rice against the bottom and sides of the mold, leaving a cavity in the center to hold most of the livers. Add about three quarters of the livers, and spoon about ½ cup tomato sauce over them. Cover with the remaining rice. Cover with a piece of buttered wax paper and press down compactly with the fingers to mold the ingredients firmly. Remove the wax paper. Invert the mold onto a plate. Carefully lift up the mold, leaving the mound of rice on the plate. Arrange the remaining livers around the rice, and spoon a little hot tomato sauce over. Serve the remaining sauce on the side.

Yield: Four servings.

Sauce aux Tomates et Champignons
(Tomato and mushroom sauce)

4 medium-size mushrooms, about ¼ pound
1 tablespoon butter
2 tablespoons finely chopped onion
1 teaspoon finely minced garlic
Salt and freshly ground pepper to taste
2 cups canned tomatoes with tomato paste
½ teaspoon chopped rosemary
¼ cup chicken broth

1. Thinly slice the mushrooms. There should be about 1½ cups.

2. Melt the butter and add the mushrooms, onion, and garlic. Sprinkle with salt and pepper and cook, stirring, about 5 minutes.

3. Add the tomatoes, rosemary, and chicken broth. Season with salt and pepper and simmer, stirring occasionally, about 10 minutes.

Yield: About two-and-a-half cups.

Salade de Brocoli et Poires d'Avocat
(Broccoli and avocado salad)

1 small bunch broccoli
Salt
1 large avocado
Juice of ½ lemon
1 teaspoon prepared mustard, such as Dijon or Düsseldorf
2 tablespoons grapefruit juice (or use lemon juice to taste)
3 tablespoons olive oil
Freshly ground pepper to taste

1. Cut the broccoli tops into "flowerets." If the pieces are

quite large, split them at the bottom and cut in half. Rinse and drain. Use the coarse or tough stems for soups or other uses.

2. Drop the broccoli pieces into boiling salted water and drain. Run briefly under cold water and drain again. Chill.

3. Cut the avocado in half. Peel each half and remove the pit. Cut each half into 8 lengthwise strips. Sprinkle with the lemon juice to prevent discoloration. Arrange alternate pieces of broccoli and avocado on each of 4 serving plates.

4. Blend the remaining ingredients and pour over the broccoli and avocado. Serve immediately.

Yield: Four servings.

THERE ARE SOME FOODS WHOSE SUCCESS AT table depends to a great extent on how rapidly they are cooked. These are foods that must be seared quickly, over very high heat, and tossed and stirred simultaneously, so they cook evenly all over.

Chicken livers, one of the best bargains in any meat counter, are another of those foods whose excellence at table depends on such a technique.

The role of chicken livers in this country seems, unfortunately, limited. They are much coveted for appetizers, such as chopped chicken livers and chicken liver pâtés, and they are widely accepted in omelets and with shirred eggs, but in many homes they are still an oddity.

The fact is that chicken livers adapt well to many seasonings and methods of cookery. They are marvelous in risottos and rice pilafs. Chicken livers go well with sage, and we recently devised a dish that includes not only that herb but also a touch of Cognac.

With the livers, I would propose a noodle dish from my childhood. Although I am a native of Burgundy, my mother often prepared noodles Alsatian style. These noodles are tossed with what is otherwise known as polonaise topping—bread crumbs, sieved egg, and parsley cooked rapidly in butter. Just how a Polish topping found its way onto a dish called Alsatian style is anybody's guess.

As usual, it would be wise to prepare and assemble all the ingredients for the chicken livers and noodles before starting to cook.

Foies de Volaille à la Sauge

(Chicken livers with sage)

4 tablespoons butter
¾ cup finely chopped onion
1 pound chicken livers
¼ cup peanut, vegetable, or
    corn oil

Salt and freshly ground
    pepper to taste
1 teaspoon ground sage, more
    or less to taste
2 tablespoons Cognac

1. Melt 2 tablespoons of the butter in a saucepan and add the onion. Toss and stir, then cover. Cook 10 minutes without browning. The onions should be quite soft.

2. Pick over the chicken livers and remove any tough veins. Quarter the livers.

3. Heat the oil in a skillet, and, when it is quite hot, add the livers. Sprinkle with salt and pepper and cook over high heat 2 to 3 minutes, shaking the skillet and tossing the livers so that they cook on all sides. Drain in a sieve.

4. Melt the remaining 2 tablespoons of butter in a skillet and, when it is very hot, add the livers and onions. Sprinkle with sage and cook, stirring, about 3 or 4 minutes. Sprinkle with the Cognac and ignite it. Serve piping hot with noodles.

Yield: Four servings.

Nouilles à l'Alsacienne
(Noodles with crumb and egg topping)

½ pound fine noodles
Salt to taste
5 tablespoons butter
Freshly ground pepper to taste

1 hard-cooked egg, peeled and put through a fine sieve
½ cup fine, fresh bread crumbs
¼ cup finely chopped parsley

1. Cook the noodles in salted water until tender. Drain and add 1 tablespoon of butter and salt and pepper to taste. Toss.

2. Quickly add the remaining 4 tablespoons of butter to a skillet, and, when it is hot and bubbling, add the egg and bread crumbs. Cook shaking the skillet and stirring, over high heat about 30 seconds. Add the parsley. Toss and pour over the noodles. Toss and serve.

Yield: Four servings.

THERE IS, OF COURSE, A GOOD DEAL OF DIFFER-
ence between food preparation in a professional kitchen
and that in a home. One of the most obvious reasons
is the number of hands and the number of hours that can be
employed in well-staffed restaurants in the preparation of what
are known in French as *les fonds de cuisine* or the bases for
cookery. These would include an assortment, some of which require hours of simmering, the tedious task of putting the sauces
through sieves, and so on.

There was a time, I think, when professional chefs were reluc-
tant to offer recipes to the public because they knew that with
rare exceptions those bases of cookery would not be used in the
home kitchen. Many chefs now realize that there are compro-
mises that can be made so that a finished product in the home,
while not made according to the "classic" pattern, may yield results that duplicate the professionally prepared dish to an admirable degree by using short cuts.

One of the best sauces in a professional kitchen is known as a
sauce madère or Madeira wine sauce. Traditionally, it is made
with one of the long-simmered brown sauces. You will find if
you prepare the chicken livers in the Madeira wine sauce outlined here, that an eminently edible variation of that sauce can
be made with mushrooms, a touch of tomato paste, chicken
broth, and, of course, Madeira. For a thickening, however, use
arrowroot instead of flour (and if you don't have any arrowroot,
use cornstarch). Flour would make the sauce starchy and heavy.

One more word of caution: Although the recipe has numerous
steps, the making of the dish is not at all complicated. The total
cooking time for the dish is half an hour or less and much of
that time is used for simmering the sauce. Plain rice or noodles
with one chopped fresh herb or another make an ideal accompaniment. Parsley is indicated here, but chopped fresh dill would
also be excellent.

Foies de Volaille et Champignons

(Chicken livers and mushrooms in Madeira wine sauce)

The sauce:
½ pound fresh mushrooms
2 tablespoons butter
Salt and freshly ground
pepper to taste
2 tablespoons finely chopped
shallots
⅓ cup plus 1 tablespoon
Madeira wine
1 cup chicken broth
2 teaspoons tomato paste

1 teaspoon arrowroot or
cornstarch

The livers:
2 pounds very fresh chicken
livers
4 tablespoons flour
Salt and freshly ground
pepper to taste
½ cup peanut, vegetable, or
corn oil
2 tablespoons butter

1. Thinly slice the mushrooms. There should be about 3 cups.

2. Melt the butter in a skillet and add the mushrooms and cook, stirring and shaking the skillet, until wilted. Add salt and pepper to taste. Cook about 5 minutes. Add the shallots and toss.

3. Add the ⅓ cup of Madeira wine and cook about 1 minute. Add the broth. Cook about 2 minutes and add the tomato paste. Simmer about 5 minutes.

4. Blend the arrowroot with the remaining tablespoon of Madeira wine and add it, stirring. Simmer 10 minutes, stirring occasionally. Set the sauce aside briefly.

5. Meanwhile, put the livers, one at a time, on a flat surface and trim and cut away every trace of thread-like veins and connecting tissues.

6. Blend the flour with salt and pepper. Coat the chicken livers in the seasoned flour.

7. Heat ¼ cup of the oil in a heavy skillet. When it is hot but

not smoking, add half the livers. Cook over high heat, shaking the skillet and turning the livers. Cook quickly so that the livers are slightly crisp on the outside. Cook about 1½ to 2 minutes in all.

8. Pour the livers and oil in which they cooked into a colander to drain well. Pour the cooked livers into the sauce and stir to coat.

9. To the skillet add the remaining ¼ cup of oil. Add the remaining livers. Cook as before until crisp outside. Drain and add to the first batch. Stir in the 2 tablespoons butter. Heat and serve with buttered noodles with parsley or with rice.

Yield: Four servings.

Nouilles Persillées
(Noodles with parsley)

½ pound wide or medium
  noodles
Salt to taste
2 tablespoons butter

Freshly ground pepper to
  taste
1 tablespoon chopped parsley

1. Cook the noodles in boiling salted water to cover.
2. Drain well and return to the kettle. Add the butter and salt and pepper to taste and toss. Add the parsley and serve hot.

Yield: Four servings.

4. Cook over high heat, shaking the pan and stirring with a fork held parallel to the bottom of the pan. When the eggs start to set, tilt the omelet pan and tap it against the stove burner. This should make the omelet slide about one inch in the direction away from the handle. This will "curve" the omelet.

5. Add a spoonful or so of the omelet filling to the center.

6. Using the fork, carefully and neatly fold the part of the omelet nearest the hand over the filling to partially enclose it.

7. Shift the handle of the omelet pan to the left hand. Hold a plate in the right. Tilt the pan so that the omelet is inverted onto the center of the plate. Garnish each end of the omelet with another small portion of the filling.

Yield: Four omelets.

Poulet Poché
(Poached chicken)

¾ pound skinless, boneless
   chicken breasts
1 cup water
   Salt to taste
1 parsley sprig

2 thin slices onion
1 small bay leaf
1 sprig fresh thyme, or ½
   teaspoon dried thyme

Combine all the ingredients in a saucepan and bring to the boil. Cover and simmer 5 minutes. Remove from the heat and let stand until ready to use. Cube the chicken if desired. Reserve the broth.

Yield: About two cups cubed chicken.

Asperges au Beurre de Muscade
(Asparagus with nutmeg butter)

12 to 16 fresh asparagus spears
  Salt to taste
3 tablespoons butter

Juice of ½ lemon
⅛ teaspoon freshly grated
  nutmeg

1. Line up the asparagus side by side on a flat surface. Using a heavy knife, cut off the tough bottoms of the asparagus. Discard the bottoms.

2. Using a swivel-bladed vegetable scraper, scrape the sides of the asparagus, starting about 2 inches from the tips. Rinse and drain if necessary.

3. Bring enough water to the boil in a skillet to cover the asparagus when added. Add salt to taste. Cook 2 to 4 minutes, depending on the size of the asparagus. Do not overcook; they will continue to cook even when drained.

4. Meanwhile, melt the butter in a saucepan. Add the lemon juice, salt, pepper, and nutmeg. Remove the saucepan from the heat and swirl the sauce around to blend it. Pour over the asparagus and serve.

Yield: Four servings.

OMELETS ARE ONE OF THE SIMPLEST DISHES IN the world to make. All it takes is a decent pan, fresh eggs, and a good dash of self-confidence.

I outlined earlier, in some detail, the steps for making an omelet. Here I have added a list of necessary equipment, and, for more adventurous cooks, two more of my own favorite omelets.

These are large omelets designed to serve two or more people at a gathering. One of them was a great favorite during the days when I served as chef at Henri Soulé's Pavillon. It is made with creamed chicken, a light tomato sauce, and cheese, and serves four to six.

Another omelet, which also serves four to six, is a classic Spanish omelet, which is to say, it is not folded in the traditional manner, but is a whole, round flat omelet turned out onto a serving dish.

For making an omelet, the utensils include, in addition to the omelet pan, one or more small mixing bowls for eggs; another fork for the butter; warm plates for the omelets. Also a spoon for adding the fillings unless, as in the case of a cheese or herb omelet, the fingers will suffice.

The ingredients for a plain omelet include eggs, salt, and pepper, and, if desired, a bit of cream. Ingredients for a filled omelet include, of course, the fillings, such as grated cheese or mixed herbs, or fillings that are cooked and ready to be added.

Just before you start cooking the omelets, break 3 eggs for each omelet into as many individual bowls as needed for the number of omelets to be made. Add salt and pepper to taste and about 2 teaspoons of heavy cream. You may also beat the eggs to expedite making the omelets.

Omelette Pavillon
(Omelet with chicken, tomato, and cheese)

7 tablespoons butter
3 tablespoons flour
1 cup chicken broth
½ cup heavy cream
3 tablespoons finely chopped
  onion
2 cups peeled, seeded, and
  chopped tomatoes
2 sprigs fresh thyme, or ½
  teaspoon dried thyme
1 bay leaf

Salt and freshly ground
  pepper to taste
1 cup finely cubed cooked
  chicken breast
1 egg yolk
¼ cup grated Swiss, Gruyère,
  or Fontina cheese
10 eggs
3 tablespoons grated
  Parmesan cheese

1. Melt 2 tablespoons of the butter in a saucepan and add the flour. Stir with a wire whisk until blended. Add the chicken broth and cook, stirring vigorously with the whisk. Add the cream and bring to the boil. Simmer about 10 minutes.

2. Meanwhile, melt another tablespoon of the butter in a saucepan and add the onion. Cook stirring, until wilted, and add the tomatoes, thyme, bay leaf, and salt and pepper. Simmer, stirring occasionally, about 10 minutes.

3. Melt another tablespoon of the butter and add the chicken. Cook, stirring about 30 seconds. Add 3 tablespoons of the cream sauce. Bring to the boil and remove from the heat. Set aside.

4. To the remaining cream sauce add the egg yolk and stir to blend. Add salt and pepper to taste and the grated Swiss cheese. Heat, stirring, just until the cheese melts. Set aside.

5. Beat the eggs with salt and pepper. Add 6 tablespoons of the tomato sauce. Melt the remaining 3 tablespoons of butter in an omelet pan or a Teflon skillet and, when it is hot, add the eggs. Cook, stirring, until the omelet is set on the bottom but moist and runny in the center. Spoon creamed chicken down

[87]

the center of the omelet and add the remaining tomato sauce. Quickly turn the omelet out into a baking dish.

6. Spoon the remaining cream sauce over the omelet and sprinkle with grated Parmesan cheese. Run the dish under the broiler until golden brown.

Yield: Four to six servings.

Omelette Espagnole
(Spanish omelet)

---

2 or 3 sweet red or green peppers	1 tablespoon finely minced garlic
2 or 3 Bermuda onions	1 cup peeled, chopped tomatoes
2 tablespoons olive oil Salt and freshly ground pepper to taste	10 eggs
	3 tablespoons butter Vinegar, optional

1. Core and seed the peppers. Cut the peppers into very fine julienne strips. There should be about 2 cups.

2. Peel the onions and cut them in half. Thinly slice the onions. There should be about 2 cups.

3. Heat the oil in a saucepan and add the onions and peppers. Season with salt and pepper and cook briskly, stirring, about 5 minutes. Add the garlic and tomatoes and cook 15 minutes.

4. Beat the eggs until frothy and add salt and pepper. Add 1¼ cups of the tomato sauce and beat lightly

5. Melt the butter in an omelet pan or in a Teflon skillet and add the egg mixture. Cook, shaking the pan and stirring with a fork. Let the omelet set on the bottom. The omelet should remain moist and runny in the center. When cooked, place a large

serving plate over the pan and quickly invert the omelet onto the plate. Spoon the remaining tomato sauce over the center of the omelet as a garnish. This omelet is normally served hot, but it is good cold. In Burgundy, it is frequently eaten with a dash of vinegar on each serving.

Yield: Four to six servings.

IT HAS BEEN NOTED THAT AN EGG, MORE THAN any other food, is probably the ultimate item for a hastily made and excellent main course. Given a few additional and inspired ingredients, such as spinach, sour cream, mushrooms, ratatouille (freshly made or leftover), ham, cheese, and so on, an egg can quickly be turned into an omelet for a feast.

Omelets, of course, take many forms. The classic and best known is the folded version, which must be made in seconds or it will become tough and rubbery. Then there is a flat omelet, with its various ingredients, which is cooked until set and served without folding.

In France, two basic methods are taught for making an omelet—à la Francesa, which is rolled and oval-shaped, and à la Espanola, which is flat.

In my childhood one of the favorite dishes was a flat omelet, a hearty, delectable preparation made with home-cured ham, cut into small cubes, and thinly sliced potatoes with onions cooked in oil until crisp. The ham and seasonings were added and the eggs cooked, stirring and lifting gently with a spatula, until set. It was all turned out onto a platter and served sliced. If any of this omelet was left over, it was often saved and served cold for outings in the country.

This makes for a substantial main course and an excellent accompaniment is quickly cooked asparagus served with a vinaigrette sauce. The significant thing to remember in making the flat omelet is to use a smooth-surfaced pan so that the omelet does not stick when transferred to a platter.

Omelette Paysanne
(A flat potato and ham omelet)

2 Idaho potatoes, about ¾ pound

3 tablespoons peanut, vegetable, or corn oil
Salt and freshly ground pepper to taste

½ cup halved, very thinly sliced onion

1 cup cooked ham, cut into ½-inch dice

4 teaspoons butter

10 eggs

2 tablespoons finely chopped parsley

1 teaspoon finely chopped tarragon

2 teaspoons finely chopped chives

1. Peel the potatoes and slice them as thinly as possible. Drop the slices into cold water to prevent discoloration. Drain and pat dry.

2. Heat a skillet and add the oil. When it is very hot, add the potatoes. Do not break the slices. Sprinkle with salt and pepper.

3. Cook, making sure the potatoes do not stick. Brown well about 10 minutes and add the onion. Continue cooking about 1 minute. Add the ham and dot with 3 teaspoons of the butter. Shake the skillet and gently turn over the ingredients so that they cook evenly.

4. Beat the eggs with a wire whisk. Add salt, pepper, and herbs. Pour the eggs over the ham and potato mixture.

5. Gently stir the mixture from the bottom, allowing the egg mixture to flow to the bottom. Cook over high heat. Lift up the edges of the omelet and let the remaining butter flow beneath the omelet. Shake the skillet to make certain the omelet is loose.

6. Invert a large plate over the skillet and quickly invert the skillet, letting the omelet fall into the plate. This omelet is best served hot, but it is also delicious at room temperature.

Yield: Four servings.

Asperges Vinaigrette
(Asparagus vinaigrette)

24 fresh asparagus spears
Salt to taste
1½ teaspoons wine vinegar
1½ teaspoons imported
    mustard, preferably Dijon
    or Düsseldorf

Freshly ground pepper to
    taste
¼ cup peanut, vegetable, or
    corn oil
1½ teaspoons finely chopped
    shallots or green onions
1½ teaspoons finely chopped
    parsley

1. Use a potato peeler and scrape the asparagus spears to within about 2 inches of the top. Cut off and discard the tough bottoms of the spears to make their lengths uniform. Place them in a skillet and add cold water to cover and salt. Bring to the boil and simmer until tender yet firm, al dente, so to speak.

2. Place the vinegar, mustard, and salt and pepper to taste in a mixing bowl and stir rapidly with a wire whisk. Gradually add the oil, stirring constantly. Stir in the shallots.

3. Drain the asparagus spears well while they are still hot. Arrange 6 spears on each of 4 serving dishes. Spoon the sauce over the tops of the asparagus, which should be lukewarm or at room temperature. Sprinkle the parsley over the tips and serve.

Yield: Four servings.

ONE OF THE ODDEST COOKING MYTHS, MORE prevalent in this country than in France, is the notion that a soufflé is the most fragile of foods. And, therefore, one of the most difficult to prepare. There seems to be a belief that it will collapse like a pierced balloon if the oven door is opened or if there is a jarring of the oven rack.

That is nonsense and so is that old wives' tale that a soufflé must be served at some magic moment of its readiness. The fact is that tastes in texture vary where soufflés are concerned. I happen to like soufflés that are quite moist (although cooked) in the center. There are those who prefer a "drier" interior texture, a point that comes about through prolonged cooking. While it is true that a soufflé must be taken from the oven and served immediately (preferably within seconds), a soufflé can remain in the oven for 5 minutes or so between the moment when it could be pronounced "ready to serve" and the time when it must be taken from the oven or be overcooked.

The basics of making a soufflé are simple. Take a cheese soufflé, for example, the best known and probably the best liked of all main-course soufflés. It consists simply of making a simple white sauce to which cubed or grated cheese is added. Egg yolks (plus cornstarch mixed with water) are added to give it body. And stiffly beaten egg whites are folded in. This is perhaps the "tricky" part for most home cooks. The best method for folding in the whites is as follows:

Stir in half the beaten whites with a whisk. Fold in the remaining egg whites and pour into a prepared dish. Bake and serve.

Soufflés have many uses in menu planning, of course. They can be served as a first course, main course, or dessert. The one I outline here—a cheese soufflé—can be served by itself as a first course or main course. To some tastes it may seem insubstantial as a main course; therefore, I have offered it along with ham in a cream sauce to be served with the soufflé. After the soufflé is put in the oven, there is ample time to prepare the ham in cream sauce. Serve with a mixed green salad and a crusty loaf of bread.

Soufflé au Fromage
(Cheese soufflé)

¼ pound Swiss or, preferably, Gruyère cheese
2 cups milk
3 tablespoons plus 2 teaspoons butter
6 large eggs
4 tablespoons flour

Salt and freshly ground pepper to taste
⅛ teaspoon freshly grated nutmeg
Pinch of cayenne pepper
2 teaspoons cornstarch
1 tablespoon water
¼ cup freshly grated Parmesan cheese

1. Preheat the oven to 375 degrees.

2. Grate the cheese or cut it into tiny cubes. There should be about ¾ cup. Set aside.

3. Bring the milk just to the boil without boiling.

4. Use 2 teaspoons of butter to grease a 5-cup soufflé dish. Set the dish aside.

5. Separate the egg yolks and whites. Put the whites into a mixing bowl.

6. Melt 3 tablespoons of the butter in a saucepan. Add the flour, stirring with a wire whisk. When blended and smooth, add the hot milk, stirring rapidly with the whisk. Add the salt, pepper, nutmeg, and cayenne and cook, stirring rapidly, about 5 minutes.

7. Blend the cornstarch and water and add it, stirring briskly.

8. Remove from the heat and add the yolks, stirring rapidly. Pour and scrape the mixture into a large mixing bowl. Add the grated Parmesan cheese. Stir to blend.

[94]

9. Beat the whites until stiff. Add half the whites to the sauce and fold them in with the whisk. Add the remaining whites and grated or cubed cheese. Fold this in with a plastic or rubber spatula. Fold over and around, top to bottom, until the whites are incorporated.

10. Pour and scrape the soufflé mixture into the prepared dish. Place in the oven and bake 20 minutes. Serve, if desired, with the ham in cream sauce.

Yield: Four servings.

Jambon à la Crème
(Ham in cream sauce)

½ pound boiled ham in one
    piece
2 tablespoons plus 1 teaspoon
    butter
2 tablespoons flour
1 cup milk

⅛ teaspoon freshly grated
    nutmeg
Salt and freshly ground
    pepper to taste
1 tablespoon finely chopped
    shallots
3 tablespoons dry sherry wine

1. Cut the ham into ½-inch or slightly smaller cubes. There should be slightly more than 2½ cups. Set aside.

2. Melt 2 tablespoons of the butter in a saucepan and add the flour, stirring with a wire whisk. When the flour and butter are blended, add the milk, stirring rapidly with the whisk. Add the nutmeg and salt and pepper. Let cool, stirring occasionally, about 5 minutes.

3. Meanwhile, melt the 1 teaspoon of butter and add the ham. Cook briefly, stirring, and add the shallots. Cook and stir briefly. Add the sherry. Heat through.

4. Add the cream sauce and turn off the heat. Serve with cheese soufflé, on toast, or put to any desired use.

Yield: Four servings.

Fish

IT IS MY BELIEF THAT ALMOST EVERY CHEF IN the world could express a preference for the type of cooking he finds more gratifying than any other. The reasons why would be as varied as the dishes he admired as a child, the dishes which personally gratify his own appetite, or the kind of cookery to which he was first subjected as a professional.

I prefer fish cookery to all others, for two reasons. In the ultimate sense, I prefer fish to many meats. Also, I was a *poissonier,* or fish cook, during my formative years in restaurants.

Curiously, in this country at least, home cooks seem to find fish to be the most complicated of foods to cook. It isn't, although more care must be used in preparing it because it can be overcooked in seconds. I have often been asked to give recipes for the basic techniques of cooking fish, and they are included here. In a sense this might be considered a primer for the basic fish dishes, but that by no means implies a lack of sophistication. Some of the simplest dishes can be foods for the gods.

The techniques and recipes offered here include a plain broiled fish in which fish fillets are simply turned in butter, seasoned, and placed under the broiler for from 2 to 8 minutes, with no turning required.

The cooking time will depend on the thickness of the fish. There is also a basic recipe for cooking fish in a skillet. The fish is simply bathed briefly in milk, coated with flour, and cooked hastily over moderately high heat, turning once.

Remember, in any of these, simply choose a fresh fish and take care not to overcook it.

Poisson Grillé
(Plain broiled fish)

---

4 skinless, boneless fish fillets, about 1¼ pounds (flounder, sole, or cod will do)

Salt and freshly ground pepper to taste
2 tablespoons butter
¼ teaspoon paprika

1. Preheat the broiler to high.
2. Sprinkle the fish with salt and pepper to taste. Set aside.
3. Select a heatproof serving dish large enough to hold the fish in one layer and add the butter. Heat under the broiler until the butter melts.
4. Add the fish fillets and turn them in it to coat in the butter. When ready for the broiling, leave the fish pieces skin side down. Hold a small sieve over the fish and add the paprika. Sprinkle the paprika over the fish and place under the broiler, about 5 inches from the source of heat. The cooking time will depend on the thickness of the fish. A very thin fish fillet, such as that of a small flounder, will cook in 2 to 4 minutes. A 1-inch-thick slice of boneless, skinless cod will require 8 minutes.

Yield: Four servings.

Poisson Meunière
(A basic sauté of fish)

4 skinless, boneless fish fillets, about 1¼ pounds (flounder, sole, cod)
Salt and freshly ground pepper to taste
3 tablespoons milk
¼ cup flour

¼ cup peanut, vegetable, or corn oil
4 tablespoons butter
Juice of ½ lemon
4 lemon slices
2 tablespoons finely chopped parsley

1. Sprinkle the fish fillets with salt and pepper to taste.
2. Pour the milk into a flat dish.
3. Dip the fillets in the milk and then dredge them in the flour, shaking to remove any excess.
4. Heat the oil in a skillet large enough to hold the fillets in one layer. Add the pieces of fish and cook about 1½ minutes, or until golden brown on one side. The fish should be cooked over a fairly high or moderately high heat. It must cook fast.
5. Turn the pieces of fish and cook until golden brown on the other side, from 1 to 2 minutes.
6. Transfer the fish to a serving dish and pour off the fat from the skillet.
7. Add the butter to the wiped-out skillet and cook over moderately high heat until the butter is foamy and then starts to brown. Sprinkle the fish with lemon juice and pour the butter over the fish. Garnish each piece of fish with a slice of lemon and chopped parsley.

Yield: Four servings.

IT IS ANOTHER OF THOSE SUPERFICIALLY EVI-
dent facts about hasty cooking—"gourmet" or otherwise
—that fish in general, and fillets of fish in particular are
tailored to the task. Although I grew up in a small town in Burgundy, a good distance from the ocean (about 350 kilometers, as
we reckoned it), we could always buy fresh fish. The fish—there
were great varieties—were shipped in iced barrels and hamp-
ers by train from Boulogne-sur-Mer, a seaport on the English
Channel.

My father and I doted on fresh fish, and I would go with
him—both of us on bicycles—to meet the train when it arrived.
If we were fortunate we would have first choice of the haul—
channel sole, turbot, herring, whiting, and a great variety of
shellfish including mussels and oysters, all depending on the
season.

Both my mother and grandmother were fine fish cooks. They
were not much schooled in the fancy sauces I learned later in
Paris restaurants, but everything they turned out was excellent in
its simplicity.

I am quite certain that in those days my mother never gave a
second thought to how long a dish would take to prepare and
cook. Cooking was simply a part of living, a thing that gave her
pleasure day by day. And although it had nothing to do with
time, one of the dishes I liked best could be conjured up in
much less than an hour.

There was no question of preheating an oven. The stove in my
home served a double purpose. It was fired with wood and char
coal and was used both for cooking and heating the small space
where we lived most of our existence. Our oven, in winter at
least, was always preheated.

When we arrived home with the fish, my father would fillet
them. My mother would roll them like turbans, sprinkle them
with butter, shallots, bread crumbs, and a little white wine and
heavy cream, and 20 minutes later we sat down to dine. With

that dish we always had steamed potatoes and a good loaf of homemade bread. And a nice white Burgundy—in my case watered down, as happened with all Burgundy children.

Filets de Poisson au Four
(Baked fish fillets)

8 skinless, boneless fillets of flounder or sole, about 1¾ pounds
Salt and freshly ground pepper to taste
3 tablespoons butter

4 teaspoons finely chopped shallots
¼ cup dry white wine
¼ cup heavy cream
¼ cup fine fresh bread crumbs
1 tablespoon finely chopped parsley

1. Preheat the oven to 400 degrees.
2. Sprinkle the fish fillets lightly with salt and pepper. Roll each of the fillets compactly.
3. Grease a baking dish large enough to hold the fish rolls in one layer. Use 1 tablespoon of the butter. Sprinkle the bottom of the dish with salt, pepper, and 3 teaspoons of shallots. Arrange the fish rolls over this bed seam side down.
4. Pour wine and cream over the fish.
5. Sprinkle the fish evenly with salt, pepper, bread crumbs, parsley, and the remaining teaspoon of shallots.
6. Melt the remaining 2 tablespoons of butter and pour over all. Place the baking dish in the oven and bake 20 minutes, or until the fish rolls are cooked and the crumbs are lightly browned.

Yield: Four servings.

Pommes de Terre au Paprika
(Paprika potatoes)

1 pound new, red, waxy
potatoes, or 2 large Idaho
potatoes

Salt to taste
1 tablespoon butter
½ teaspoon paprika

1. Peel the potatoes. If they are new potatoes, there should be at least eight. Leave them whole. If they are large Idaho potatoes, quarter them, which is to say cut each potato into four equal-size pieces.

2. Place the potatoes in a saucepan and add water to cover and salt to taste. Bring to the boil and simmer until tender, 15 or 20 minutes, depending on size. Do not overcook.

3. Drain and add the butter and paprika, shaking the saucepan until the potatoes are coated.

Yield: Four servings.

BROILED FOODS, FISH IN PARTICULAR, ARE IDE-ally suited to good but hasty cookery. And yet home cooks seem more perplexed by broiling techniques than almost any other. It's true that broiling may embrace the simplest yet most confusing of cooking procedures. To broil properly, numerous variables are involved—including source of heat, intensity of heat, and the thickness of the food to be cooked.

Here are two recipes for broiled fish, the first a "perfectly" broiled fillet that will have a naturally browned surface. To prepare this dish I often use tilefish, a little-known fish that is becoming increasingly available and popular in this country along the Atlantic Coast. I could also use striped bass, flounder, or whatever.

To aid in browning, the fish—which is placed in a buttered baking dish—should be brushed often with butter as it cooks. For this particular dish I used melted butter with a little anchovy paste for flavor. To prevent the fish from drying out, it is essential that it be cooked under very high heat. In this case the flame is at its highest point.

The fish is best cooked relatively close to the flame or other source of heat—say 2½ to 3 inches away. There is probably less danger of the fish burning than one would think, but mind it carefully as it cooks. Cooking time will depend on the thickness of the fillets. Tilefish fillets, slightly less than an inch thick, require about 12 to 15 minutes to cook. If your fillets are half that size, they should cook in about half that time, given a minute or two one way or the other.

A second method of broiling fish is considered here. In this one, the cook "cheats" a bit and gives the surface of the fish a light dusting with a mixture of bread crumbs and paprika. This, most assuredly, will aid in "browning."

The fillets are placed in a buttered baking dish, then sprinkled with the bread crumb and paprika mixture. The fillets are then placed under a hot broiler, not quite full flame, and they are broiled about 6 inches from the source of heat. In this case, the heat must be slightly less intense than otherwise stipulated and the fish broiled at a greater distance from the source of heat. If the broiler heat is too high or if the crumb-covered food is too close to the heat, the crumbs will burn.

Filets de Poisson Grillés au Beurre d'Anchois
(Broiled fish fillets with anchovy butter)

2 pounds fish fillets, such as tilefish, sea bass, fluke, and so on
5 tablespoons butter

Salt and freshly ground pepper to taste
1 teaspoon anchovy paste
Lemon wedges
Parsley sprigs, optional

1. Preheat the broiler to full heat.
2. Some fillets of fish have a small bone line running the length of the center. If there is, use a sharp knife and cut on both sides of this line to remove and discard it. Cut the fish fillets into 4 to 6 pieces of approximately the same size.
3. Generously butter a baking pan with about 1 tablespoon of butter. Sprinkle with salt and pepper.
4. Arrange the fish pieces over the pan.
5. Melt the remaining 4 tablespoons of butter and stir in the anchovy paste. Brush the top of the fish with some of this.
6. Run the fish under the broiler, about 2½ to 3 inches from the source of heat. As the fish cooks, brush it occasionally with more of the anchovy butter. Cook 12 to 15 minutes. Transfer the fish to a hot platter or hot individual serving dishes. Serve with lemon wedges and, if desired, garnish with parsley sprigs.

Yield: Four servings.

Filets de Poisson Grillés
(Broiled fish fillets)

4 fish fillets, about ½ pound each
8 tablespoons butter
Salt and freshly ground pepper to taste

1 cup fresh bread crumbs
1 teaspoon paprika

1. Preheat the broiler to high. Just before cooking the fish, reduce the broiler heat by a fraction.

2. Select a baking dish just large enough to hold the fish fillets in one layer. Grease the bottom of the dish with 1 tablespoon of the butter. Sprinkle it with salt and pepper.

3. Arrange the fillets skin side down on the dish and sprinkle with salt and pepper to taste.

4. Scatter the bread crumbs on a piece of wax paper. Hold a small sieve over the crumbs. Put the paprika through the sieve and blend the paprika and crumbs. Sprinkle the fish fillets with the crumbs and dribble the remaining butter over all. Broil about 6 inches from the heat until golden brown. Broil 10 minutes.

Yield: Four servings.

LIKE MOST PROFESSIONAL CHEFS, I TEND TO pride myself on the ability to detect the ingredients of almost any dish that is set before me, plus the ability to recreate, in fairly accurate detail, a reproduction of that dish, within the confines of my own kitchen. Perhaps I should qualify that to add that I am speaking of foods of the Western world. Much of the cooking of the Orient is infinitely more complex in some preparations and many of the ingredients are—for better or for worse—foreign to my Western palate.

All that is said to preface a confession. Two or three years ago I was invited into the home of friends to feast on a meal, one of the dishes of which had very fresh flounder as its base. It was a simple dish of broiled fish but the flavor was a bit piquant and there was a golden brown topping. The only two ingredients of which I was absolutely certain were, in addition to the fish and the parsley garnish, the flavor of lemon and mustard.

I must admit that I was a bit flustered, and volunteered the thought that the topping of the fish was perhaps a hollandaise flavored with the mustard. I was both amused and abashed when the hostess—an excellent cook—told me that she had simply smeared the fish with a mustard mayonnaise before putting it under the broiler. That's all there was to it. The fish with its mustard coating had been placed about 3 or 4 inches from the source of heat and allowed to broil for a minute or so until the topping became a golden brown.

This is conceivably the most easily made and quick dish appearing in this book.

Because of the speed with which this dish—it can well serve as a main course—is prepared and cooked, there is ample time to spend on accompanying vegetable. An excellent choice is zucchini, sliced and cooked in a skillet with assorted fresh herbs, if available, including parsley, chives, dill, tarragon, and basil. If the fresh are not available, use a small amount of dried herbs.

Filets de Flet à la Moutarde
(Broiled flounder fillets with mustard)

8 small, skinless, boneless
flounder fillets, about 1
pound
Salt and freshly ground
pepper to taste
1 tablespoon peanut,
vegetable, or corn oil
2 tablespoons mayonnaise,
preferably homemade,
although bottled mayonnaise
may be used

1 tablespoon imported
mustard, such as Dijon or
Düsseldorf
2 teaspoons finely chopped
parsley
4 lemon or lime wedges

1. Preheat the broiler to high.

2. Place the fillet halves on a flat surface. Sprinkle with salt
and pepper and brush with oil.

3. Arrange the fillets on a baking sheet or dish. Blend the
mayonnaise, mustard, and parsley. Brush it evenly over the
fillets.

4. Place the fillets under the broiler, about 3 or 4 inches from
the source of heat. Broil about 1 minute, or until golden brown
on top and the fish is just cooked through. Serve with lemon
wedges.

Yield: Four servings.

Courgettes aux Herbes d'Été

(Zucchini with summer herbs)

1½ pounds zucchini
4 tablespoons olive oil
   Salt and freshly ground
   pepper to taste
2 tablespoons butter
2 teaspoons chopped garlic

1 tablespoon chopped parsley
1 tablespoon chopped chives
1 tablespoon chopped dill
1 teaspoon chopped tarragon
1 tablespoon finely chopped
   fresh basil

1. Rinse the zucchini and pat them dry. Trim off the ends but do not peel. Cut the zucchini into thin slices about ⅛ inch thick. There should be about 6 cups.

2. Heat the oil in a skillet and, when it is quite hot, add the zucchini. Cook over relatively high heat, shaking the skillet, tossing and stirring gently with a spatula to turn the slices. Add salt and pepper to taste. Cook about 5 to 7 minutes. Drain in a sieve. Do not wipe out the skillet.

3. To the skillet add the butter. When melted and hot, return the zucchini. Add the garlic and herbs. Add salt to taste. Toss and serve hot.

Yield: Six servings.

THE COOKING TIME FOR MOST STUFFED DISHES is fairly extended and hard to embrace within the time space of an hour or less. One of the great, easily made and hastily cooked dishes, however, is stuffed sole fillets. In case you wonder, it is true that many fish are sold over the fishmonger's counter and labeled sole. It is confusing, for the list may consist of such things as grey sole, lemon sole, flounder, and so on.

The important thing in preparing the stuffed sole outlined here is the quality, which is to say, the freshness of the fish and the size of the fillets. To prepare the dish properly, you must ask your fishman to sell you small, skinless, boneless fish fillets and they must be approximately the same size. The reason for this is obvious. To prepare the dish you place the fillets on a flat surface and sprinkle with salt and pepper. You add a small mound of filling atop half the fillets. You then cover each of the "stuffed" fillets with a second fillet so that the contours of the fillets match all around.

The preparation of the stuffing is simplicity itself. You simply blend crabmeat (that has been picked over to remove all chance bits of shell and cartilage) with an egg yolk and seasonings plus a minimum amount of fresh bread crumbs to lighten the texture.

The cooking of the dish is nearly as quick as abracadabra. When the fillets have been filled and are ready, you arrange them in a buttered baking dish. You sprinkle dry white wine and a few chopped shallots all around the fish and bring the wine to the boil on top of the stove. This is to expedite the cooking. The dish is then placed under a preheated broiler and cooked just until the top of each fillet is golden and the fish flakes easily. The total oven time is about 6 to 8 minutes.

This is a dish of such simplicity and ease that it allows more than ample time to prepare an accompaniment. Zucchini with summer herbs (you could also use dried) is an excellent side dish for the fish (see page 107).

Sole Farcie au Crab
(Sole or flounder stuffed with crab)

8 skinless, boneless fillets of sole or flounder, each of approximately the same size, about 1¼ pounds total weight
Salt and freshly ground pepper to taste
1 cup crabmeat, preferably lump crabmeat, picked over to remove all traces of shell and cartilage

1 egg yolk
2 tablespoons finely chopped parsley
1 tablespoon fine, fresh bread crumbs
4 tablespoons melted butter
2 tablespoons finely chopped shallots
½ cup dry white wine

1. Preheat the broiler.

2. Place 4 fillets skinned side up on a flat surface. Sprinkle with salt and pepper.

3. Blend the crab, egg yolk, parsley, bread crumbs, and salt and pepper in a bowl. Center equal portions of this filling on the top of the fillets on the flat surface. Smooth the filling over, leaving a slight margin around it.

4. Sprinkle the remaining fillets with salt and pepper. Arrange them skinned side down over the filling. Press lightly around the sides.

5. Rub the bottom of a heatproof baking dish with half the butter. Arrange the stuffed fish over it. Sprinkle the shallots around the fish.

6. Melt the remaining butter and brush the fillets with it. Pour the wine around the fillets.

7. Place the baking dish on the stove. Bring the wine to the boil and let simmer about 15 seconds. Place under the broiler about 7 or 8 inches from the source of heat. As it cooks, watch closely to prevent burning. Turn the baking dish so that the fish broils evenly. The total broiling time is about 6 to 8 minutes.

Yield: Four servings.

[109]

IT WOULD BE DIFFICULT TO THINK OF ANY MAIN course that offers itself more readily—and tastefully—to hasty cooking in a so-called gourmet style than a well-made fish soup. There are literally countless thousands of ways to make a palatable, indeed an eminently edible and hearty, fish soup. Techniques and ingredients for making these soups differ, of course, from country to country and region to region.

Along the Mediterranean, fish soups are almost invariably based on olive oil, garlic, onions, tomatoes, and such herbs as thyme or bay leaf. The fish bear such names as rascasse, saint-pierre, congre, rouget, rouquier, and the end result is robust.

The classic example is bouillabaisse. In Paris, fish soup tends to be based on butter and cream and to be made with a more delicate fish. Some fish soups incorporate the elements of both the Paris and Mediterranean areas, including both tomatoes and cream.

A basic fish soup, quickly and easily made, is offered here. Almost any white-fleshed, non-oily fish can be used—obviously the fresher the better. Although scallops are included in this recipe, they are not essential. Instead of scallops, you might simply increase the quantity of the basic fish used. Recipes are and should be flexible.

The soup, by the way, is made more substantial and given a more interesting texture by the addition of croutons—crisply broiled slices of French bread, rubbed lightly with garlic and sprinkled with a little olive oil before cooking. These, too, are optional.

The recommended way to proceed with the recipe is to prepare all the ingredients in advance. The most time-consuming thing is the preparation of the fish and vegetables, the onion, garlic, green pepper, leeks, potatoes, and parsley. These foods must be chopped, cubed, or sliced. The remainder of the ingredients come out of bottles or tins. The croutons may be prepared after the soup has been put on to simmer.

The menu could include, as a second course, the usual salad with cheese and, if desired, a final course of fresh fruit or a purchased or previously made dessert.

Soupe de Poisson
(Fish soup)

3 tablespoons olive oil
¼ cup finely chopped onion
1 teaspoon finely chopped garlic
½ cup chopped green pepper
½ cup chopped leeks, optional
½ cup finely chopped carrot
1 hot red pepper, crumbled
1 bay leaf
2 teaspoons fresh thyme sprigs, or ½ teaspoon dried thyme
1 cup dry white wine
1 cup chopped fresh or canned tomatoes

⅓ pound potatoes
1 cup water
1¼ pounds white-fleshed, non-oily fish, such as cod, tilefish, or a combination of two or more fish
½ pint bay scallops
1 cup heavy cream
¼ cup finely chopped fresh parsley
Salt and freshly ground pepper
16 toasted croutons (see recipe)

1. Heat the oil in a kettle and add the onion, garlic, green pepper, leeks, and carrot. Cook, stirring often, until the onions are wilted.

2. Add the crumbled red pepper, bay leaf, thyme, wine, and tomatoes. Bring to the boil.

3. Peel the potatoes and cut them into ½-inch cubes. Drop into cold water briefly. Drain. Add the potatoes to the soup.

4. Cover closely and cook 10 minutes.

5. Add the water. Uncover and cook 5 minutes.

6. Add the fish and scallops and simmer 2 or 3 minutes. Do

not overcook or the fish will fall apart. Add the cream and bring to the boil. The soup must be piping hot.

7. Gently stir in the parsley and add salt and pepper to taste. Add 1 or 2 croutons to each serving and serve the remainder on the side.

Yield: Four servings.

Croûtons

Half a loaf of French bread	**¼ cup olive oil**
1 clove garlic, peeled and left whole	

1. Rub the outside crust of the bread all over with the garlic.
2. Cut the bread into 16 thin slices. Arrange the slices on a baking sheet and sprinkle with oil.
3. Broil until golden on one side. Turn and brown lightly on the other side.

Yield: Sixteen croutons.

SOME THINGS SEEM MADE FOR EACH OTHER LIKE Moët and Chandon, Lea and Perrins, and Cross and Blackwell. That lengthy list would also include a couple of plentiful foods from American waters, shad and shad roe. Separately either would make good feasting. Cooked together with a bit of shallots, a touch of heavy cream, and a final sprinkling of chopped parsley and/or chives, this is food to appease the appetite of the most sluggish connoisseur. And the entire kitchen proceedings—minus the eating, of course—can be accomplished in far less than an hour.

In fact, the actual cooking time is approximately 20 minutes, leaving ample time for the preparation of the sundry accompaniments. Speaking of things that go together, steamed potatoes are in order for this dish, although steamed rice would be an agreeable substitute. A chilled salad of Belgian endive plus sliced tomatoes and a simple oil and vinegar dressing would be ideal. In the days and weeks prior to the arrival of the first honestly vine-ripened tomatoes, it may be best to choose cherry tomatoes, which seem to have more flavor than the run-of-the-mill hothouse varieties.

When this dish was prepared in my own kitchen, we sat down to dine with a nice chilled bottle of Burgundy at hand, specifically a Chassagne-Montrachet. A bottle of Mosel or Rhine wine, however, would not have been out of place, nor a good, light dry California wine.

Alose à la Crème

(Shad and shad roe in cream)

2 boned shad fillets, about 2 pounds
2 pairs shad roe
Salt and freshly ground pepper to taste
4 tablespoons butter

2 tablespoons finely chopped shallots
1 cup heavy cream
Juice of ½ lemon
2 tablespoons finely chopped parsley or chives

1. Cut the fillets in half lengthwise. Sprinkle the fillets and roe on all sides with salt and pepper.

2. Melt the butter in one or two heavy skillets and add the shad and roe in one layer. Sprinkle the shallots between the pieces of fish and roe. Add ½ cup of heavy cream and cover. Bring to the boil and cook 10 to 15 minutes.

3. Uncover and remove the fish to a serving platter. Split the roe in half and top each portion of fish with a piece of roe. Keep warm.

4. Add the remaining ½ cup of heavy cream to the skillet and bring to the boil. Put the sauce through a fine sieve into a saucepan. Bring to the boil and simmer 5 minutes. Add lemon juice and salt and pepper to taste. Pour the sauce over the fish and roe and serve sprinkled with parsley. Serve with steamed potatoes.

Yield: Four servings.

Pommes Vapeur
(Steamed potatoes)

1 pound red, new, waxy
  potatoes
Salt to taste

2 tablespoons butter, optional
Freshly ground pepper to
taste

1. Rinse and drain the potatoes and put them in a small kettle or deep saucepan.

2. Cover with water and add salt to taste. Bring to the boil and simmer 20 minutes, or until tender. Drain and, when cool 'gh to handle, peel.

Melt the butter in a heavy saucepan and add the pota-'prinkle with salt and pepper to taste. Cover and heat thor-

I: Four servings.

FROM MY APPRENTICESHIP AS A CHEF IN PARIS more than forty years ago, one of the things I remember most profoundly is the occasional trip to the old markets at Les Halles with my mentor and guide, the chef of the Restaurant Drouant, at that time one of the most celebrated restaurants in the city.

He was a man obsessed with the quality of fresh produce, and we would arrive before dawn, going from produce stall to produce stall, walking between what seemed like mountains of scarlet-red radishes, snow white and deep green leeks, new celery and green hills of parsley, thyme, and chervil. We would visit the displays of freshly slaughtered veal and beef and spend a long time at the fish merchants.

Through him I had it pounded into my brain that food is best when purchased and cooked in its purest and most recently gathered or harvested state. And this applies, of course, to the home as well as the restaurant.

I thought of this while visiting the fish market in Amagansett, Long Island, where they had on display several dozen mackerel that had just come in from the sea. I used four of them to make a fine supper for four in much less than an hour, and you could not have dined on fish much fresher than that. There are those who complain that they don't like mackerel because it has an oily flavor. Not if they are newly caught.

The recipe here is for mackerel Portuguese-style, which is to say with tomatoes and sweet peppers, and, optionally, a touch of saffron. It is an easy dish to prepare. It requires about 30 minutes of baking time. As the fish cook, there is ample time to prepare such side dishes as you may require. Plain boiled potatoes—known in French as pommes vapeur—are excellent with it.

The menu could include as a second course that usual salad with cheese and, if desired, a final course of fresh fruit or previously made dessert.

Maquereaux Portugaise
(Mackerel with tomato and pepper sauce)

4 very fresh mackerel, about ½ pound each, cleaned, gills removed but with the head and tail left on
¼ cup olive oil
2 teaspoons finely minced garlic
1 onion, sliced wafer thin, about 1 cup
½ teaspoon hot red pepper flakes
1 cup sliced, seeded sweet green pepper
Salt and freshly ground pepper to taste
1 bay leaf
½ teaspoon loosely packed leaf saffron, optional
2 large unblemished ripe tomatoes, cored and coarsely chopped, about 3 cups
4 anchovies, chopped

1. Preheat the oven to 450 degrees.

2. Using a pair of kitchen scissors, trim off the back and side fins of the fish if this has not been done by the fisherman. Rinse well and drain.

3. Heat 3 tablespoons of the oil in a skillet and add the garlic. Cook briefly and add the onion. Cook until wilted and add the pepper flakes and cook until the onion starts to brown lightly. Add the green peppers and salt and pepper and continue cooking, stirring occasionally, until the peppers start to brown lightly. Add the bay leaf, saffron, and tomatoes. Cook, stirring occasionally, about 5 minutes.

4. Grease an oval baking dish (a dish measuring about 10 by 16 inches was used to test this recipe) with the remaining tablespoon of oil. Arrange the fish side by side in the dish. Sprinkle with salt and pepper. Pour the sauce on top and sprinkle with salt and pepper. Dot with the chopped anchovies. Place in the oven and bake 30 minutes.

5. Run quickly under the broiler and serve hot or cold.

Yield: Four servings.

Merlan au Plat avec Herbes

(Breaded baked whiting with herbs)

4 whiting, about ½ pound each

3 slices French bread

1 tablespoon finely minced shallots

1 tablespoon finely minced onion

2 tablespoons finely chopped parsley

¼ cup butter

½ cup dry white wine

1. Preheat the oven to 400 degrees.

2. Arrange the bread slices in a baking dish. Bake until golden brown and as crisp as Melba toast. Let cool. Rub through a sieve or process until fine in a blender or food processor. There should be about ⅓ cup of crumbs.

3. Combine the crumbs, shallots, onions, and parsley.

4. Butter a baking dish large enough to hold the fish in one layer with 1 tablespoon of the butter. Sprinkle about 3 tablespoons of the crumb mixture over the bottom. Arrange the fish over the crumbs. Sprinkle the fish with the remaining crumbs and dot with the remaining butter.

5. Pour the wine around the fish and bake 30 minutes. Baste and bake 5 minutes longer.

Yield: Four servings.

Courgettes au Four avec Tomates

(Baked zucchini with tomatoes)

1 zucchini, about ½ pound
2 medium-size tomatoes, about ½ pound
1 medium-size green pepper, cored, seeded, and chopped
1 cup finely chopped onion
Salt and freshly ground pepper to taste
¼ cup olive oil

1. Preheat the oven to 400 degrees.

2. Trim off the ends of the zucchini and core the tomatoes. Cut each into 10 ½-inch slices. Arrange them, edges slightly overlapping, alternating the zucchini with the tomato.

3. Sprinkle with green pepper, onion, and salt and pepper. Sprinkle evenly with the oil.

4. Broil about 5 minutes. Take care that the vegetables do not burn on top.

5. Place in the oven and bake about 25 minutes. Serve hot.

Yield: Four servings.

THERE IS A DISH THAT DOVETAILS NICELY WITH an old American custom. It is the New England tradition of offering guests fresh salmon, peas, and new potatoes in celebration of the Fourth of July.

In this case, however, there is a slight departure from tradition. The custom, particularly around Boston and in Connecticut, is to serve a whole steamed salmon with peas and potatoes.

A whole salmon properly steamed (poached is more like it) requires a good deal of time and effort. The preparation proposed here is for grilled salmon, and the procedure is no more complicated and time-consuming than marinating the fish fillets in a mixture of oil, dill, salt, and pepper before cooking briefly on a preheated grill.

To tell the truth, the inspiration for this dish is of Scandinavian origin, notably gravlax, although the curing time is dispensed with. This is another of those dishes whose preparation and cooking time, start to finish, is so rapid that the better part of scheduling is to concentrate on the vegetable accompaniment —in this case, potatoes in a light cream sauce with fresh or frozen peas. The potatoes must be cooked in their jackets before the dish is finished. The cooking time is about 20 minutes.

When the potatoes are peeled and sliced into rounds, they are cooked briefly with milk and cream and seasonings. If fresh peas are to be blended with the potatoes, they should be cooked separately. If the peas are really fresh from the garden, the cooking time could almost be measured in seconds. If the peas are frozen, however, they can simply be added to the potatoes at the last minute and cooked until piping hot throughout.

If you really wanted to complete a Fourth of July meal, New England-style, you would end the meal with strawberry shortcake, but that, of course, would require more time.

Saumon Grillé à la Danoise
(Grilled dilled salmon fillets)

2 pounds boneless fillets, preferably with the skin left intact

¼ cup peanut, vegetable, or corn oil

3 tablespoons finely chopped dill

Salt and freshly ground black pepper to taste

4 tablespoons melted butter

4 thin lemon slices for garnish

Parsley sprigs for garnish

1. Cut the salmon into 4 pieces of approximately the same size and weight. Put the pieces in a dish and add the oil, dill, and salt and pepper. Blend well.

2. Refrigerate briefly, turning the pieces in the marinade several times.

3. Preheat the broiler.

4. Arrange the pieces of fish in one layer or on an unheated broiler tray. Place the fish under the broiler about 2 or 3 inches away from the source of heat.

5. Broil about 4 minutes, or just until the pieces are cooked through. It is not necessary to turn the pieces. Brush with melted butter. Garnish with lemon slices and parsley sprigs.

Yield: Four servings.

Pommes de Terre et Pois à la Crème
(Potatoes with peas in cream)

4 potatoes, about 1¼ pounds
Salt to taste
1 cup milk
½ cup heavy cream
Freshly ground pepper to taste

⅛ teaspoon freshly grated nutmeg
2 cups fresh or frozen green peas
¾ cup chopped scallions

1. Put the potatoes in a saucepan with water to cover and salt to taste. Bring to the boil and simmer 20 minutes or longer, or until the potatoes are tender without being mushy.

2. When cool enough to handle, peel the potatoes and cut them into ¼-inch rounds. There should be about 4 cups.

3. Put the slices in a saucepan and add the milk and cream.

4. Place on the heat and add salt, pepper, and nutmeg. Bring to the boil and simmer over high heat about 5 minutes.

5. Meanwhile, if fresh peas are to be used, cook them in boiling salted water until tender. Drain and add them to the potatoes in cream. Add the scallions and stir. Cook about 1 minute.

Yield: Four servings.

DURING THE SUMMER THERE ARE FEW FRENCH restaurants throughout the country that do not have cold poached fish served with one kind of sauce or another on the menu. It is warm weather fare, the kind of dish that is ideal for cooking.

It requires a minimum of care, for poached fish must be cooked for a short period or it loses its texture. But more about that later.

It is possible, naturally, to cook a fish in only water with salt and peppercorns. It is far preferable, however, to cook the fish in an easily made cooking liquid called a court bouillon. This consists of water and wine blended with herbs and spices plus one or two vegetables, such as carrots and onions.

The best thing about poached fish in terms of care and time is that once the fish is brought to the boil there is nothing more to be done until it is cooked. Simply let it simmer gently for a short, specified time. The 3-pound striped bass called for here will cook perfectly in 10 minutes.

One of the best of all sauces to go with a poached fish is a sauce verte or green sauce that can be whipped up in seconds using a food processor or blender. For a summer menu, a tomato and hard-cooked egg garnish is very much in order. To extend the menu you might want to cook a few potatoes (cook them separately but simultaneously with the fish) and add a cold sliced cucumber salad.

Bar Rayé Poché
(Poached striped bass)

1 3-pound striped bass, with head on but gills removed
24 cups water
1 cup dry white wine
½ cup carrot rounds
¾ cup coarsely chopped onion
8 sprigs fresh parsley
1 teaspoon dried rosemary
1 bay leaf
10 peppercorns
Salt to taste
1 hot red pepper
Lemon wedges for garnish
Sauce verte (see recipe)
Tomato and hard-cooked egg garnish (see recipe)

1. Rinse the fish well and pat it dry. Set aside.

2. Combine all the remaining ingredients except the lemon wedges, sauce verte, and tomato and hard-cooked egg garnish in a fish poacher or other oval casserole or pot large enough to hold the fish. Bring to the boil and simmer 10 minutes.

3. Carefully lower the fish into the liquid. If desired, the fish may be wrapped in cheesecloth to facilitate its removal, but if a fish poacher with a rack is used, this is not necessary.

4. Bring the liquid to the boil and simmer gently exactly 10 minutes. Remove the cooker from the heat and let stand until ready to serve. The fish may rest in the liquid for up to half an hour without detriment.

5. To serve, place the fish on a serving dish and carefully remove and discard the skin. Garnish with lemon wedges and serve the sauce verte and tomato and hard-cooked egg garnish separately.

Yield: Four servings.

Sauce Verte
(Green sauce)

⅓ cup loosely packed parsley, coarsely chopped

⅓ cup coarsely chopped raw onion

2 tablespoons coarsely chopped chives

1 teaspoon chopped fresh tarragon

1 clove garlic, finely minced

½ cup olive oil

3 tablespoons wine vinegar

1 tablespoon imported mustard, such as Dijon or Düsseldorf

1 hard-cooked egg, quartered

1. Combine the parsley, onion, chives, tarragon, garlic, olive oil, vinegar, and mustard in the container of a food processor or electric blender. Blend until the herbs are finely chopped. Do not overblend, however. The ingredients should retain some texture.

2. Add the egg and blend briefly until coarsely chopped.

Yield: About one-and-a-quarter cups.

Garniture d'Oeufs Durs
(Garnish of hard-cooked egg)

1 large ripe tomato

Salt to taste

2 hard-cooked eggs, peeled

Freshly ground pepper

Mayonnaise, optional

1. Remove the core and cut away a small slice from the bottom of the tomato. Cut the tomato into 8 wedges and sprinkle with salt.

2. Quarter the eggs. Arrange four pairs of two tomato wedges, centers touching. Arrange quartered eggs neatly in the center to fit. Serve with salt and pepper on the side. And, if desired, serve with a spoonful of mayonnaise on each serving.

Yield: Four servings.

ONE OF THE OBVIOUS ADVANTAGES OF LIVING in coastal areas is the relative abundance of fresh fish. Perhaps the most abundant fish is that sold over the counter as "sole." The truth of the matter is that the sole found in American markets may well be fluke or flounder, grey sole or lemon sole, among others. Just why the word sole became a sort of catch-all is not known, but the ultimate consideration in buying sole, as any other fish, is its fresh quality.

Fillet of sole is admirable for hasty cooking, for overcooked fish becomes dry and fibrous. One of the most appetizing preparations for sole is sole grenobloise, which is to say in the style of Grenoble, France. The fish is first cooked meunière (lightly coated with flour and sautéed quickly). It is then given a grenobloise garnish, which is lemon and capers.

Since capers have a character all their own and they are a bit assertive, the dish is best complemented by a vegetable dish of substantial flavor, and an excellent idea for this is cherry tomatoes provençale, in which you use a touch of garlic and parsley. That, plus the classic accompaniment for fish meunière or any of its variations, buttered, boiled or steamed potatoes.

The best method of approaching such a menu is to get all the ingredients prepared before starting to cook. Both dishes, once the ingredients are assembled and made ready, can be cooked in a very few minutes.

Filets de Sole Grenobloise
(Sautéed sole with capers and lemon)

4 individual servings fish
  fillets, about 1¼ pounds
  total weight
¼ cup milk
  Salt and freshly ground
  pepper to taste
1 small lemon

½ cup flour
½ cup peanut, vegetable, or
  corn oil
¼ cup butter
1 tablespoon drained capers
1 tablespoon finely chopped
  parsley

1. Place the fillets in a dish large enough to hold them in one layer. Pour the milk over them and add salt and pepper. Turn the fish in the milk so that they are coated on all sides.

2. While they stand, peel the lemon, cutting away and discarding all the white pulp as well as the yellow skin. Cut the lemon into thin slices and discard the seeds. Cut the slices into small cubes. Set aside.

3. Scatter the flour over a large pan and add salt and pepper to taste. Blend well.

4. Heat the oil and 1 tablespoon of the butter in a large skillet.

5. As the oil heats, remove the fillets from the milk but do not drain. Coat the fish on all sides in seasoned flour, shaking to rid the fillets of excess flour.

6. When the oil is quite hot but not smoking, add the fillets (this might have to be done in two steps) and cook until nicely browned on one side. Turn and brown on the other. The total cooking time for each fillet should be from 4 to 5 minutes. As the fillets are cooked, transfer them to a warm platter.

7. Melt the remaining butter in a small skillet and cook, shaking the skillet until the butter foams up and takes on an appetizing hazelnut-brown color. Remove from the heat. Add the cubed

lemon and capers. Pour this evenly over the fillets. Sprinkle with chopped parsley and serve.

Yield: Four servings.

Tomates Cerises à la Provençale
(Cherry tomatoes with garlic and parsley)

24 ripe unblemished and firm cherry tomatoes
2 tablespoons olive oil

1 teaspoon finely chopped garlic
2 tablespoons finely chopped parsley

1. Remove the stems from the tomatoes. Rinse and pat the tomatoes dry.
2. Heat the oil in a skillet large enough to hold the tomatoes in one layer. Add the tomatoes and cook, shaking the skillet so that the tomatoes are distributed and cook evenly. Cook about 1 or 2 minutes, or just until tomatoes are heated through. Do not overcook or the skins will split and the tomatoes will become mushy.
3. Sprinkle with garlic, toss briefly, and serve sprinkled with parsley.

Yield: Four servings.

SOME OF THE FINEST DINING IN THE UNITED States can occur right in the middle of winter because some of the finest, freshest fish come from the cold winter waters of the Atlantic.

And since most fish cookery is designed for hasty cooking, a hot platter of halibut, cod, or other seasonal fish is timely.

It is odd that in French cooking so many of the best-received dishes stem directly from the countryside rather than from the cities. Fish boulangère could be counted as one of those dishes. Boulangère means in the style of the baker's wife. It is called that because the dish is baked and one of its characteristics is a final sprinkling of the baker's bread crumbs before it is put in the oven.

Fish boulangère—it is delicious made with fresh halibut or cod fillets—consists of fillets folded and baked with potatoes and onions sliced wafer-thin.

It is a simple dish, for after the fillets are surrounded by the vegetables and sprinkled with crumbs and butter, it simply requires half an hour of baking.

In essence, halibut or cod boulangère could easily serve as a meal in itself, but, personally, I prefer it with another vegetable, such as vichy carrots or perhaps with a well-dressed green salad made a trifle piquant with the addition of a good grade of imported mustard.

The preparation of such a meal is simplicity itself. Once the dish is in the oven, there is half an hour for preparing salad greens, salad dressing, or whatever else strikes your fancy.

Flétan Boulangère
(Halibut baked with bread crumbs)

1¼ pounds potatoes, peeled and sliced as thinly as possible, about 4 cups
1 onion, about ⅓ pound, peeled and sliced wafer thin
12 tablespoons butter
4 halibut or cod fillets, about 2½ pounds total weight
Salt and freshly ground pepper to taste
¼ cup chopped parsley
1 clove garlic, finely minced
½ cup bread crumbs
½ cup dry white wine

1. Preheat the oven to 425 degrees.
2. Prepare the potatoes and keep covered with cold water.
3. Prepare the onion rings and set aside.
4. Rub the bottom of an oval baking dish with 6 tablespoons of the butter.
5. Fold each halibut fillet over itself and arrange down the center of the baking dish. Sprinkle with salt and pepper.
6. Drain the potatoes and put them in a bowl. Add the onions, parsley, garlic, and salt and pepper to taste. Blend well.
7. Arrange the vegetable mixture around the fillets. Dot with the remaining butter. Sprinkle the fish with bread crumbs. Add the wine.
8. Bring the dish to a boil on top of the stove and place in the oven. Bake 30 minutes. As the fish bakes, tilt the baking dish and spoon the liquid over the fish.

Yield: Four servings.

Carottes Vichy
(Steamed carrots)

1 pound carrots
1 cup water
2 tablespoons butter

1½ teaspoons sugar
Salt and freshly ground
pepper to taste

1. Trim and scrape the carrots and cut them into very thin rounds.

2. Put the carrot rounds in a deep casserole and add the water. It should barely cover the carrots. Add the butter, sugar, and salt and pepper.

3. Cook about 10 minutes and uncover. Cook over high heat about 15 to 20 minutes, or until all the water has evaporated. Toss and stir the carrots so that they cook evenly. Cook until the carrots are nicely glazed and lightly browned.

Yield: Four servings.

Shellfish

MOST COOKS TEND TO CATALOGUE DISHES IN their mind in two categories—those for the everyday table and those for the special occasions. In many cases—dishes requiring elaborate and tediously prepared dough; dishes with costly ingredients, such as truffles and foie gras—such divisions are justified. There are some dishes, however, so easily made and of such special character they can serve well as one or the other.

For years, at least as long as I can remember, the Spanish rice and seafood dish has been considered very much a dish for special functions. And, of course, in its most elaborate form—garnished with cut-outs of pimientos, egg, and so on—it can be time-consuming. That is not to pretend that the dish recommended here is an absolutely authentic paella. It is, however, an excellent dish of seafood with rice, which is what a paella essentially is.

And it is certainly easily made within the space of 60 minutes. It helps, of course, if the seafood can be purchased ready-cleaned and ready for the kettle—the shrimp peeled, the mussels scrubbed, the clams washed, and so on—and the best fish dealers, in most metropolitan centers, sell their shellfish in such fashion.

Other than that, the only steps that are time-consuming are the chopping of a few vegetables, such as onion, garlic, green peppers, and tomatoes, and the cooking of rice, which any reasonably intelligent ten-year-old child can do with small effort.

Rice requires less than 20 minutes cooking time—if it is cooked longer than that it becomes mushy and unpalatable. In this recipe, seasoned rice is cooked separately from the shellfish; and not the least important thing about prepared seafood where rapid cookery is concerned, it must be cooked in haste for maximum flavor and texture. Thus, while the rice cooks, the seafood preparations should be in progress, the two operations timed to be ready for serving simultaneously. More or less. Once the rice is cooked less than its alloted time, it can be removed from the heat and allowed to stand for several minutes or longer without detriment to its texture.

Fruits de Mer au Riz
(Mixed shellfish with rice)

The rice:
2 tablespoons olive oil
¼ cup finely chopped onion
¼ cup diced green pepper
1 clove garlic, finely minced
½ teaspoon loosely packed saffron stems
1 cup rice
1¼ cups water
Salt and freshly ground pepper to taste

The seafood:
¼ cup olive oil
1 cup finely chopped onion
2 cloves garlic, finely minced

1 hot dried red pepper, optional
1½ cups diced, peeled fresh or canned tomatoes
1½ cups dry white wine
1 teaspoon dried oregano
Salt and freshly ground pepper to taste
18 small littleneck clams, the smaller the better, rinsed well
1½ quarts well-scrubbed mussels, about 6 cups
½ pound shrimp, shelled and deveined
½ pound sea scallops, halved or quartered

1. To begin, prepare and measure out all the ingredients for the rice. To save time, chop an extra cup of onions and 2 extra cloves of garlic for the seafood mixture. Set these aside.

2. Heat the 2 tablespoons of oil for the rice in a saucepan and add ¼ cup of onion, green pepper, and 1 clove of garlic and cook until wilted. Add the saffron and cook about 2 minutes longer.

3. Add the rice, water, and salt and pepper and cover closely. Cook about 17 minutes, or just until the rice is tender. As the rice cooks, prepare the seafood. Remember that when the rice is cooked, remove it from the heat. It can stand several minutes, covered, without damage.

4. In a kettle, heat the ¼ cup oil and add the 1 cup of onion and 2 cloves of garlic. Stir and cook until wilted. Add the red pepper, tomatoes, wine, and oregano. Add salt and pepper. Cover and cook about 10 minutes.

5. Add the clams and mussels to the kettle and cover again. Cook about 3 minutes and add the shrimp, scallops, and salt and pepper to taste. Cover and cook about 5 minutes.

6. There are several ways to serve this dish. Use a large, deep serving dish and make a border of rice with a "well" in the center. Add the shellfish with their juices to the center and serve. Or you may blend the rice and the shellfish and serve as a paella.

Yield: Four servings.

THERE IS NO DOUBT THAT TASTES IN FOOD ARE sometimes cyclical. During the 1930s when I was an apprentice and then a young chef at the Restaurant Drouant in Paris, there were numerous dishes that appeared on Paris menus that contained or centered on cooked oysters. And then for a long time cooked oysters were seldom heard of on French menus.

There is a story, although I don't believe a word of it, that when Georges Auguste Escoffier was the reigning chef of Europe and presided over the kitchen of the Ritz, he was asked by a wealthy American lady who lived at the hotel to prepare a turkey with an oyster stuffing for one of her holiday meals. He refused on the grounds that turkey or any other kind of fowl and oysters were incompatible if not "cannibalistic."

Within recent memory, however, I have noticed that more and more cooked oysters are appearing on the menus of some of the most famous restaurants both in this country and abroad.

Actually, cooked oysters—if they are not overcooked—are quite special, and I like to use them in a dish contrived with smoked salmon and a julienne of vegetables with a light white wine and cream sauce. The oysters and salmon are served on a bed of fine noodles, and it is recommended as an easily made dish for special occasions.

As a vegetable accompaniment, I propose a lukewarm salad of green beans vinaigrette with chopped fresh dill.

The order of cooking would be to prepare all the ingredients for the creamed oyster dish and set them aside until the last moment. The water should be kept at the simmer in a kettle to cook the noodles. The noodles cook in about 5 minutes.

Prepare the salad and keep the same separate and warm. Start cooking the oysters with salmon and, as they cook, drop the noodles into the water to simmer for 5 minutes or less. Assemble the foods in a logical manner.

[137]

Huîtres et Saumon Fumé à la Crème avec Nouilles

(Creamed oysters and smoked salmon with noodles)

2 pints shucked, raw oysters
4 pieces of fresh leeks, each about 2 inches long
2 carrots
4 large mushrooms
½ pound smoked salmon
½ cup dry white wine
Salt and freshly ground pepper to taste
½ cup oyster liquor or bottled clam juice
1½ cups heavy cream
6 tablespoons butter
2 tablespoons finely chopped shallots
½ pound fine noodles
Juice of 1 lemon

1. Pour the oysters into a sieve placed over a mixing bowl. Let drain. Reserve the oyster liquor.

2. Cut the pieces of leeks in half. Rinse and drain well. Cut the pieces lengthwise into very thin strips (julienne). There should be 1 cup, loosely packed. Set aside.

3. Scrape and cut the carrots into 2-inch lengths and cut each length into very thin strips like the leeks. There should be about 1 cup. Set aside.

4. Cut the mushrooms into thin strips. There should be about 1 cup. Set aside.

5. Cut the salmon into 1-inch squares or diamond-shaped pieces. Set aside.

6. Combine the carrots, leeks, and mushrooms in a saucepan and add the wine. Add a little salt and pepper. Add the oyster liquor if there is any; otherwise, add the clam juice.

7. Simmer partly covered about 5 minutes and add the cream. Add any more liquor that may have accumulated from the oysters. Cook about 5 minutes.

8. Melt 2 tablespoons of the butter and add the shallots. Cook briefly and add the oysters and salmon pieces. Sprinkle with pep-

per, no salt. When sizzling, cover and cook 30 seconds, no longer. Strain any liquid that accumulates and add it to the vegetables. Continue to add any liquid that accumulates.

9. Cook the noodles in boiling salted water about 3 to 5 minutes, or until tender. Drain quickly and add 2 tablespoons of the butter. Add salt and pepper and stir.

10. To the vegetable mixture, swirl in the remaining butter and the lemon juice.

11. Spoon equal amounts of noodles onto each of 4 to 6 hot plates. Spoon equal portions of oysters and salmon over the noodles and spoon the sauce over all. Serve hot.

Yield: Four to six servings.

ONE OF THE RECURRENT QUESTIONS IN MY LIFE is whether any "new" dishes have been created in the last century, and the answer, of course, is yes. If that question were phrased differently—Have any new principles of cookery been developed in the last hundred years?—the answer would probably be no. The creation of new dishes is limitless, and yet they are based on the same inevitable laws known to Antonin Carême and La Varenne. Techniques have been refined, but the principles remain the same. The so-called 60-minute dish that appears here has, to my knowledge, never been duplicated before the day it came out of my skillet. It came about because fresh scallops, one of the finest seafoods to be found in American waters (or the world, for that matter), had recently come into season and were available at the local fish market.

On arriving home I found the remaining ingredients in the refrigerator—cream, white wine, shallots, butter, mushrooms, tomatoes, and parsley. You simply add them all together (a manner of speaking) and they turn out to be coquilles St. Jacques façon du chef—chef's fashion is a much used and easy method for naming dishes that are otherwise nameless.

Scallops, like many fish and seafoods, depend on rapid-fire cooking—a term not used loosely—for their goodness and delicacy. You should cook them as quickly as possible over very high heat. Low heat and slow cooking will cause their valuable juices to flow from within and thereby cause dryness and tastelessness.

Note, too, that you must never cook too many scallops at one time, which is to say they should never be crowded in a skillet. In fact, they should not even touch except as they are stirred or the skillet is shaken.

To go about preparing this less-than-60-minute meal with scallops, cook the recommended rice accompaniment. As it cooks, prepare the ingredients for the scallops. Cook the scallops at the very last minute before serving.

Coquilles St. Jacques Façon du Chef
(Scallops and mushrooms in cream sauce)

3 tablespoons butter
2 pints scallops
  Salt and freshly ground
  pepper to taste
2 tablespoons finely chopped
  shallots

2 cups quartered or sliced
  fresh mushrooms
12 cherry tomatoes
¼ cup dry white wine
1 cup heavy cream
1 tablespoon finely chopped
  parsley

1. Melt 2 tablespoons of the butter in one large or two medium skillets. Take care that the scallops when added will not be crowded in either pan or pans. If they are too close together they will not "sear" properly and the juices will flow.

2. When the butter is quite hot and before it browns, add the scallops. Cook over high heat, shaking the skillet and stirring. Sprinkle with salt and pepper. Cook about 1 or 2 minutes, or until lightly golden all over. The less cooking time the better.

3. Using a slotted spoon, remove the scallops and keep them warm.

4. Add the shallots to the skillet and cook briefly. Add the mushrooms and cherry tomatoes and cook, stirring often, about 1 minute. Add the wine and reduce the liquid by half.

5. Add the cream and salt and pepper to taste. Cook down over high heat about 3 minutes. Add the scallops. Swirl in the remaining tablespoon of butter. Sprinkle with chopped parsley and serve with rice.

Yield: Four servings.

Riz au Four avec Pignolats
(Baked rice with pine nuts)

2½ tablespoons butter
2 tablespoons minced onion
¼ teaspoon minced garlic
1 cup uncooked rice
1½ cups chicken broth
2 sprigs parsley

1 sprig fresh thyme, or ¼
teaspoon dried thyme
½ bay leaf
⅛ teaspoon cayenne pepper or
Tabasco sauce to taste
¼ cup toasted pine nuts

1. Preheat the oven to 400 degrees.

2. Melt 1 tablespoon of the butter in a heavy saucepan and cook the onion and garlic, stirring with a wooden spoon, until the onion is translucent. Add the rice and stir briefly over low heat until all the grains are coated with butter.

3. Stir in the chicken broth, making sure there are no lumps in the rice. Add the parsley, thyme, bay leaf, and cayenne. Cover with a close-fitting lid and place in the oven.

4. Bake the rice exactly 17 minutes. Remove the cover and discard the parsley and thyme sprigs and bay leaf. Using a two-pronged fork, stir in the remaining butter and the pine nuts. If the rice is not to be served immediately, keep covered in a warm place.

Yield: Four servings.

AN ACQUAINTANCE ONCE SAID THAT THE TIME to start to cook is before you start to cook. The notion isn't all that nonsensical. A few mental gymnastics—anticipation of what must be done to prepare a meal—are highly in order.

With a little foresight, the body of the meal recommended here can be accomplished in less than half an hour.

The principal dish is scallops meunière, and these must be cooked in seconds or they will be overcooked and chewy and lose some of their natural flavor. They are to be served with pommes nature or "natural" potatoes, which is to say simmered, drained and served as simply as possible with butter.

And again there are cherry tomatoes provençale, and these take the least effort of all. The stems are removed from the tomatoes and the tomatoes are cooked rapidly in butter and sprinkled with a touch of garlic.

A point to be made a hundred times is organization. Before you start to cook, chop what has to be chopped and measure what has to be measured. Bring out such pots and pans as are necessary for cooking—in this case two skillets (one for the scallops, one for the tomatoes) and a saucepan (for the potatoes).

Coquilles St. Jacques Meunière
(Scallops quick-fried in butter)

1 pint (1 pound) scallops
¼ cup milk
   Flour for dredging
   Salt and freshly ground
   pepper to taste

5 tablespoons peanut,
   vegetable, or corn oil
4 tablespoons butter
   Juice of ½ lemon
2 tablespoons finely chopped
   parsley

1. Put the scallops into a bowl and add the milk, stirring to coat them. Let stand briefly.

2. Place the flour in a dish and add salt and pepper to taste. Blend well. Drain the scallops. Dredge them in flour and add them to a large sieve. Shake to remove excess flour. Scatter them onto a sheet of foil or wax paper so that they do not touch or they might stick together.

3. The scallops must be cooked over high heat without crowding. Heat 3 tablespoons of the oil and 1 tablespoon of butter in a large skillet. When the mixture is quite hot but not smoking, add half of the scallops, shaking and tossing them in the skillet so that they cook quickly and evenly until golden brown on all sides.

4. Use a slotted spoon and transfer the scallops to a hot platter. Add the remaining 2 tablespoons of oil to the skillet and when it is quite hot, add the remaining scallops, shaking and tossing them in the skillet as before. When brown, transfer them to the platter with other scallops. Wipe out the skillet, add the remaining butter and cook until lightly browned or the color of hazelnuts. Sprinkle over the scallops. Then sprinkle the scallops with the lemon juice and chopped parsley.

Yield: Four servings.

Pommes Nature
(Steamed potatoes)

---

8 to 12 small new, waxy potatoes, or use 3 or 4 medium Idaho or Maine potatoes	Salt to taste 2 or 3 tablespoons melted butter

1. Peel the potatoes. If the potatoes are small and new, leave them whole. If they are large, cut them into thirds or quarter them.

2. Put the potatoes in a saucepan and add water to cover and salt to taste. Bring to the boil and simmer until the potatoes are tender, about 10 to 15 minutes, depending on size.

3. Drain and pour melted butter over them. Serve hot.

Yield: Four servings.

Tomates Cerises à la Provençale
(Cherry tomatoes with garlic)

---

1 pint cherry tomatoes
2 tablespoons butter

Salt and freshly ground
pepper to taste
1 clove garlic, finely minced

1. Pluck off and discard the stems from the tomatoes.

2. Melt the butter in a skillet and, when it is quite hot, add the tomatoes, tossing and shaking them in the skillet so that they cook evenly. Sprinkle with salt and pepper to taste and the garlic. Continue cooking briefly, just until the tomatoes are heated through. If they cook too long, they will become mushy in the center. It is better to undercook than overcook these tomatoes. Pour onto a platter and serve hot.

Yield: Four servings.

FOOD PATTERNS IN AMERICA ARE CURIOUS. There are wide taste differences between the North and South. Northerners can't understand the Southern passion for hominy grits and to many Southern palates, the bread known as a bagel is an oddity.

I think about these differences every time I indulge myself in one of the greatest foods from the sea. It would be hard to recall when I didn't prize mussels as one of the finest foods for feasting ever put in a kettle and steamed. Mussels, or moules as they are known in France, are choice fare. They are highly esteemed throughout Europe and for some reason are particularly associated with Belgium. Walk down any street in Brussels and you'll find yourself smelling the fine scent and aromatic, herbed steam from kettles of mussels which will be served in deep dishes with frites or French fried potatoes on the side.

Like many another food spoken of in this book, mussels depend for their inherent goodness on quick cooking. They should be cooked just until all the shells are open, no longer, or they will become poorly textured and lose part of their natural savor. Generally speaking, there are two liquids used for "steaming" mussels—dry white wine or just a touch of vinegar. Mussels give up a good deal of their own liquor as they cook and this is one of the finest broths known to any cook. Or to anyone who dines on them. A bit of water could also be used for the steaming but there will be a touch less flavor in the broth.

Mussels are, of course, more popular and available now than ever. A few years ago, most of the mussels cooked in this country were those used in restaurant kitchens, or those sold to European immigrants and their descendants.

Fortunately, today almost all the best fish markets on much of the East Coast have an abundant supply of mussels.

Mussels, as the French and Belgians long ago discovered, are quite adequate for a meal unto themselves. Serve steamed mussels with a few crisp slices of garlic toast made with a crusty French or Italian loaf and olive oil, and the combination is a joy.

Moules Poulette
(Mussels in cream and egg sauce)

---

3 quarts cleaned, well-scrubbed mussels
3 tablespoons butter
¼ cup finely chopped onion
2 tablespoons finely chopped shallots
Salt and freshly ground pepper to taste

½ cup dry white wine
¼ cup finely chopped parsley
1 bay leaf
4 sprigs fresh thyme, or ½ teaspoon dried thyme
½ cup heavy cream
1 egg yolk
Garlic toast (see recipe)

1. Drain the mussels and set aside.

2. Melt 3 tablespoons of butter in a heavy kettle or deep skillet and add the onion and shallots. Cook, stirring, until wilted.

3. Add the mussels, salt and pepper, wine, parsley, bay leaf, and thyme. Cover closely and bring to the boil. Cook about 10 minutes, shaking and tossing the mussels in the kettle to redistribute them. Cook only until the mussels are opened.

4. Beat the cream and yolk together until well blended.

5. Turn the heat off under the kettle and add the cream to the mussel liquid, stirring. Cover and let stand briefly.

6. Serve the mussels and liquid in hot soup bowls and sprinkle with parsley. Serve with garlic toast on the side.

Yield: Four servings.

Toast à l'Ail
(Garlic toast)

12 slices French bread   1 large clove garlic
2 tablespoons olive oil

1. Preheat the broiler.
2. Brush the bread slices on both sides with oil.
3. Arrange the slices on a baking sheet and broil first on one side, then the other, until golden brown.
4. Remove the toast. Rub on both sides with garlic.

Yield: Twelve slices.

THERE MAY JUST POSSIBLY BE SOME SAVANTS in this world who can explain the phenomenon of flavors that marry other flavors. Why, for example, is lime better suited to tropical foods than lemons? It's true whether it's a langouste grilled on the beach or a tropical drink. Why do those flavors and foods indigenous to Provence—tomatoes, garlic, and thyme—seem so natural in a dish? And why does that Mediterranean drink, the anise-flavored pastis, seem made to add a final fillip to the fish soups of Marseilles?

The thought was logical as applied to the dish on the next page, stuffed lobsters, the liver and coral scraped away and blended with butter, bread crumbs, and tarragon. Tarragon goes with lobster like a rich consommé with port wine, or fresh foie gras with a well-chilled sauternes. It is, to put it one way, a marriage made in culinary heaven. And it was not without reason that this was for many years one of the most admired and widely ordered items on the menu of Le Pavillon Restaurant, respected at the time as one of the greatest French restaurants in America. I must have prepared the dish a thousand and more times during my twenty-five years as a chef.

I am amused to think that not one customer among those who ordered the dish knew how incredibly easy the dish is to prepare. Truth to tell, the only difficult thing about the dish is in the initial preparation of the lobsters. There are those who seem a bit squeamish about splitting a lobster down the back. The fact is, however, this can easily be done by the fish merchant although it should be done not too far in advance of the lobster being taken into the kitchen and made ready for the broiler. Should you have this done outside the home kitchen, by all means caution the butcher to save every morsel of the coral and liver (the soft, greenish or darker mass found in the chest cavity of the crustacean).

It is no exaggeration to state that the tarragon filling for the lobsters can be made in approximately 10 minutes. The baking

[149]

time is less than half an hour, and you and your guests can feast like kings. Such a simple thing as corn on the cob can be an excellent match for the dish.

Homards Farcis à l'Estragon
(Tarragon stuffed lobsters)

4 lobsters weighing from about 1½ to 1¾ pounds
¼ pound butter cut into chunks
1 cup bread crumbs
Salt and freshly ground pepper to taste

2 tablespoons finely chopped fresh tarragon, or ½ tablespoon dried tarragon
⅓ cup peanut, vegetable, or corn oil, approximately
Lemon wedges for garnish
4 tablespoons melted butter

1. Preheat the oven to 500 degrees or its highest setting.
2. Split the lobsters in half and remove the intestinal tract and the small hard sac near the eyes of the lobsters. Arrange the halves split side up in a baking dish.
3. Remove and reserve the coral and liver (all the soft, edible interior portions of the lobster except the meat). Put them in a mixing bowl. Cut off the claws of each lobster. Arrange these in a separate baking dish.
4. To the coral and liver add the butter, bread crumbs, and salt and pepper. Beat the mixture with a spoon or whisk until finely blended. Beat in the tarragon.
5. Spoon the mixture inside the cavities of each lobster. Do not cover the tail meat. Sprinkle the tail meat with salt and pepper.
6. Drizzle 2 teaspoons of oil over each lobster half.
7. Place the pans in the oven and bake 20 to 30 minutes.

8. Serve hot with lemon wedges and spoon the melted butter over all.

Yield: Four servings.

Maïs en Épi au Beurre de Poivre Vert
(Corn on the cob with green peppercorn butter)

---

8 ears fresh corn, shucked
4 tablespoons butter at room temperature

1 teaspoon chopped green peppercorns, available in specialty shops where fine imported foods are sold

1. Drop the corn into boiling salted water. Cover. When the water returns to the boil, remove from the heat. Let stand 5 minutes or longer, until ready to serve.

2. Meanwhile, beat the butter with the green peppercorns. Drain the corn and serve with the peppercorn butter.

Yield: Four servings.

DURING MY MANY YEARS AS CHEF AT THE late Pavillon Restaurant in New York, I was as fascinated by the food preferences of *le patron,* Henri Soulé, as by the tastes of any of the clientele. Cost in that kitchen meant very little in those bygone years; there was always a count or a duke or an emperor with an appetite to be appeased by grouse or breast of guinea hen or fresh foie gras or turbot freshly flown in from France.

Oddly, Mr. Soulé shunned the luxury foods and ate very simply, generally in mid-afternoon after the last customer had departed. I remember well that one of his favorite dishes was one of the simplest to make. And it was rich. This was fresh crabmeat cooked in a cream sauce and served over lightly broiled Smithfield ham on toast. There was good reason why he admired this dish. The crab was in a cream sauce lightly flavored with sherry wine, and although rich, it was easy to digest, and the Smithfield ham (when I make the dish today I generally use thinly sliced prosciutto which is more widely available) offered a highly complementary contrast in textures and flavor.

This is the sort of dish that, many years ago, would have been thought of as chafing-dish cookery. It is done with great haste and little effort. To prepare it, cream is cooked down with a touch of chopped shallots and dry sherry. The crabmeat (already cooked, of course) is sautéed quickly in a little butter and the two elements are combined. Once toast is made and the prosciutto run under the broiler for a matter of seconds, the dish is ready to be assembled and served.

As with many fish and seafood dishes, lightly cooked cucumbers make an excellent foil for the crab dish. These, too, can be prepared in haste.

It almost goes without saying that this is an expensive dish, the cost of crab in most areas being somewhat elevated. It is best to buy the fresh crab in 1-pound tins rather than the frozen kind which is more costly—perhaps because of the package. Either version will do. And if you don't have prosciutto, use a good grade of cooked ham, preferably Smithfield.

Fondue de Crabe avec Prosciutto sur Canapé
(Creamed crab with prosciutto on toast)

1 pound fresh crabmeat
2 tablespoons butter
2 tablespoons finely chopped shallots
5 tablespoons dry sherry wine
1 cup heavy cream

1 egg yolk, lightly beaten
1 teaspoon Worcestershire sauce
4 slices toast
8 thin slices prosciutto or other ham

1. Pick over the crab to remove all traces of shell and cartilage, if necessary. Drain well.

2. Melt half the butter in a heavy skillet and add the shallots. Cook, stirring, until wilted. Add 4 tablespoons of the wine and cook down. Reduce the liquid to about half.

3. Add the cream and cook down about 5 minutes over high heat.

4. Meanwhile, melt the remaining butter and add the crabmeat. Add 1 tablespoon of wine and heat thoroughly. Remove from the heat.

5. Add a few spoons of the hot cream to the egg yolk and stir to blend. Return this mixture to the cream, stirring rapidly. Remove from the heat.

6. Spoon and scrape the sauce over the crabmeat.

7. Prepare the toast and keep warm.

8. Heat the prosciutto under the broiler.

9. Place the ham slices on the toast slices and top with the crabmeat in cream sauce.

Yield: Four servings.

Concombres Sautés
(Sautéed cucumbers)

1 or 2 cucumbers, about 1 pound
2 tablespoons butter

Salt and freshly ground pepper to taste
1 tablespoon finely chopped dill

1. The new so-called "gourmet" or "burpless" cucumber is good for this. Trim off the ends of the cucumbers.
2. Cut the cucumbers into 1½-inch lengths. Cut each length in half. Peel the cucumber and cut away the soft center, leaving batons. Set aside.
3. Melt the butter in a skillet and add the cucumber batons. Sprinkle with salt and pepper. Cook, tossing and stirring, so that the pieces cook evenly. Cook for a total of about 2 minutes. Sprinkle with dill and serve hot.

Yield: Four servings.

ONE OF THE MOST INTRIGUING ASPECTS OF INternational cooking are the variations on themes. To my mind, there isn't a western country that does not have what we know in French as a sauce verte or green sauce.

Green sauce, the name, derives, of course, from the use of green herbs which give the color—and freshness—to the sauces. The green herbs generally contain chopped parsley, chives, scallions, and tarragon. In French, more often than not, we also include chervil (which flourishes in my garden on Long Island), but oddly the herb is not much known on these shores.

I thought of this once while dining at a very plain but excellent restaurant in Puerto Rico, La Fragua in San Juan. There we dined on an elegant dish of mero or pollock in green sauce, Spanish-style. This green sauce was unlike the traditional French green sauce. It was cooked quickly with the fish, which had been dusted in flour.

Recently this dish was reproduced in my own kitchen, but substituting clams (the chef of La Fragua told me that clams are often served with the sauce) for the fish. The salsa verde in this case contains chopped garlic (the flavor should be somewhat pronounced), parsley, and scallions, plus white wine and a touch of hot red pepper.

This is a dish that must cook in seconds. The only time-consuming aspect is the opening of the clams, but this could be done by the market. These clams go well with rice cooked with green peppers. The rice, which cooks in less than 20 minutes, requires more time to prepare than the clams.

Almejas con Salsa Verde
(Hot clams with green sauce)

24 to 32 littleneck clams, the smaller the better
Freshly ground pepper to taste
¼ cup oil
1 tablespoon finely chopped garlic
¼ cup finely chopped scallions
½ cup plus 1 tablespoon dry white wine
¾ cup fresh or bottled clam juice
⅛ teaspoon hot dried red pepper flakes
1 tablespoon arrowroot or cornstarch
Salt to taste
¼ cup chopped parsley

1. Open the clams on the half-shell, discarding the top shell. Leave the clam attached by its muscle to the bottom shell. Be sure to collect all the liquid that accumulates. There should be about ¾ cup.

2. Heat the oil in a large skillet and, when it is very hot, add the garlic and clams on the half-shell. Cook, stirring, over very high heat about 30 seconds—no longer. If they cook longer, the clams will toughen. Add the scallions and ½ cup of wine. Add the clam juice and pepper flakes. Let boil.

3. Quickly blend the remaining tablespoon of wine and arrowroot and stir it into the clams and sauce, stirring until thickened. Add a little salt. Sprinkle with parsley and stir. Toss and serve in small soup bowls or small bowls with rims. Serve with rice.

Yield: Four servings.

Riz aux Piments

(Rice with peppers)

1 tablespoon butter
3 tablespoons finely chopped
   onion
½ cup diced pimiento or
   roasted, peeled sweet pepper

1 cup rice
1½ cups water
Salt to taste

1. Melt the butter in a saucepan and add the onion. Cook until wilted and add the diced pepper, rice, water, and salt.

2. Bring to the boil and cover closely. Cook exactly 17 minutes. Remove from the heat and keep warm until ready to serve.

Yield: Four servings.

IF I WERE TO NAME THE ONE INGREDIENT THAT IS more often than not elaborately overcooked in American kitchens—be they in private homes or in restaurants—it would certainly be shrimp. It is beyond my concept how any home cook and certainly any professional chef refuses to understand that only the briefest simmering, a minute or two, to keep their texture firm and intact—not soggy, flabby, and fibrous—is necessary.

It is not only their brief cooking time that should give shrimp a special appeal to those who would cook in a hasty time period. Shrimp happen to be one of the great food delicacies of the world. I can recall several happy occasions when in mid-summer we have dined on a shrimp feast with family and friends, generally out of doors, at a table covered with newspapers to receive the shells, and with only a hot butter and lemon sauce in which to dip the shrimp—freshly steamed with beer and seasonings—as they were peeled.

Shrimp, cooked and left in the shell, can be prepared in a thousand different ways when cold. From a basic shrimp cocktail with a typical American cocktail sauce (ketchup, lemon juice, Worcestershire sauce, horseradish, and hot pepper sauce) to blendings with mayonnaise or vinaigrette sauces. One of the best of these sauces is the one known as rémoulade. This sauce, incidentally, is not the same as that in Louisiana or New Orleans cooking. That sauce, although tasty and excellent, is made with oil, lemon or vinegar, chopped celery, and green onions. The classic rémoulade has a mayonnaise base and contains chopped small sour pickles, chopped anchovy, capers, parsley, and tarragon.

Crevettes à la Bière
(Shrimp with beer)

3 pounds shrimp in the shell
4 cloves garlic, peeled
6 allspice
1 dried hot red pepper
Salt and freshly ground
pepper to taste

1 bay leaf
6 sprigs fresh parsley
2 sprigs fresh dill
1 12-ounce can beer

1. Combine all the ingredients in a heavy skillet and cover closely. Bring to the boil.

2. Let the shrimp simmer 2 minutes and remove from the heat. Serve in the shell, letting each guest peel his own. Serve hot with individual portions of melted lemon butter.

Yield: Eight servings.

Beurre au Citron
(Lemon butter)

¼ pound butter
Juice of ½ lemon
1 teaspoon Worcestershire
sauce

Salt and freshly ground
pepper to taste
1 clove garlic, unpeeled but
lightly crushed

1. Heat the butter until quite hot and almost bubbling.

2. Add the remaining ingredients and stir. Serve hot with shrimp steamed in beer.

Yield: About half a cup.

Crevettes Rémoulade

(Shrimp in mayonnaise sauce)

1½ pounds shrimp cooked in the shell (see recipe for shrimp cooked in beer)
1 egg yolk
1 teaspoon imported mustard
2 teaspoons tarragon vinegar
Salt and freshly ground pepper to taste
1 cup peanut, vegetable, or corn oil
1 tablespoon finely chopped drained capers
3 tablespoons finely chopped, drained cornichons (small, imported sour pickles)

1 tablespoon anchovy paste or chopped flat anchovy fillets
2 tablespoons finely chopped parsley
2 teaspoons chopped fresh tarragon, or ½ teaspoon dried tarragon
Juice of ½ lemon
8 leaves Boston lettuce
2 hard-cooked eggs, peeled and quartered
8 cherry tomatoes

1. Peel and devein the shrimp. Leave them whole or cut them in half. Set aside.

2. Put the yolk into a bowl and add the mustard, vinegar, and salt and pepper. Start beating with a wire whisk and gradually add the oil, beating vigorously with the whisk.

3. Squeeze the capers in a clean cloth to extract their liquid. Add the capers to the mayonnaise. Add the cornichons, parsley, and tarragon. Blend well.

4. Put shrimp in a bowl and sprinkle lemon juice over them. Add the sauce and blend well.

5. Arrange 2 lettuce leaves on each of 4 plates. Spoon equal portions of the shrimp onto the lettuce. Garnish with hard-cooked eggs and cherry tomatoes.

Yield: Four servings.

THE FIRST ANECDOTE I EVER HEARD ABOUT American cooking after I came to this country in 1939 had to do with that hastily made preparation called shrimp, lobster, or crabmeat Newberg. It is a story I have heard in several versions since then, but basically it concerns a customer named Wenberg who dined often at the old Delmonico's restaurant in Manhattan during the last quarter of the nineteenth century. Some say he created a dish with cream and egg yolks and sherry which he offered the chef and which subsequently was listed on menus as seafood Wenberg.

For years, it was said, Mr. Wenberg enjoyed a considerable rapport with the management and his name became famous and synonymous with the dish. Then one day he became involved in a heated argument with the restaurant's owner. He was banned from the premises and the dish was rechristened Newberg.

That history may be a bit of a fabrication, but the dish itself is excellent. Much of its success depends on quick cooking. There are actually two ways of making it, one with flour as a thickening agent, the other with only egg yolks used to thicken. I prefer the latter.

Not too many decades ago, chafing-dish cookery was a fad in this country, somewhat akin to fondue cookery today. It isn't surprising that the Newberg dishes were among the best known of the chafing-dish creations.

Although lobster or crabmeat may be used in preparing this dish, I find that shrimp are more conveniently cooked in the sauce from the raw state. In the long run, the shrimp provide more flavor. Note that the cooking time for the dish is reckoned in minutes, thus it will be best to start to prepare an accompaniment, such as rice, which requires longer cooking, a few minutes in advance.

Crevettes "Newberg"
(Shrimp in cream sauce)

2 tablespoons butter
1½ pounds shelled and deveined shrimp (1¾ pounds with shells on)
Salt and freshly ground pepper to taste

1 tablespoon paprika
1 tablespoon finely chopped shallots
⅓ cup dry sherry wine
1½ cups heavy cream
2 egg yolks

1. Melt the butter in a large heavy skillet and add the shrimp. Cook briefly and sprinkle with salt, pepper, and paprika.

2. Sprinkle with the shallots and stir. Add the wine and stir. As soon as the shrimp have lost their raw look, after a minute or so, transfer the shrimp to another skillet and cover. Keep warm.

3. Reduce the pan liquid by half and add 1¼ cups of cream. Cook about 5 minutes over high heat.

4. Beat the yolks with the remaining heavy cream and add it to the cream sauce, stirring rapidly. Bring almost but not quite to the boil. Add the shrimp and reheat.

Yield: Four servings.

Riz avec Pois et Persil
(Rice with parsley and peas)

3 tablespoons butter
2 tablespoons chopped onion
1 cup raw rice
1½ cups water
1 bay leaf

Salt and freshly ground pepper to taste
Tabasco sauce to taste
1 cup frozen peas
2 tablespoons finely chopped parsley

1. Melt 2 tablespoons of the butter in a saucepan and add the onion. Cook until wilted. Add the rice and stir briefly.

2. Add the water, bay leaf, salt and pepper, and Tabasco.

3. Bring to the boil. Cover and simmer 20 minutes.

4. Meanwhile, combine the peas with the remaining butter, and salt and pepper to taste—no liquid. Heat, shaking the saucepan to redistribute the peas so that they cook evenly, about 1 minute.

5. Add the peas and parsley to the rice and stir to blend.

Yield: Four servings.

WE HAVE DISCUSSED THE VIRTUES OF SHRIMP for cooking *à la minute*. Shrimp should be cooked at relatively high heat, whether in a skillet or in the oven, so that they change from a grayish, translucent state to achieve a red outer coating and a snow-white interior as rapidly as possible. The moment they become piping hot throughout, they are ready to be served, although a minute or two beyond that point will probably not make them unsavory.

I have had pointed out to me on several occasions various regional recipes across the United States that call for cooking shrimp half an hour or even longer. Like most things in cooking, I presume these recipes are designed for people who don't really care about food. They are, in my opinion, in much the same category as people who prefer their prize beef well-done.

Shrimp have a wholly admirable versatility. They adapt—in the best of taste—to a multitude of herbs, spices, and other seasonings.

Shrimp, like many fish soups of France, are totally complemented with the addition of a spoonful or so of the anise-flavored liqueur known as pernod or ricard. Either liqueur gives a curious and compelling flavor that is almost exotic and certainly welcome.

Shrimp in almost any form are also complemented by rice and that is recommended here. It is best to go about the preparation and cooking of the rice accompaniment before you tackle the shrimp.

Crevettes au Pernod
(Shrimp sauté with pernod)

1½ pounds shrimp
3 tablespoons butter
2 tablespoons finely chopped
  shallots

2 tablespoons pernod, ricard,
  or other anise-flavored
  liqueur
¾ cup heavy cream
  Salt and freshly ground
  pepper to taste

1. Peel the shrimp but leave the last tail segment intact. Split the shrimp down the back. Wash the shrimp under cold running water to remove the black vein down the back. Drain well.

2. Melt the butter in a skillet and add the shrimp and shallots. Cook, shaking and stirring and tossing the shrimp in the skillet. Cook quickly until the shrimp are pink all over, 3 or 4 minutes.

3. Add the pernod and stir. Using a slotted spoon, remove the shrimp to a warm dish. Add the cream to the skillet and cook over high heat about 1 minute. Add salt and pepper to taste. Return the shrimp to the sauce and cook just to heat through. Serve with rice.

Yield: Four servings.

Riz au Four

(Baked rice)

2½ tablespoons butter
2 tablespoons minced onion
¼ teaspoon minced garlic
1 cup uncooked rice
1½ cups chicken broth
2 sprigs parsley

1 sprig thyme, or ¼ teaspoon
  dried thyme
½ bay leaf
⅛ teaspoon cayenne pepper or
  Tabasco sauce to taste

1. Preheat the oven to 400 degrees.

2. Melt 1 tablespoon of the butter in a heavy ovenproof saucepan and cook the onion and garlic, stirring with a wooden spoon, until the onion is translucent. Add the rice and stir briefly over low heat until all the grains are coated with butter.

3. Stir in the broth, making sure there are no lumps in the rice. Add the parsley, thyme, bay leaf, and cayenne. Cover with a close-fitting lid and place in the oven.

4. Bake the rice exactly 17 minutes. Remove the cover and discard the parsley and thyme sprigs. Using a two-pronged fork, stir in the remaining butter.

Yield: Four servings.

THERE IS ONE ARTICLE OF FOOD, OFTEN FOUND on menus and much admired in America, that is almost if not impossible to define with any sense of total accuracy. That food is scampi. It is generally agreed that they are prawns, another name that is used loosely in this country to describe large shrimp.

European encyclopedias sometimes state that scampi is the Italian word for what are known in Ireland as Dublin Bay prawns, and then add that the Italian version is twice as large as the Dublin Bay version.

For simplicity's sake it seems reasonable to conclude that any recipe calling for "scampi" or "prawns" in this country can be properly made with shrimp, the larger the better.

The most frequent preparation of scampi in Italian restaurants in America is a hastily made dish in which the shrimp (or prawns or scampi) are bathed in a blend of olive oil, garlic according to the chef's conscience, plus parsley and oregano. And, at times, a sprinkling of fresh bread crumbs to contribute a bit of texture.

Once the mixture is blended (the shrimp, oil, and seasonings), there only remains the necessity to arrange the shellfish in a single layer in a baking dish (along with the marinating ingredients) and to broil—without even turning them—until the shrimp have lost their raw, grayish-white look and turn bright red on the exterior. Incidentally, the shrimp and marinade could easily be blended several hours in advance (not overnight) and refrigerated until ready to run under the broiler.

An excellent accompaniment for broiled scampi are curried sweet red peppers (bell peppers or "frying" peppers). This is a dish, too, that requires only a few brief minutes for cooking. While these two elements could easily suffice for a supper, the addition of rice would round out the meal rather nicely.

Crevettes "Scampi"
(Shrimp broiled in olive oil and seasonings)

2 pounds shrimp, the larger the better
½ cup olive oil
2 teaspoons finely chopped garlic
2 tablespoons finely chopped parsley
⅛ teaspoon hot red pepper flakes
½ teaspoon crushed dried oregano
2 tablespoons fine fresh bread crumbs
Salt and freshly ground pepper to taste

1. Preheat the broiler to high.
2. Split the shrimp down the back side. Rinse and pat dry. Or peel them but leave the last tail segment intact. Rinse and drain well.
3. Add the remaining ingredients to the shrimp and toss to coat evenly and well.
4. Line a baking dish with foil and arrange the shrimp over it.
5. Place the shrimp under the broiler about 3 to 4 inches from the source of heat. Broil 5 to 6 minutes. It is not necessary to turn the shrimp as they cook. Baste the shrimp and serve hot with curried sweet peppers and rice.

Yield: Four servings.

Julienne de Poivrons au Kari
(Curried sweet pepper strips)

2 pounds sweet green or red peppers
4 tablespoons olive oil
Salt and freshly ground pepper to taste
1 to 2 tablespoons curry powder

1. Cut the peppers in half. Scrape away and discard the seeds, white inner veins, and core. Place each pepper half, cut side down, on a flat surface and cut into ½-inch crosswise strips (julienne). There should be about 8 cups.

2. Using a very large skillet, heat the oil and, when it is hot but not quite smoking, add the pepper strips, salt and pepper and curry powder.

3. Cook, stirring, over high heat about 4 to 6 minutes, or until barely cooked. When ready, the pepper strips should be crisp-tender.

Yield: Four servings.

Riz au Four
(Baked rice)

3 tablespoons butter
⅓ cup minced onion
1½ cups uncooked rice
2¼ cups water
2 sprigs parsley

Salt and freshly ground
pepper to taste
2 sprigs thyme, or ½ teaspoon
dried thyme
½ bay leaf
Tabasco sauce to taste

1. Preheat the oven to 400 degrees.
2. Melt half the butter in a saucepan and add the onion. Cook, stirring, until wilted. Add the rice and stir to blend.
3. Add the water, stirring to make certain there are no lumps in the rice. Add the remaining ingredients. Cover with a close-fitting lid and, when the water boils, place the pan in the oven.
4. Bake exactly 17 minutes. Remove the cover and discard the parsley, bay leaf, and thyme sprigs. Using a two-pronged fork, stir in the remaining butter. If the rice is not to be served immediately, keep covered in a warm place.

Yield: Four to six servings.

MOST PROFESSIONAL CHEFS THAT I KNOW ARE amused with the idea that the Creole cooking of Louisiana in general, and of New Orleans in particular, has a solid French foundation. While it is indisputable that the French influence is present in that highly specialized form of American cookery, it is, in some of its terminology and practices, anything but a carbon copy of the French.

That is by no means to disparage Creole cookery. Far from it. The gumbos, the fabulous assortment of oyster dishes, such as Rockefeller and Bienville, and the trout Marguery as made in New Orleans are excellent. But they are regional and admirable creations. Consider one classic case. A true rémoulade sauce in French cookery is made with a mayonnaise base to which is added mustard, anchovy paste, capers, chopped cornichons, and herbs. The most popular rémoulade sauce in New Orleans is served on shrimp rémoulade. That version is made with an unthickened oil and vinegar base—a salad dressing really—to which is added chopped scallions, celery, parsley, Creole mustard, and paprika—and, sometimes, anchovy paste. Perhaps it is nitpicking, but that, in basic French terminology, is more a ravigote than a rémoulade.

One of the best, tastiest, and most easily made of Creole dishes is shrimp Creole. This starts with a combination of chopped onion, green pepper, and celery (the base of a good many Creole dishes), plus tomatoes. It is definitely not French although it could be vaguely related to the Midi or Provence in France where ripe tomatoes abound.

Shrimp Creole is an ideal dish for 60-minute cookery. After the vegetables have simmered briefly (they must retain their texture), the tomatoes are added and cooked for a short time. The shrimp are cooked separately, the two elements are combined, and that—with the addition of that traditional Southern seasoning, hot pepper sauce—is all there is to it. Serve with a platter of simply made boiled buttered rice (in French kitchens we call it Riz Créole) and that is a very good balance.

Crevettes à la Créole
(Shrimp in Creole sauce)

1¼ pounds raw shrimp in the shell
4 tablespoons butter
2 cups finely chopped onion
2 teaspoons minced garlic
1 cup chopped celery
2 cups green pepper, cored, seeded, and cut into 1-inch cubes

Salt and freshly ground pepper to taste
3 cups fresh tomatoes cut into small cubes, or use an equal amount of canned imported tomatoes
4 tablespoons finely chopped parsley
1 bay leaf
Tabasco sauce to taste

1. Peel the shrimp and remove the intestinal tract down the back. Set the shrimp aside.

2. Melt half the butter in a saucepan and add the onion and garlic. Cook about 5 minutes without browning. Add the celery and green pepper. Add salt and pepper to taste.

3. Cook about 4 minutes, stirring often. Do not overcook. The vegetables should remain crisp.

4. Add the tomatoes, parsley, and bay leaf. Cover. At the boil cook about 10 minutes. Add Tabasco sauce to taste.

5. In a skillet, melt the remaining butter and add the shrimp. Sprinkle with salt and pepper. Stir. Cook only about 1 minute, or until the shrimp lose their gray color.

6. Spoon the tomato mixture over the shrimp and stir. Bring to the boil. Serve piping hot with Creole rice.

Yield: Four servings.

Riz Créole
(Boiled rice)

4 cups water
Salt and freshly ground
pepper to taste

1 cup long grain rice
1 tablespoon butter
1 teaspoon lemon juice

1. Bring the water to a boil in a saucepan and add the salt and rice. When the water returns to the boil, let the rice boil vigorously in the water.

2. Let cook exactly 17 minutes. Drain in a colander and run hot water over it.

3. Add the butter, salt and pepper to taste. Sprinkle with lemon juice and toss until the grains are coated.

Yield: Four servings.

IT IS AN EASILY OBSERVED FACT IN THE WORLD of food that most people have a special liking for foods that are "stuffed." It might be the roast turkey, a breast of veal, peppers, onions, zucchini, clams, mussels, lobsters, or oysters. After all, oysters Rockefeller are, in a sense, "stuffed" with a spinach filling.

The reasons are as numerous as they are obvious. A "filling," "stuffing," "dressing," or "farce," call it what you will, offers an appealing contrast both in flavors and textures. And almost anything within reason can go into a well-made filling, from ground or chopped leftover meats and vegetables to whole sausage. (One of the most interesting "stuffed" foods I've ever sampled was cooked by a Cuban acquaintance several years ago, a roast loin of pork stuffed with chorizos, a fleshy garlic sausage.)

The cooking time for stuffed foods, of course, can vary from what amounts to seconds to an hour and longer. If cooking time is a factor, raw shrimp would be an excellent food for a well-seasoned stuffing.

In the following recipe, the cleaned shrimp are "butterflied," which is to say, split part way down and flattened lightly. The stuffing consists of a few additional raw shrimp, chopped mushrooms, celery, garlic, and parsley. There is a small amount of fresh bread crumbs and egg to bind the filling together. A small amount of filling is heaped onto each flattened shrimp. The dish is dotted with butter and it is placed under the broiler until cooked, about 5 minutes. The dish must not cook for an extended time or the shrimp will dry out. One word of caution: You should heat the shrimp in the baking dish on top of the stove before broiling. This will hasten the cooking time.

An excellent accompaniment for the shrimp are cherry tomatoes bordelaise, and these, too, of necessity, must be cooked in short order for more obvious reasons. If the tomatoes are overcooked their skins burst. They must be cooked in hot butter for a matter of moments. Their seasoning is chopped shallots and parsley, the traditional bordelaise flavors.

Crevettes Farcies
(Shrimp-stuffed shrimp)

---

22 to 32 medium to large
    shrimp, about 1¼ pounds
5 tablespoons butter
4 large mushrooms, slightly
    less than ¼ pound
⅔ cup finely chopped onion
⅔ cup finely chopped celery

½ teaspoon finely minced garlic
    Salt and freshly ground
    pepper to taste
¾ cup plus 1 tablespoon fine
    fresh bread crumbs
¼ cup finely chopped parsley
1 egg, lightly beaten

1. Preheat the broiler.

2. Peel and devein the shrimp or buy them already prepared. Set aside 16 large or 24 medium shrimp. Chop the remaining shrimp coarsely. There should be about ½ cup. Set aside.

3. Slice and finely chop the mushrooms. There should be about 1 cup. Set aside.

4. Melt 2 tablespoons of the butter in a saucepan and add the onion, celery, and garlic. Cook until wilted and add the mushrooms, salt, and pepper. Stir. Cook about 3 minutes.

5. Remove the saucepan from the heat and add the chopped shrimp. Stir. Add ¾ cup of the bread crumbs, parsley, and egg. Stir to blend. Add salt and pepper to taste.

6. Butterfly the shrimp. That is to say, split them down the back almost but not all the way through. Open up the shrimp split side down on a flat surface.

7. Spoon equal portions of the stuffing on top of each shrimp as ''stuffing.''

8. Use 1 tablespoon of the butter to grease a baking dish large

enough to hold the shrimp in one layer. Arrange the shrimp over the dish.

9. Sprinkle the shrimp with the tablespoon of bread crumbs and dot with the remaining 2 tablespoons of butter. Place the baking dish on top of the stove and bring the juices around the shrimp to the boil and heat thoroughly. (The butter will melt.)

10. Place the shrimp under the broiler about 5 inches from the source of heat. Cook about 5 minutes, or until the shrimp are heated through and are nicely browned.

Yield: Four servings.

Tomates Cerises Bordelaise
(Cherry tomatoes sautéed with shallots)

---

1 quart ripe but firm cherry tomatoes	1 tablespoon finely chopped shallots
2 tablespoons butter Salt and freshly ground pepper to taste	1 tablespoon finely chopped parsley

1. Pick over the tomatoes and discard the stems. Rinse and drain the tomatoes.

2. Melt the butter in a large skillet and when it is quite hot but not brown add the tomatoes and salt and pepper. Cook, shaking the skillet so that the tomatoes cook evenly.

3. Cook about 2 minutes. They should just be heated through. If they are overcooked they will collapse. Add the shallots and parsley and cook, shaking the skillet, about 15 seconds.

Yield: Four servings.

ONE OF THE FALSE CONCLUSIONS ASSUMED BY hundreds and thousands of amateur cooks is that the preparation time for any given recipe is in exact ratio to the number of ingredients it contains. It is an unfortunate conclusion and a pity, for you cannot equate the length of time to make a dish with what is known in the newspaper field as "column inches."

To choose an obvious example, many dishes in Indian cookery may call for as many as a dozen or more dried spices, most of which will come in jars with screw tops. Their use simply involves going to a pantry shelf, collecting the spices, and measuring out the amounts required. It is an act that can be performed in minutes. In opposition to that, consider the French preparation known as a salade russe. Basically it involves a very few vegetables—carrots, turnips, and so on—but the dish is a bit tedious to make because it isn't the numbers of vegetables involved. It is what has to be done to them—the careful dicing, for example—that can require a great deal of time to arrive at a finished product.

It may come as a surprise to numerous readers to know that one version of the well-known Spanish dish called paella can easily be made within the confines of an hour. Basically it consists of cooking sausage and chicken pieces together before adding a few chopped vegetables, herbs and spices, rice, and liquids that include canned tomatoes. Seafood in the form of clams and shrimp is added and the dish is covered and simmered until it is ready for the table.

If you plot the timing and preparation carefully, it is a dish that can be made, start to finish, in about 45 minutes. As the chicken and sausages cook, for example, there is ample time to chop the onion, green pepper, and so on for the second step. As these cook together, the seafood can be rinsed and peeled as a last addition to complete the dish.

A good paella is a meal unto itself but there is one salad that complements it admirably. This is a hastily made orange and black olive salad that is tossed together with an oil and vinegar dressing, with paprika and finely minced garlic.

Paella

2 tablespoons olive oil
4 sweet or hot Italian sausages
4 small chicken thighs (or use 2 thighs and 2 legs, separated to make 4 pieces), about 1 pound
1 green, unblemished sweet pepper, cored, seeded, and cut into 1-inch cubes
1 cup finely chopped onion
1 teaspoon finely minced garlic
1 dried hot red pepper, optional
½ teaspoon stem saffron

1 large bay leaf
1 sprig fresh thyme, or ½ teaspoon dried thyme
1 cup undrained canned tomatoes
1 cup rice
¾ cup water
Salt and freshly ground pepper to taste
8 littleneck clams, the smaller the better
8 shrimp, peeled and deveined
Finely chopped parsley

1. Heat the oil in a large skillet. Prick the sausages with a fork and add them. Cook, turning often, about 5 minutes.

2. Add the chicken pieces skin side down and continue cooking the sausages and chicken until the chicken skin is browned, about 5 minutes. Turn the pieces often and continue cooking about 10 minutes, or until the sausages have cooked, a total of 20 minutes, and the chicken 15 minutes.

3. As the sausages and chicken cook, prepare the pepper, onion, and garlic. Add these to the skillet.

4. Add the saffron, bay leaf, and thyme. Stir.

5. Add the tomatoes, rice, water, and salt and pepper. Cover closely. Cook 15 minutes.

6. As the mixture cooks, rinse and drain the clams. Peel and devein the shrimp.

7. Add the clams and shrimp to the rice mixture. Cover again and let cook about 8 minutes longer. Serve sprinkled with chopped parsley.

Yield: Four servings.

Salade d'Oranges et Olives Noires
(Orange and black olive salad)

---

2 seedless navel oranges, about 1¼ pounds total weight

8 black olives, preferably imported

1 teaspoon paprika

½ teaspoon finely minced garlic

1 teaspoon red wine vinegar

3 tablespoons olive oil
Salt and freshly ground pepper to taste

2 tablespoons finely chopped parsley

1. Trim off the ends of the oranges. Peel the oranges and cut them into ¼-inch slices. Put them in a mixing bowl.

2. Add the olives.

3. Blend the paprika, garlic, vinegar and oil, and salt and pepper. Blend well and pour this over the oranges and olives. Blend well.

4. Sprinkle with parsley and serve.

Yield: Four servings.

Lamb

MORE AND MORE IN THIS DAY AND AGE, people are learning that some of the simplest dishes have a grand and justified appeal.

Here is an outline in detail for two of the quickest and simplest methods for cooking lamb chops. One will be the chops cooked under the broiler flame. The other will be the chops pan broiled, which is to say, cooked in a skillet. I will all but ignore the use of a grill in cooking the chops.

Should you choose to cook lamb chops under the broiler of your home stove, the cooking time will depend primarily on two things. One consideration is how hot the source of heat is. That temperature will vary from one make of stove to the other, even when the heat is set at its highest setting. The second thing is how close the meat is placed to the source of heat. The primary choice is this: If you want the meat to be quite rare inside (*bleu* we say in French), you should put the meat quite close to the flame, turning once and browning well and quickly on both sides. In any event, the oven door should be left open at all times while broiling, or the meat will "steam."

Should you wish to pan broil your chops, the most important thing is the skillet. It should be heavy. A black iron skillet is ideal. Do not add any form of fat but heat the skillet until almost "smoking" or red hot. Add the chops and cook about 3 or 4 minutes to a side, longer if you want the meat well done. Turn the lamb chops and cook until they are nicely browned.

Côtes d'Agneau Grillées
(Broiled lamb chops)

8 lamb chops, about ½ pound each and about 1½ inches thick

Salt and freshly ground pepper to taste

1. Preheat the broiler to high.
2. Sprinkle the chops with salt and pepper. Arrange the chops on a baking rack and place under the broiler about 5 or 6 inches from the source of heat. Leave the broiler door open. Broil about 5 minutes on one side and turn.
3. Continue broiling the second side. If you want to speed up cooking for a rarer interior, move the broiling pan closer to the source of heat, about 3 inches away. Cook about 3 minutes. If you want a medium or well-done interior, leave the broiler in its original position and broil about 5 to 10 minutes.

Yield: Four servings.

Côtes d'Agneau Poêlées
(Pan-broiled lamb chops)

8 lamb chops, each about ½ pound and 1½ inches thick
Salt and freshly ground pepper to taste
4 tablespoons butter

1 teaspoon finely chopped garlic
2 tablespoons finely chopped parsley

[180]

1. Sprinkle the chops with salt and pepper on all sides.

2. Use one or two heavy skillets, such as a black iron skillet, large enough to hold the chops in one layer.

3. Heat the skillet until almost smoking. Do not add any oil or other fat. Add the chops and cook on one side about 4 minutes until well browned. The chops should be cooked at all times over moderately high heat. Turn the chops and pour off the fat from the skillet or skillets.

4. Continue cooking the chops on the second side about 3 minutes.

5. Turn the lamb chops on the sides to cook the rim of fat. It may be necessary to let them rest against the side of the skillet to keep them upright. Let cook about 2 minutes and return them to the second side and continue cooking about 1 minute.

6. Remove the chops to a warm platter and pour off the fat from the skillet. Add the butter and, when it is hot, add the garlic. Cook briefly and pour over the chops. Serve sprinkled with chopped parsley.

Yield: Four servings.

Pommes de Terre à Cru
(Skillet-fried potatoes)

4 large Idaho potatoes, about 1½ pounds
¼ cup peanut, vegetable, or corn oil
2 tablespoons butter

Salt and freshly ground pepper to taste
1 clove garlic, finely minced
2 tablespoons finely chopped parsley

1. Peel the potatoes and cut them into very thin slices, using a hand slicer. As they are sliced drop them into cold water to pre-

vent discoloration. Or wait until the last moment before the potatoes are to be cooked to peel and slice them. There should be about 3 cups loosely packed sliced potatoes.

2. Heat the oil in a skillet, preferably one with rounded sides. Dry the potatoes with paper towels. When the oil is hot, add the potatoes, tossing and shaking the skillet to prevent sticking. Cook about 15 minutes, or until golden, turning them gently to prevent breaking the slices.

3. Drain the potatoes in a colander, pouring all the oil from the skillet. Add the butter to the skillet and, when it is hot, add the potatoes and salt and pepper. Add the garlic and parsley and continue cooking, stirring and tossing gently, about 3 minutes.

Yield: Four servings.

QUICKLY MADE MEAL AND A DINNER WITH style are by no means mutually exclusive, and one of the most concrete expressions of that proposition is the following pair of recipes. The heart of this meal is one of America's choicest and most elegant cuts of meat—a tender, succulent rack of lamb.

The cost of a rack of lamb is, admittedly, somewhat elevated, but when this meal is thought of as a somewhat special dinner for four, the cost may not seem all that abhorrent.

When the lamb is purchased, it is best to have the butcher prepare it for cooking precisely as indicated in the recipe. Remember that fast cooking is essential to a proper rack of lamb. The total cooking time from the moment the lamb is placed under the broiler until it is taken from the oven should be from 12 to 16 minutes. This should ensure that the center of the meat ranges from pink to red. If the meat is overcooked, it will become grayish and not be so moist and succulent.

Grilled tomatoes go well with the lamb. Toss a salad at the last moment to be served with the main course or afterward. Serve pears and cheese at the conclusion of the meal.

Carré d'Agneau Persillé
(Parsleyed rack of lamb)

---

2 racks of lamb, about 2½ pounds combined weight	½ cup bread crumbs
Salt and freshly ground pepper to taste	3 tablespoons chopped parsley
	1 clove garlic, finely minced
4 tablespoons butter	1 shallot, finely minced
	1 teaspoon olive oil

1. Have the butcher hack or saw off the chine bone (the flat,

continuous bone at the top of the ribs), leaving the meat exposed.

2. Preheat the broiler to high. If the oven is heated separately, preheat it also to 500 degrees.

3. Using the fingers and a sharp knife, pull and slice off the top thick layer of fat from the racks of lamb. When ready, the loins and ribs should be almost clean of fat. Hack off the ends of the ribs, leaving about 1½ inches of the ribs intact and extending from the loin meat.

4. Rub with butter a baking dish large enough to hold the racks of lamb in one layer and close together. Place the racks meat side down in the dish and dot the ribs with 2 tablespoons of the butter.

5. Meanwhile, combine the bread crumbs, parsley, garlic, shallot, and olive oil in a bowl.

6. Place the racks of lamb under the broiler and cook about 2 or 3 minutes. Turn and cook about 2 or 3 minutes.

7. Sprinkle the meaty side of the ribs with the bread crumb mixture. Melt the remaining 2 tablespoons of butter and pour it over the ribs. Place in the oven and bake 8 to 10 minutes, depending on the degree of doneness desired.

Yield: Four to six servings.

Tomates Grillées à la Provençale
(Grilled tomatoes with garlic and rosemary)

---

2 ripe, firm, and unblemished
   tomatoes
3 cloves garlic, each cut into 4
   or 6 slivers

1½ teaspoons rosemary leaves
Salt and freshly ground
   pepper to taste
3 tablespoons olive oil

1. Preheat the broiler to high.

2. Split the tomatoes in half and arrange them cut side up in a baking dish just large enough to hold the four halves compactly.

3. Stud the surface of each half with equal amounts of slivered garlic and rosemary leaves. Sprinkle with salt and pepper to taste. Spoon the olive oil over the tomatoes.

4. When ready to serve, place the tomatoes under the broiler and cook until the surfaces are blistered, bubbling, and piping hot. Quickly remove and discard the garlic and rosemary and serve immediately.

Yield: Four servings.

WHEN IT COMES TO WHAT MIGHT BE CALLED cooking *à la minute,* the virtues of ground meat are immediately apparent. Chief among them is their cooking nature. Toss a quarter pound of first-quality ground beef on a hot grill or into a lightly oiled (or even unoiled) skillet, add a touch of salt, a sprinkling of pepper, and a dollop of butter and the results are almost foolproof.

Trouble is, a diet of ground beef can be cloying to the appetite, and fortunately there are numerous other ground meats to resort to, among them lamb and pork (ground chicken and fish can also be delicious).

Ground lamb patties are easily made and even more expeditious to cook. One thing to remember is that ground lamb should be cooked to the well-done stage—well-done, that is, but still moist inside—for most palates.

In the following recipes, the patties are flavored with dill and a touch of onion, plus bread crumbs to make them tender and one egg to bind them together. Dill is one of those herbs that are particularly complementary to lamb, thus it is also used in the quickly made light cream and mushroom sauce to accompany the patties once they are cooked. The total advance preparation of these patties can be reckoned in 15 minutes or less and, if it seems more profitable, may be done several hours prior to cooking.

An ideal side dish for the meat are easily made broiled tomatoes, which can be assembled in a very brief while once the lamb patties have been shaped. If you wish a starch to accompany this meal, buttered fine noodles—plain or tossed with poppy seeds—are recommended.

Bitoks d'Agneau
(Broiled lamb patties)

1½ pounds ground lean lamb
3 tablespoons plus 1 teaspoon butter
⅓ cup finely chopped onion
½ cup fresh bread crumbs
3 tablespoons plus 2 teaspoons finely chopped dill or parsley
1 egg, lightly beaten

Salt and freshly ground pepper to taste
¼ pound mushrooms, quartered or sliced
1 tablespoon finely chopped shallots
¼ cup dry white wine
½ cup heavy cream

1. Place the lamb in a mixing bowl.

2. Melt 1 teaspoon of butter in a skillet and add the onion. Cook, stirring until wilted. Add this to the lamb.

3. Add the bread crumbs, 3 tablespoons chopped dill, 1 egg, and salt and pepper to taste. Blend well and divide into 8 portions. Shape each portion into a patty.

4. Melt 2 tablespoons of butter in a skillet and cook the lamb patties, 3 or 4 minutes to a side.

5. Remove the patties and wipe out the skillet. Add the remaining 1 tablespoon of butter and the mushrooms. Cook until lightly browned. Add the shallots and wine. Cook until the liquid evaporates almost entirely. Add the cream. Cook about 5 minutes and add the remaining dill. Serve the hot sauce poured over the patties.

Yield: Four servings.

Tomates Grillées
(Broiled tomatoes with garlic and marjoram)

4 small-to-medium ripe but
   firm tomatoes
8 slivers garlic
   Salt and freshly ground
   pepper to taste

4 teaspoons dried marjoram
   or oregano, crumbled
8 teaspoons olive oil

1. Preheat the broiler to high.

2. Cut the tomatoes in half width-wise. Arrange them cut side up in a baking dish. Insert 1 sliver of garlic in the center of each half.

3. Sprinkle with salt and pepper. Sprinkle with equal amounts of marjoram. Sprinkle each with 1 teaspoon of oil. Place under the broiler for 8 to 10 minutes, until bubbling and the tips of the garlic start to brown. Remove the garlic and serve.

Yield: Four servings.

ONE OF THE QUESTIONS THAT SEEMS TO LOOM large in the home cook's mind is whether or not foods can be cooked with equal success under a broiler or on top of the stove, using a skillet. It is an understandable dilemma, for foods cooked under the broiler generate a good deal of smoke and odors in small facilities without proper ventilation.

Chops, as I have noted previously, are ideal for a meal to be cooked in less than an hour for obvious reasons. To my mind, pan-broiling in the home would be far preferable to cooking over or under a high heat for the reasons outlined above.

One of the pleasures of lamb chops is that they adapt well to so many seasonings, such as herbs and spices and sauces. They are excellent, of course, simply grilled and served with only melted butter. They can take on an added dimension when served with or on a provençale "garnish." This would be a quickly made, savory garnish with a base of tomatoes but including green and black olives, onion, garlic, and a bit of rosemary.

The lamb chops listed here weigh in the vicinity of 1 pound each. They require about 45 minutes cooking if they are to be served medium-rare. They must be cooked longer, of course, if you wish to serve them well-done. Serve the chops and the provençale garnish, if desired, with rice cooked according to package directions.

The fact is that skillet cookery is sometimes far preferable for certain dishes that are usually broiled under direct heat. For example, foods that have a high fat content (such as chops that are rimmed with fat) or those that must be cooked for an extended period are best "pan-broiled." (Pan-broiled is a curious phrase, incidentally; in its most basic sense, broiling involves cooking food under or over direct and intense heat, such as hot coals or a flame.)

When fat is exposed to direct heat, it tends to flame up, which creates both smoke and odors. Foods that require long cooking also may burn under direct and intense heat.

The lamb chops in the recipe for the "hasty" meal outlined here are a case in point. It is a question of personal taste, but I prefer one thick lamb chop to a couple of chops with half the thickness.

Côtes d'Agneau à la Provençale
(Lamb chops with Provençale garnish)

4 thick lamb chops, about 1
   pound each
   Salt and freshly ground
   pepper to taste
1 tablespoon oil

1 teaspoon dried rosemary
   Provençale garnish (see
   recipe)
   Chopped parsley

1. Sprinkle the chops with salt and pepper.
2. Heat the oil in a heavy skillet and add the chops. Cook until well browned on one side, about 10 minutes. Turn and cook 7 or 8 minutes. Turn onto the side and cook to brown the fat well, about 10 minutes.
3. Turn the meat meat side down and cook 15 to 18 minutes, or until the chops are nicely browned all over. Five minutes before the chops are done, sprinkle both sides with the rosemary. This produces a medium-rare chop. Cook 15 minutes longer for well-done meat.
4. Arrange the garnish over the bottom of a serving dish. Arrange the chops over and sprinkle with chopped parsley.

Yield: Four servings.

Garniture Provençale
(Provençale garnish)

2 tablespoons olive oil
2 tablespoons chopped onion
1 teaspoon chopped garlic
1¼ pounds fresh tomatoes (about 3) cored, peeled, and cut into 1-inch cubes, about 2 to 3 cups

Salt and freshly ground pepper to taste
1 teaspoon dried rosemary, chopped
⅓ cup drained imported black olives
½ cup drained pitted green olives

1. Heat the oil in a skillet or casserole and add the onion and garlic. Cook briefly until wilted.

2. Add the tomatoes, salt and pepper, and rosemary.

3. Let cook about 5 to 10 minutes. Do not overcook. The tomatoes should not be mushy. Add the olives and heat through.

Yield: Four servings.

WHEN IT COMES TO "GOURMET" COOKERY, there is no chef in the world who would put a price on the ingredients. That is to say that a finely made omelet when eggs are at a peak of freshness can be just as seductive in flavor as a truffled pâté or nightingales' tongues (a legendary dish which I never hope to try).

The dishes printed in this book range from a humble sauerkraut to filet mignon; from hamburger creations to a richly endowed crabmeat in cream sauce.

Fine lamb is one of the great—and expensive—American delicacies. Lamb has limited qualities where cooking in less than 60 minutes is concerned. No choice where roast legs and saddles of lamb and stews are concerned.

Among the few dishes—variations on simply grilled or broiled chops—that require a brief period in preparation and cooking, is a dish—admittedly costly—called noisettes d'agneau à l'anglaise, boneless lamb chops English-style.

The name *à l'anglaise* is used in several ways in a French kitchen. At times it means foods cooked in water. In this case it implies a breaded dish sautéed in oil with hazelnut brown butter poured over when ready to serve.

The noisettes made from the choicest parts of loin lamb chops are fork-tender and eminently edible. The total cooking time for the noisettes or medallions is less than 5 minutes. It may be added that there is a final culinary conceit in the preparation of this dish. The butter is delicately scented with chopped tarragon, a flavor that marries admirably well with lamb.

The lamb itself could be accompanied by a simple platter of boiled parsley potatoes. An excellent salad for the meal would be cold string beans with a well-seasoned vinaigrette sauce.

Noisettes d'Agneau à l'Anglaise
(Breaded lamb medallions)

8 loin lamb chops, each about 6 ounces and about 1 inch thick
Salt and freshly ground pepper to taste
2 tablespoons flour
1 large egg, beaten
1 tablespoon water

1½ cups bread crumbs
3 tablespoons peanut, vegetable, or corn oil
¼ cup butter
1 tablespoon chopped fresh tarragon, or 1 teaspoon dried tarragon

1. Hack off, or have the butcher hack off, the top chine bone and cut away the rib bone of each chop. Trim away all but a light layer of fat from around the chop. Using a flat mallet, lightly flatten each chop. When flattened, the meat should be about ½ inch thick.

2. Sprinkle the medallions on both sides with salt and pepper. Dredge lightly in flour and shake off any excess. Beat the egg with the water. Dip the medallions in the egg mixture to coat well. Place in the crumbs and dredge to coat thoroughly on both sides. Pat lightly with the side of a heavy knife to help the crumbs adhere.

3. Heat the oil in a heavy skillet large enough to hold the medallions in one layer. Add the medallions and cook about 1½ minutes, or until golden brown, on one side. Continue cooking until golden brown on the other side, about 2 minutes. Remove to a warm serving dish.

4. Heat the butter in a skillet until it is foamy and turns a hazelnut brown. Do not let it burn. Remove from the heat and add the tarragon. Stir quickly and pour the sauce over the medallions.

Yield: Four servings.

Haricots Verts Vinaigrette
(String beans with vinaigrette sauce)

¾ pound string beans   ½ cup vinaigrette sauce

1. Trim or snap off the ends of the beans. Otherwise, leave the beans whole. Drop them into boiling water and cook until crisp-tender, about 5 minutes. Do not overcook.
2. Drain and run the beans briefly under cold running water. Drain again, and while the beans are still warm, pour the sauce over the beans.

Yield: Four to six servings.

Sauce Vinaigrette
(Vinaigrette sauce)

1 teaspoon imported mustard, such as Dijon or Düsseldorf
1 tablespoon finely chopped shallot
½ teaspoon finely minced garlic

2 tablespoons finely chopped parsley
1 tablespoon red wine vinegar
¼ cup peanut or olive oil
Salt and freshly ground pepper to taste

1. Put the mustard, shallot, garlic, parsley, and vinegar in a mixing bowl.
2. Gradually add the oil while stirring with a wire whisk. Add the salt a little at a time. Add the pepper. Stir until well blended.

Yield: About half a cup.

INDIAN COOKERY, FOR THE MOST PART, IS ONE of the most intricate—as well as most versatile—of foreign cuisines. Over the years I have dined at numerous Indian tables, both professionally and socially. And while I have never tried to master that country's cooking in depth (the curry that I prepare is almost a study in French adaptation), I do enjoy preparing skewered kebabs with a basic assortment of "traditional" spices—turmeric (which gives curry powder its yellow color), coriander, and cumin. And happily, I almost invariably have at my disposal fresh ginger and (invariably) fresh garlic.

I am also keen on a kind of "chutney" taught me by an Indian friend, a chilled cucumber and yogurt relish that is simple and quick to prepare, a dish that makes a happy foil for the "spiciness" of the kebabs.

The preparation of the kebabs and their arrangement on skewers requires but a nick in time, and this is another of those dishes that may be done at the last moment, or perhaps the evening before. Some people aver that it is preferable to prepare the meat in its marinade the evening before, but it isn't essential. The cooking time for the kebabs is about 10 minutes when cooked under a home broiler.

The classic accompaniment for such a dish is plain rice, which could be cooked in 15 to 20 minutes. The best way to set about such a meal is, in my mind, to prepare the meat in its seasonings. Put the rice on to boil and prepare the cucumber relish. Skewer the meats and place them under the preheated broiler.

Brochettes d'Agneau à l'Indienne
(Lamb kebabs)

24 cubes of lean lamb, about 1¾ pounds, preferably meat from the leg
1 teaspoon finely chopped garlic
2 teaspoons finely chopped ginger
2 tablespoons lemon juice
¼ cup peanut, vegetable, or corn oil
½ teaspoon ground turmeric
½ teaspoon ground coriander
½ teaspoon ground cumin
⅛ teaspoon cayenne pepper
Salt and freshly ground pepper to taste
1 tablespoon grated onion

1. It will expedite the preparation if you have the butcher cube the lamb.

2. Put the lamb in a bowl and add the remaining ingredients.

3. Preheat the broiler to high.

4. When ready to cook, arrange equal amounts of the meat on 4 skewers.

5. Place the skewered lamb about 4 or 5 inches from the source of heat. Cook, turning so as to cook the meat evenly, about 10 minutes. Serve with rice and cucumber with yogurt sauce.

Yield: Four servings.

Sauce de Concombres à l'Indienne

(Cucumber with yogurt sauce)

1 cucumber, about ¾ pound
¾ teaspoon whole cumin seeds
2 teaspoons chopped, seeded, hot fresh green chiles, optional
1 cup yogurt
Salt to taste
1 teaspoon peanut, vegetable, or corn oil
½ teaspoon finely chopped garlic

1. Use the coarse blade of a grater to grate the cucumber coarsely. Put it in a bowl and set aside.

2. Put the cumin seeds in a small saucepan and cook until "toasted." Do not burn. When they start to crackle, remove from the heat, shaking the skillet.

3. Combine the yogurt with the cucumbers, cumin seeds, chiles, salt, oil, and garlic. Blend well and chill.

Yield: About two cups.

Veal and Calf's Liver

THERE IS A SMALL MAGAZINE, EDITED AND PUB-lished in Manhattan, that is little known to the world at large, but is admired and respected by many chefs in the United States. It is the official publication of the Vatel Club, to which most of the finest French chefs in this country belong, and the editors declare that it is "the only culinary review in the French language published in North America."

I was much amused, in a recent issue, to read about the origins of one of the best and most quickly made veal dishes in the French repertory. The dish is called côtes de veau Foyot or veal chops in the style of Foyot. The magazine outlines the history of the Café Foyot, in its heyday one of the greatest restaurants in Paris. It was still in existence during the siege of Paris in 1870, until, I believe, shortly after World War I.

The dish is made as follows: You take a fine, pink-textured veal chop and cook it on both sides in butter. It takes only 2 minutes to a side, if the skillet is heavy enough and the heat is high enough.

You combine fresh bread crumbs with grated Parmesan cheese and a portion of butter at room temperature. This mixture is "workable." That is to say, it is firm enough to be shaped by hand. You shape the mixture in 4 flat portions, just large enough to cover each chop, arrange the chops in the skillet containing chopped shallots, and pour in a touch of dry white wine. Then you bake it 10 minutes uncovered and then loosely covered with foil, for about 30 minutes in all.

That's all there is to it. The dish is, to me, a classic example of how great French cooking need not take hours and days of preparation to be brought to simple perfection. Côtes de veau Foyot is a dish suitable for a gathering of your most discriminating friends. It is worthy of a good wine, too, perhaps a fine Burgundy of good vintage. An easily made and excellent accompaniment for the dish would be noodles with a quick, simple, and freshly made tomato sauce.

Côtes de Veau Foyot
(Veal chops with Parmesan cheese in white wine)

---

4 veal chops, about ¾ pound each
Salt and freshly ground pepper to taste
6 tablespoons butter at room temperature

½ cup fresh bread crumbs
½ cup freshly grated Parmesan cheese
2 tablespoons finely chopped shallots
¼ cup dry white wine

1. Preheat the oven to 400 degrees.
2. Sprinkle the chops on both sides with salt and pepper.
3. Melt 2 tablespoons of butter in a heavy skillet and add the chops. Cook over high heat until golden brown on one side, about 2 minutes. Turn the chops and cook 2 minutes longer, or until golden brown on the other side. Transfer the chops to a platter and keep warm.
4. Meanwhile, mix the bread crumbs, cheese, and remaining 4 tablespoons of butter with the hands, until thoroughly worked together and blended. Divide the mixture into 4 portions of equal size.

5. Sprinkle the shallots over the bottom of the skillet in which the chops cooked. Return the chops to the skillet.

6. Work the bread crumb mixture into flat sheets to fit the top of each chop. Place on the tops of the chops.

7. Pour the wine around the chops.

8. Place, uncovered, in the oven and bake about 10 minutes, or until the tops are appetizingly brown. Place a layer of foil on top, letting it rest loosely over the veal. Return to the oven and continue baking about 20 minutes.

9. When ready to serve, do not spoon the sauce over the veal. Spoon it around the veal.

Yield: Four servings.

Nouilles à la Sauce Tomate
(Noodles with fresh tomato sauce)

2 tablespoons butter
¼ cup finely chopped onion
1 small clove garlic, finely minced
1 14-ounce can imported tomatoes with tomato paste
1 bay leaf
Salt and freshly ground pepper to taste
½ pound medium-width noodles

1. Melt half the butter in a saucepan and add the onion and garlic. Cook, stirring briefly, and add the tomatoes. Add the bay leaf, and salt and pepper and cover.

2. Let simmer about 10 minutes. Remove the bay leaf. Swirl in the remaining butter.

3. Cook the noodles to the desired degree of doneness. Drain well and serve hot with the sauce.

Yield: Four servings.

BELGIAN ENDIVE IS, TO MY TASTE, ONE OF THE finest of cooked vegetables when braised. It does require an extended cooking time, time in which the other ingredients for a meal can be assembled, chopped, heated, and so on.

There is an exception to that lengthy cooking time for the vegetable (which also, uncooked, makes a fine addition to a salad bowl). If the endive is shredded, the cooking time is greatly reduced.

One of the meats that is enormously complemented when served or cooked in tandem with endive is a nice cut of pink, tender veal. When placed in combination with braised endive, which has an uncommon, subtle flavor that is at once slightly bitter and slightly sweet, the veal should not be overpowering. The simpler the better.

One of the simplest ways of cooking veal (other than grilling it, of course) is a simple sauté, topping it off with a sauce consisting of nothing more than a few tablespoons of chopped shallots, a dash of white wine, and a little veal or chicken broth to thin and increase the quantity of the juice.

Incidentally, the sauce for the veal calls for swirling in butter as a last step before serving. I have often been asked why this is done. It is for the simple reason that butter, in effect, tends to thicken if it is swirled in. Care must be taken, however, not to boil the sauce after the butter is added or it will separate.

Both the veal and endive in these recipes are cooked quickly and may be put on the stove to cook simultaneously. There will be ample time for preparing a mixed green salad as an accompaniment.

Côtes de Veau aux Endives
(Veal chops with braised endives)

4 loin veal chops, ½ pound
  each
  Salt and freshly ground
  pepper
4 tablespoons butter

2 tablespoons chopped shallots
¼ cup dry white wine
½ cup fresh or canned chicken
  broth
  Braised endives (see recipe)

1. Sprinkle the chops on both sides with salt and pepper.

2. Melt 3 tablespoons of the butter in a heavy skillet large enough to hold the chops in one layer. Add the chops and cook on one side about 5 minutes, or until golden brown.

3. Turn the chops and cook on the other side about 6 minutes, or until cooked through. Do not overcook or the veal will be dry.

4. Remove the chops to a serving platter and cover with foil to keep warm.

5. Add the shallots and cook briefly, stirring. Add the wine and cook down to half the quantity. Add the broth and cook down quickly until reduced to about half the original quantity. Swirl in the remaining butter.

6. Spoon the sauce over the chops and serve with braised endives.

Yield: Four servings.

Endives Braisées
(Braised endives)

1¼ pounds fresh Belgian endives
 2 tablespoons butter
  Juice of ½ lemon or lime

  Salt and freshly ground
  pepper to taste
¼ teaspoon sugar

1. Trim off the ends of each endive. Place the endives on a flat surface and cut on the diagonal into very thin strips. There should be about 6 cups of shredded endives.

2. Melt the butter in a heavy skillet and add the endives. Add the lemon juice, salt and pepper, and sugar.

3. Cook, stirring often, about 3 minutes, or until wilted. Cover and cook about 8 minutes. Uncover and continue cooking, stirring often, about 3 or 4 minutes, or until lightly browned.

Yield: Four servings.

Salade Panachée
(Mixed green salad)

1 bunch watercress
1 head Boston lettuce
1 ripe tomato, cored and cut into eighths
6 radishes, trimmed and thinly sliced
2 tablespoons tarragon vinegar

1 clove garlic, finely minced
1 tablespoon imported mustard, such as Dijon or Düsseldorf
6 tablespoons olive oil
Salt and freshly ground pepper to taste

1. Trim off the tough stems of the watercress. Core the Boston lettuce and separate the leaves. Rinse the greens and shake off the excess moisture. Put the greens in a mixing bowl and add the tomato and radishes.

2. Blend the vinegar, minced garlic, and mustard in a mixing bowl. Stir with a whisk, gradually adding the oil. Add salt and pepper to taste.

3. Toss the greens with the dressing.

Yield: Four servings.

ONE OF THE BEST, TASTIEST, AND FASTEST ground meat dishes in the French repertory is known as veal cutlets Pojarski. Like bitoks, it is a kind of hamburger. The story of the origin of the name is well known. There was a tavern in a Russian town called Torjok, and the proprietor of the inn was named Pojarski. Legend has it that he created one or more of the ground beef dishes that bear his name, and these he served to passengers who passed his way in their carriages.

There are numerous basic ingredients other than veal that may be used in making Pojarski. It can be made, for example, with ground chicken and salmon.

To prepare veal Pojarski, the meat is twice ground (or it may be ground in a food processor). The meat is mixed with bread crumbs and cream and seasoned lightly with nutmeg, salt, and pepper. This is divided into equal portions and each portion shaped into "cutlets," that is to say, in the shape of chops such as pork or lamb chops. The cutlets are cooked in butter and served with a bit of noisette butter poured over.

Fresh peas have been used as an accompaniment for the veal Pojarski, the peas combined with cooked potatoes.

To go about it, cook the potatoes in their jackets, and peel them when cool enough to handle. As the potatoes cook, prepare the peas. Meanwhile, blend the veal with the other ingredients. Blend the potatoes with the peas.

Côtes de Veau "Pojarski"
(Ground veal cutlets with bread crumbs and cream)

1½ pounds lean veal, ground twice
1 to 1¼ cups fine fresh bread crumbs
¼ teaspoon freshly grated nutmeg

Few drops of Tabasco sauce
Salt and freshly ground pepper to taste
¾ cup heavy cream
4 tablespoons butter
Lemon wedges, optional

1. The veal may be ground by the butcher or it may be ground in a food processor. Place the veal in a mixing bowl and add ½ cup of the bread crumbs, nutmeg, Tabasco, and salt and pepper. Beat vigorously with a wooden spoon or blend in the food processor.

2. Gradually beat in the cream. (Eggs are not required in this recipe.)

3. Divide the mixture into 4 portions and shape into ovals. Roll the ovals lightly in the remaining crumbs. Flatten the ovals to make "chops" about ½ inch thick. Actually, the "chops" should be shaped by hand to resemble pork chops.

4. Melt half the butter in a skillet and add the chops. Brown about 5 minutes on each side, or until cooked.

5. Transfer the patties to a warm serving dish. Heat the remaining butter in another skillet until it is hazelnut brown. Pour over the patties and serve hot. If desired, serve with lemon wedges.

Yield: Four servings.

Pommes de Terre et Pois au Printemps
(Potatoes and peas in cream sauce)

8 new, red, waxy potatoes, about 1 pound
Salt
¾ cup freshly shelled green peas, about ¾ pound in the shell
1 tablespoon butter
1 very small white onion, peeled and thinly sliced
1 large leaf Boston lettuce, finely shredded
Freshly ground pepper to taste
¼ teaspoon sugar
¼ cup heavy cream
¼ cup milk

1. Place the potatoes in a saucepan and add water to cover and salt to taste. Bring to the boil and cook about 20 minutes. Drain.

2. In another saucepan, combine the peas, butter, onion, shredded lettuce, salt and pepper to taste, and sugar. Cover closely and simmer about 5 to 10 minutes, depending on the age of the peas. Cook until tender.

3. Meanwhile, peel and cut the potatoes into ¼-inch-thick slices. Add the potatoes to the peas. Add the cream and milk and salt and pepper to taste. Cook down about 5 minutes. Serve hot.

Yield: Four servings.

ONE OF THE BEST, MOST EASILY MADE, AND least costly of fine dishes is the one known in France as escalopes de veau viennoise. Escalopes de veau are simply scallopine of veal. Viennoise means in the style of Vienna, and the dish is the French version of wiener schnitzel.

It is a dish that offers a good lesson in one of the basics of cookery, which is to say the technique of breading. The meat—a quarter of a pound per person is sufficient—is first pounded lightly and then, in classic fashion, dipped first in flour, then in beaten egg, and finally in bread crumbs. The breaded scallops are cooked in oil until golden brown on both sides and served with a garnish, and, more often than not, with beurre noisette, or butter that is heated until it takes on the color of hazelnuts.

The garnishes for escalopes de veau viennoise are anchovies, capers, sieved and/or chopped hard-cooked egg, and parsley. The preparation time for the dish is approximately 15 minutes; the cooking time less than 10. A good accompaniment for the breaded veal are cooked potatoes, sliced and browned in a skillet. Logically, the potatoes should be put on to simmer and, as they cook, the veal should be made ready.

The main course should be followed by a salad; watercress and Belgian endive are an excellent combination. The dessert—purchased, perhaps—should be as simple as fresh fruit or a fruit compote.

Escalopes de Veau Viennoise
(Breaded veal with lemon and caper garnish)

4 veal scallopine, about ¼ pound each
Salt and freshly ground pepper
2 eggs, lightly beaten
3 tablespoons water
Flour for dredging
1 cup fresh bread crumbs

1 hard-cooked egg
¼ cup finely chopped parsley
4 thin slices lemon, seeded
4 flat anchovy fillets, drained
¼ cup drained capers
¼ to ½ cup peanut, vegetable, or corn oil
6 tablespoons butter

1. Place the scallopine, one at a time, between sheets of plastic wrap and pound them with a flat mallet or the bottom of a heavy skillet until quite thin.

2. Sprinkle the meat on all sides with salt and pepper.

3. Beat the eggs with the water and season with salt and pepper. Add this mixture to a large flat plate.

4. Have ready two other large flat plates, one containing the flour, the other containing the bread crumbs.

5. Coat the slices on both sides with flour. Dip the slices, one at a time, in egg until well coated, and then in bread crumbs until uniformly coated. As the slices are prepared set them aside. Tap each slice lightly with a flat spatula to help the crumbs adhere.

6. Before cooking the meat, prepare the garnishes.

7. Slice the egg in half. Chop the white and put the yolk through a fine sieve. Set them aside in separate batches. Have the chopped parsley ready.

8. Arrange the lemon slices on a plate. Shape each anchovy fillet into a round band and arrange one band on each lemon slice. Fill each anchovy band with capers.

9. Heat ¼ cup of oil in one large skillet or use two skillets, if

necessary, and add more oil. Cook the meat until nicely browned on one side. Turn and cook on the other side until browned.

10. Arrange the slices on each of four hot plates. Heat the butter in a skillet, swirling it around until it foams up and becomes hazelnut brown. Do not burn the butter. When the foam subsides, pour equal portions of butter over each meat slice.

11. Garnish each slice with a slice of anchovy-topped lemon. Garnish the ends of each slice with neat spoonfuls of chopped egg white, chopped yolk, more capers, and chopped parsley.

Yield: Four servings.

Pommes de Terre Sautées
(Skillet potatoes)

4 medium-size potatoes, about 1¼ pounds
Salt to taste
3 tablespoons peanut, vegetable, or corn oil

1 tablespoon butter
Freshly ground pepper to taste

1. Place the unpeeled potatoes in a saucepan and add cold water to cover. Add salt to taste and bring to the boil. Simmer 15 to 20 minutes, or until tender. Do not overcook. The potatoes must remain firm. This may be done a day in advance.

2. Peel the potatoes and cut them into slices ¼ inch thick or slightly thicker.

3. Heat the oil and butter in a heavy skillet and add the potato slices. Add salt and pepper. Cook, shaking and tossing the skillet to redistribute the potatoes. Cook until the potatoes form a crisp outside crust and are nicely browned. Serve hot.

Yield: Four servings.

A GOOD, EASILY MADE REDUCTION OF TOMAtoes—an essence of tomatoes to use another phrase—can be one of the greatest boons to rapid cooking. The reduction can be added to soups and sauces, and turned into a fine spaghetti sauce simply by heating it in oil with garlic, oregano, and chopped parsley. The essence will also keep well if stored tightly covered in the refrigerator, particularly if a light layer of oil is spooned over the top to help preserve it. It can also be frozen.

One example of its use is demonstrated here in a scallopine dish made with the sauce plus scallopine and mozzarella cheese. It is simply a rolled version of veal parmigiana but a trifle more fancy, perhaps.

Veal scallopine, of course, is almost by its nature a meat that should never require prolonged cooking. The longer it cooks the drier it becomes, whether it is a quick sauté as in veal scallopine Marsala, veal francese, or veal piccata.

In the dish outlined below, the veal is wrapped around fingers of mozzarella cheese, cigarette fashion. These rolls are browned quickly in hot oil and a rapid-fire tomato sauce is prepared in the same skillet with garlic and wine. The scallopine rolls, the sauce, parsley, and Parmesan cheese are layered and baked until piping hot.

This is the kind of dish that would be compatible with almost any form of pasta, and one interesting form, available in Italian markets, is called bavette. Serve with a crusty loaf of bread and a good dry Italian red wine, such as Valpolicella or Bardolino.

Unless otherwise indicated, it is recommended that this menu include the usual salad with cheese as a second course and, if desired, a final course of fresh fruit or a purchased or previously made dessert.

Escalopine de Veau au Mozzarella Parmigiana
(Scallopine and mozzarella Parmigiana)

1 2-pound, 3-ounce can imported tomatoes, about 4 cups
8 slices veal scallopine, about 1¼ pounds
Salt and freshly ground pepper to taste
½ teaspoon finely chopped rosemary
¼ pound whole-milk mozzarella cheese
2 tablespoons olive oil
2 cloves garlic, finely minced
¼ cup dry white wine
3 tablespoons finely chopped parsley
¼ cup grated Parmesan cheese

1. Place the tomatoes in a heavy saucepan and bring to the boil. Let cook until thickened and reduced to 3 cups.

2. Pound the meat lightly with a flat mallet without breaking the fibers. Place the slices on a flat surface and sprinkle with salt, pepper, and rosemary. Cut the mozzarella into 8 thin "fingers" of equal size. Arrange one finger in the center of each veal slice. Fold over the edges, then roll, envelope fashion, to enclose the cheese. Tie each roll neatly with string in two places.

3. Preheat the oven to 400 degrees.

4. Heat the oil in a heavy skillet and brown the rolls quickly and evenly over high heat, about 4 minutes. Transfer the rolls to a baking dish. Remove the string.

5. To the skillet add the garlic and cook briefly. Add the wine and stir to dissolve the brown particles that cling to the bottom and sides of the pan. Add the cooked-down tomatoes, salt, and pepper. Cook 5 minutes and add the parsley.

6. Pour the sauce over the meat rolls and sprinkle with Parmesan cheese. Bake 10 to 15 minutes, or until piping hot. Serve with cooked buttered imported Italian noodles, such as bavette.

Yield: Four servings.

WHEN IT IS A QUESTION OF SPEED-COOKING, that is to say in less than an hour, the advantages of boneless cuts of meat are obvious. And of all those boneless cuts, there are few with more flavor than veal. Veal, on the other hand, requires a bit more knowledge of meat cookery than does, let us say, beef, lamb, or pork. Although beef and lamb may be cooked rare or well-done or some point in between, according to taste, the cooking time is fairly easy to manipulate. Pork, of course, must be cooked to a fairly well-done state because of the nature of the meat (and there is sometimes something to be said, even, for pork that has been long cooked until it is fork-tender).

Undercooked veal is a trifle unappetizing. Overcooked veal has a tendency to be dry and chewy. But veal that is cooked to the exact point of doneness, cooked so that the center is moist yet no longer pink, is one of the choicest morsels that any cook could bring to the table.

Choice veal for the most part doesn't require a great deal of embellishing to be good, although the meat does adapt well—because of its basically neutral nature—to a variety of herbs and spices including rosemary or sage (very Italian) or tarragon (very French). It is excellent Hungarian-style (or my idea of what that style is) with a touch of paprika and a smattering of sour cream. The total cooking time for an individual veal steak (preferably taken from the leg of the animal) is approximately 10 minutes. The final sauce demands not more than another 10 minutes or so.

Like almost any dish made with a sour cream sauce, this veal goes extremely well with noodles, and can be given an added fillip with a bit of caraway seed. The preparation and cooking time for broccoli, another good side dish, and noodles is scarcely more than 15 minutes, if that. And with the proper coordination and organization, all the dishes may be prepared simultaneously.

[212]

Steak de Veau Hongroise
(Sautéed veal steak with paprika)

4 boneless veal steaks, preferably taken from the leg, about 1½ pounds total weight
Salt to taste
Freshly ground pepper to taste
2 tablespoons flour
3 tablespoons butter
⅓ cup finely chopped onions
1 teaspoon garlic
⅓ pound sliced or quartered mushrooms, about 3 cups
1 tablespoon paprika
½ cup dry white wine
½ cup sour cream

1. Sprinkle the meat on both sides with salt and pepper. Dredge on both sides in flour.

2. Melt the butter in a heavy skillet and cook the meat on one side until golden brown, about 5 minutes. Turn and cook on the other side about 5 minutes.

3. Remove the meat and keep it warm.

4. To the skillet add the onions and garlic. Cook until the onion is wilted. Add the mushrooms and paprika and cook until the mushrooms are wilted, about 5 minutes. Sprinkle with salt and pepper. Add the white wine and cook until it has almost evaporated. Add salt and pepper to taste.

5. Stir in sour cream and heat without boiling. Return the meat to the skillet. Turn it in the skillet and serve with the sauce spooned over. Serve with buttered noodles.

Yield: Four servings.

[213]

THE VIRTUES OF VEAL SCALLOPINE AS THE basis for hasty dishes have been elaborated on at considerable length. One of the most interesting aspects of veal is the remarkable manner in which it is complemented by other foods and flavors. Almost any sweet herb or spice goes agreeably well with veal, whether it be a sweetly perfumed herb like basil or tarragon or something as pungent and assertive as curry powder.

Veal is, admittedly, one of the most expensive of meats as well as one of the choicest in its versatility. There is another virtue in the fact that scallopine can be "stretched" by combining it with other complementary foods, such as mushrooms, ham, and cheese. And, in fact, the four ingredients go well together in one dish, as demonstrated in the quickly cooked one outlined here.

This dish has Italian origins, and ideally it is made with prosciutto although plain boiled ham could be used. Similarly, the traditional cheese for this dish is Fontina, although Gruyère or Swiss also work well.

Because the dish involves fresh mushrooms in a cream sauce, buttered noodles make an admirable accompaniment—plain buttered noodles or buttered noodles with seeds such as caraway, as indicated below.

Once the ingredients for this dish are assembled, the final preparation is child's play.

Almost any well-made tossed green salad would go well with this meal. A bowl of arugola blended, perhaps, with pieces of crisp romaine and tossed with oil and vinegar would be excellent. A bottle of dry red Italian wine or chilled dry white wine would make a good accompaniment. For dessert try chilled, ripe, unblemished pears and cheese.

Escalopes de Veau à la Crème
(Veal with mushrooms in cream)

1½ pounds veal, cut into 8 thin
  slices
3 tablespoons butter
1 tablespoon finely chopped
  shallots
½ pound mushrooms, thinly
  sliced, about 3 cups

Salt and freshly ground
  pepper to taste
2 tablespoons dry white wine
1 cup heavy cream
8 thin slices prosciutto or
  boiled ham
8 thin slices Fontina, Gruyère,
  or Swiss cheese

1. Pound the veal lightly with a flat mallet to make it thinner. Set aside.

2. Melt 2 tablespoons of the butter in a saucepan and add the shallots. Cook briefly and add the mushrooms and salt and pepper to taste. Sprinkle with wine and cook about 10 seconds. Add the cream. Cook down over high heat until the cream has a saucelike consistency, about 3 minutes. Set aside.

3. Melt the remaining 1 tablespoon of butter in a heavy skillet and add the veal. Cook to brown lightly on one side, about 2 minutes. Turn and cook to brown the other side, about 2 minutes.

4. Transfer the veal to a platter.

5. Cover each slice of veal with a slice of prosciutto. It should be trimmed to fit the veal neatly or fold the slice over.

6. Spoon equal portions of creamed mushrooms on the ham. Arrange one piece of cheese on each serving. Run briefly under the broiler just until the cheese melts. Serve immediately.

Yield: Four servings.

Nouilles au Carvi
(Buttered noodles with caraway seeds)

½ pound broad noodles
Salt to taste

2 tablespoons butter
½ teaspoon caraway seeds

1. Drop the noodles into boiling salted water to cover and stir until the water returns to the boil. Cook until the noodles are tender, 7 minutes or longer.

2. Drain and return the noodles to the pot. Add the butter and caraway seeds and toss until well coated.

Yield: Four servings.

IF EVER THERE WAS A DISH TAILOR-MADE FOR quick cooking—and pure enjoyment—it is of the sort known in French as an *émincé*, a word for which there is no exact English equivalent. An *émincé* consists of any sort of meat cut into shreds and cooked quickly with liquids and seasonings added to make a sauce. Next to an omelet, perhaps, there are few dishes to be cooked in such a hurry.

There is no accounting of why an émincé of veal is so characteristically Swiss, although, like watches and yodeling, it is. It is the sort of dish that would, of necessity, be included in any comprehensive Swiss cookbook.

A traditional accompaniment for the dish are rosti potatoes, a recipe for which is given here. Untypically, the potato side dish requires a touch more effort than the main course.

A meal of émincé of veal and rosti potatoes plus a salad, followed by a cheese with new apples, would be sufficient for a meal unto itself. If you insist on a dessert, however, an apple tart or pie—purchased to conserve time—would be ideal.

By all means, start this menu with the potatoes, and, as they cook, occupy yourself with the meat and accompaniments.

Émincé de Veau à la Crème
(Veal in cream sauce)

1 pound thin veal slices, preferably taken from the leg

¼ pound thinly sliced prosciutto or boiled ham

2 cups thinly sliced mushrooms

2 tablespoons butter
Salt and freshly ground pepper to taste

1 tablespoon finely chopped shallots

½ cup dry white wine

1½ cups heavy cream

1. Cut the veal into the thinnest possible (julienne) strips. Set aside.

2. Stack the prosciutto slices and cut them into the thinnest possible strips. Set aside.

3. Prepare the mushrooms and set aside.

4. Melt the butter in a skillet and, when it is hot without browning, add the veal, stirring rapidly. Sprinkle with salt and pepper and cook about 45 seconds over very high heat, stirring. Add the prosciutto, cook about 10 seconds and, using a slotted spoon, remove the meats. Set aside.

5. Add the mushrooms to the skillet and cook until wilted. Add the shallots, cook about 30 seconds, stirring, and add the wine. Cook until almost completely reduced and add the cream. Cook about 5 minutes over high heat. Add the meats and any liquid they give up. Cook briefly until piping hot. Sprinkle with salt and pepper and serve immediately with rosti potatoes.

Yield: Four servings.

Galette de Pommes de Terre
(Rösti potatoes)

5 or 6 Maine potatoes, about
   1½ pounds
   Salt to taste
¼ cup oil

7 tablespoons butter,
   approximately
   Freshly ground pepper to
   taste

1. Place the potatoes in a kettle and add cold water to cover and salt to taste. Bring to the boil and simmer about 15 minutes. Do not cook fully.

2. Drain the potatoes and let them cool.

3. Peel the potatoes and grate them using the coarse blade, or slice the potatoes thinly and cut into julienne strips.

4. Meanwhile, cure a black iron skillet by heating ¼ cup oil to the smoking point. Let stand half an hour or so. Pour out the oil and wipe out the skillet with paper towels.

5. Melt 2 tablespoons of butter in the skillet and add the potatoes in one thick layer. Sprinkle with salt and pepper. Cook, pressing down with the flat side of a spatula. When golden brown on one side, after about 10 minutes, carefully but quickly invert a plate over the potatoes and turn the "pancake" out onto the plate. Slip the pancake, uncooked side down, back into the skillet. Add another 2 tablespoons of butter, letting it melt around the pancake. If necessary, add more butter. Cook, pressing down occasionally, until golden brown on the other side. Serve sliced in wedges.

Yield: Four servings.

THERE ARE A DOZEN OR SO QUESTIONS THAT seem inevitable in casual conversation in any chef's life. Things like, "What's your favorite food?" "Do you ever eat junk food?" and "Do you have to watch your weight?"

A fourth recurrent query is whether or not the chef can recreate a particular dish after a single sampling. A dish, that is, heretofore not encountered. The answer to that one is an almost unqualified yes. Provided it is a dish within the Western tradition. It stands to reason that cooks and chefs of the Middle East and Far East—in places like India and Thailand and Korea—indulge in spices and seasonings that are generally unknown to French and American kitchens.

One of the trickiest foods, one that required more than a little amount of time to figure out, came about while having dinner at a small Italian restaurant in Boston a few years back. The dish in question was a boneless chicken filled with an incredibly light "custard" that seemed to melt in the mouth.

How, one wondered, could an uncooked custard mixture, a blend of eggs and cream and seasonings, be inserted inside the cavity of a bird without having the custard seep out the enclosure. We even tried sewing up the cavity with very tight stitches using a trussing needle and thread. To no avail. A short while later, by accident, I was faced with a batch of leftover scrambled eggs, untouched by a house guest. Suddenly it dawned on me that if this were used as a filling, it might—just possibly—come out smooth and custard-like. I tried it and it worked.

Since then I've discovered that scrambled eggs make a fine filling for many things, including the hastily made dish that follows, rollatine of veal, the kind that is sometimes called in French "veal birds." The egg filling is easily made and seasoned with a touch of cream and herbs. The preparation of the dish is quick and simplicity itself. Because the veal is cut in the form of scallopine, it cooks quickly. The dish is accompanied in an ideal sense with a very simple and good quick fresh tomato sauce.

Rollatine de Veau

(Rollatine of veal with egg filling)

8 pieces veal scallopine, about
¾ pound
Salt and freshly ground
pepper to taste
2 large eggs
2 tablespoons heavy cream

1 tablespoon finely chopped
herbs, such as tarragon,
chives, parsley, or a
combination of two or more
3 tablespoons butter
Flour for dredging
Fresh tomato sauce (see
recipe)

1. Place the veal slices between slices of plastic wrap and pound lightly. Do not make holes in the meat. Sprinkle with salt and pepper.

2. Break the eggs into a mixing bowl and add the cream, herbs, and salt and pepper to taste. Beat lightly to blend.

3. Melt 1 tablespoon of the butter in a saucepan and add the egg mixture. Cook, stirring gently from the bottom using a rubber or plastic spatula. Cook to the soft-cooked but not too-runny stage. Remove from the heat. Let cool briefly.

4. Spoon equal portions—about 1 tablespoon per slice—of scrambled eggs in the center of each slice. Roll the veal slices to enclose the egg in the center. Tie the rolls with string, or skewer them with toothpicks. Tying with string is a bit more tedious but it is preferable.

5. Sprinkle the rolls with salt and pepper and dredge on all sides in flour. Shake off any excess.

6. Melt the remaining 2 tablespoons of butter in a small skillet and add the veal rolls. Cook about 5 or 6 minutes.

7. If you are to serve a fresh tomato sauce (see recipe), do not wipe the skillet out. Use it to make the sauce. Serve the rollatine with the sauce spooned over. Serve with ziti, penne, or rigatoni tossed with melted butter and grated Parmesan cheese.

Yield: Four servings.

Coulis de Tomates
(Fresh tomato sauce)

2 cups tomatoes, cored and
   cut into 1-inch cubes
2 tablespoons butter
¼ cup finely chopped onion
½ teaspoon finely minced garlic

⅓ cup dry white wine
3 fresh basil leaves, or 1
   teaspoon dried basil
Salt and freshly ground
   pepper to taste

1. Prepare the tomatoes and set aside.

2. If you are to serve this dish with the rollatine of veal (see recipe), you will not have to use additional butter. Use the same skillet with drippings. Otherwise, add the butter to a skillet.

3. Add the onion and garlic and cook briefly. Add the wine and cook to reduce by about half. Add the tomatoes, basil, and salt and pepper to taste. Cook about 5 minutes.

4. Pour the mixture into the container of a food processor and blend to a purée. Reheat and serve.

Yield: About two-and-one-half cups.

IF I HAD TO NAME ONE SINGLE ULTIMATE CUT OF meat that would produce the finest quickly cooked dishes of which any cook is capable, it would probably be scallopine of veal. Veal scallopine (sometimes called cutlets) have all the qualities to be desired for a hastily produced and excellent main course.

First of all, quick cooking is essential with scallopine. If they cook too long, they tend to dry out or to lose their moist inner goodness. Second, the nature of the veal is such that it marries well with a multitude of flavors. It is the perfect foil for such bland foods as mushrooms in cream sauce (veal with morels à la crème is one of the sublime dishes of the world). It is complemented by tomato sauce in almost any form. It takes well to spicy things like mustard and is oddly complemented by fish and seafood—consider vitello tonnato with tuna and anchovies, and veal à la Oskar with crayfish, shrimp, or crabmeat.

One of the finest and most basic of scallopine dishes is scallopine of veal with *fines herbes*. As pointed out on numerous occasions, the traditional *fines herbes* in French kitchens are parsley, tarragon, chervil, and chives. Chervil is not all that common in America and may be omitted. The preparation of the dish consists in cooking veal scallopine—thin slices that have or should be pounded lightly with a flat mallet—in very hot butter. The cooking takes only about 45 seconds to a side. Only an omelet can cook that quickly to such advantage. And omelets can be boring. Veal, properly cooked, is never boring. The herbs are added along with a bit more butter and the dish is ready to serve.

It is a dish so simple that more attention may be paid to an accompanying vegetable dish. An excellent accompaniment for this would be a savory Italianate ratatouille, this one baked with mozzarella cheese—a bit tangy and good. Prepare the vegetable dish before turning your attention to the veal.

Escalopes de Veau aux Fines Herbes
(Scallopine of veal with herbs)

16 pieces thin veal scallopine, about 1¼ pounds
Salt and freshly ground pepper to taste
6 tablespoons butter

1 tablespoon finely chopped parsley
2 teaspoons finely chopped tarragon
2 teaspoons finely chopped chives

1. Place the meat on a flat surface and pound lightly. Sprinkle on both sides with salt and pepper to taste.

2. Melt 4 tablespoons of the butter in one or two large skillets and, when it is very hot, add the meat. This may be done in one skillet in two steps. Add the pieces of veal and cook briefly, about 45 seconds on each side. As the pieces brown, transfer them to a warm platter.

3. Add the remaining butter to the skillet and add the parsley, tarragon, and chives. Pour the sauce over the veal and serve hot.

Yield: Four servings.

Légumes à la Napolitaine

(A baked mélange of vegetables with mozzarella)

3 tablespoons olive oil
¾ cup finely chopped onion
1 tablespoon finely minced garlic
3 cups peeled eggplant cut into 1-inch cubes
2 cups trimmed, unpeeled zucchini cut into 1-inch cubes
2 sprigs fresh thyme, or 1 teaspoon dried thyme

1 bay leaf
Salt and freshly ground pepper to taste
1½ cups cored tomatoes cut into 1-inch cubes
4 slices mozzarella cheese, each slice about ¼ inch thick
2 tablespoons grated Parmesan cheese

1. Preheat the oven to 400 degrees.

2. Heat the oil in a large heavy skillet and cook the onion and garlic until the onion is wilted.

3. Add the eggplant and zucchini and stir. Cook about 1 minute and add the thyme, bay leaf, and salt and pepper to taste. Cook, stirring as necessary to prevent sticking, about 5 minutes.

4. Add the tomatoes and cook about 5 minutes longer, shaking the skillet to prevent sticking.

5. Spoon the mixture into a baking dish and cover with slices of mozzarella cheese. Sprinkle with Parmesan cheese. Place on a baking sheet to catch any drippings. Bake 10 minutes.

Yield: Four servings.

I HAVE OFTEN REFLECTED ON THE DIFFERENCES, as I see and remember them, between home kitchens, those of my childhood and those in this country.

I was brought up in a rural community in Burgundy, and we literally lived off the land. Our home garden was not vast, but it was copiously planted and carefully tended. There was one small quarter given over to sweet green herbs and that was my grandmother's pride. She grew an abundance of parsley, chives, tarragon, and chervil. Those were the basics, not only of her herb plot but also of her kitchen.

It was years later, as an apprentice in a Paris restaurant, that I learned that these were the most traditional herbs of the classic French kitchen. These four herbs are what are known as *les fines herbes,* and they are the requirements for a few thousand dishes, the best known of which is in an omelette aux fines herbes.

I have discovered, happily, that more and more Americans are making use of these herbs, except for chervil, which, for some reason, has never been very popular here. More often than not, it can be easily dispensed with.

One of the best uses for *les fines herbes* is with a sauté of liver, which demands a quick treatment if it is to be served with maximum flavor and texture. Long-cooked liver (and minutes in this case can matter) is dry, tasteless, and dull.

The preparation of foie de veau aux fines herbes is simplicity itself. The liver is lightly floured and seasoned and cooked hastily on both sides in oil. The slices are removed, the skillet wiped clean and butter added. Shallots are cooked quickly, and a dash of vinegar is added. The hot sauce is poured over and all of it is sprinkled with the herbs. Grilled tomatoes and steamed potatoes are classic accompaniments for the dish.

Foie de Veau aux Fines Herbes
(Calf's liver sautéed with herbs)

8 thin slices calf's liver, about 1½ pounds
Salt and freshly ground pepper to taste
¼ cup flour
2 tablespoons peanut, vegetable, or corn oil
6 tablespoons butter
2 tablespoons finely chopped shallots
1 tablespoon red wine vinegar
2 tablespoons finely chopped parsley
2 tablespoons finely chopped chives
1 teaspoon finely chopped fresh tarragon

1. Place the liver slices on a flat surface and sprinkle on both sides with salt and pepper. Dredge on both sides in flour and shake off any excess.

2. Heat the oil in a large skillet and cook as many pieces of liver at one time as will fit comfortably in the skillet. Cook about 1 minute or longer until nicely browned. The cooking time will vary depending on the thickness of the slices. Turn and cook about 1 minute or longer to the desired degree of doneness.

3. Remove the slices to a warm platter and continue adding slices in one layer. As the slices cook, remove them and add more. Continue until all the slices are cooked. Cover the liver on the platter and keep it warm.

4. Pour off any fat that is left in the pan. Wipe out the pan with a clean cloth or paper toweling. Add the butter and cook over high heat until the butter is hazelnut brown. Add the shallots, stirring, and cook about 5 seconds. Add the vinegar and pour the hot butter over the liver. Sprinkle with parsley, chives, and tarragon.

Yield: Four servings.

Tomates Grillées
(Grilled tomatoes)

2 large ripe tomatoes
1 tablespoon plus 4 teaspoons peanut, vegetable, or corn oil

1 large clove garlic, cut into slivers
Salt and freshly ground pepper to taste

1. Preheat the broiler.
2. Core the tomatoes and slice them in half.
3. Grease a baking dish large enough to hold the tomato halves with 1 tablespoon of oil. Arrange the halves in the dish cut side up. Insert slivers of garlic inside the cut side of the tomatoes.
4. Sprinkle each half with salt and pepper. Sprinkle about 1 teaspoon of oil over each half and place them under the broiler. Broil about 5 minutes. Quickly remove the garlic slivers and serve.

Yield: Four servings.

Pommes Vapeur
(Steamed potatoes)

8 small red, new, waxy potatoes, about ¾ pound

Salt to taste

1. Peel the potatoes and put them in a saucepan. Add water to cover and salt to taste.
2. Bring to the boil and simmer about 12 minutes, or until the potatoes are tender. Drain and serve. These potatoes are frequently served without butter or other garnish.

Yield: Four servings.

HISTORIANS CONTEND, OF COURSE, THAT Italy was actually the cradle of French cooking (I have yet to find a French chef, including myself, willing to admit to the truth of that claim) and that it all began with the arrival of Catherine de Médicis, who came to France to wed Henry II in the sixteenth century. To be sure, there are certain dishes in French cooking that are dead ringers for those produced in Italian kitchens and vice versa. One of the most conspicuous of these is the dish known in France as foie de veau lyonnaise, or calf's liver and onions, and in Italy as fegato alla veneziana. The former is "in the style of Lyon," the latter, "in the style of Venice."

The two dishes are remarkably similar in their traditional preparations. The liver in both is cooked with a considerable amount of onions and both have just a trace of vinegar added to the skillet before serving.

Origins aside, calf's liver lyonnaise is a tasty, excellent dish, easily prepared and quickly cooked. Ideal for cooking in less than an hour.

The most difficult part of preparing such a meal, if indeed it could be called complicated, is in cutting the liver and onions to the required size. The liver should be cut into very thin strips, the onions sliced wafer thin.

The onions take far more time to cook than the liver; as a matter of fact, they should cook until they become slightly more than golden, almost caramel colored. This long cooking (and they must be stirred often to prevent sticking) brings out the natural sugars or sweetness of the onions. Thus, prepare and start to cook the onions. As they cook, prepare the remaining ingredients.

The liver should not take more than 5 minutes for the entire batch to cook.

As the onions cook, the potatoes should also be put on to boil.

Potatoes with parsley are the traditional accompaniment for calf's liver lyonnaise.

Foie de Veau Lyonnaise
(Calf's liver and onions)

2 large onions, about 1½ pounds total weight
4 tablespoons peanut, vegetable, or corn oil
1 bay leaf

Salt and freshly ground pepper to taste
1 pound calf's liver
2 tablespoons butter
2 tablespoons vinegar
Chopped parsley for garnish

1. Peel the onions and quarter them. Slice them thinly. There should be about 5 cups.

2. Heat 2 tablespoons of the oil in a skillet and add the onions, bay leaf, and salt and pepper. Cook, stirring as necessary, until the onions are golden brown, about 20 minutes. Set aside.

3. Meanwhile, cut the liver into thin strips about ½ inch wide or slightly less. Sprinkle with salt and pepper.

4. Heat the remaining oil in a skillet and, when it is hot and almost smoking, add half the liver, stirring rapidly and turning the pieces as necessary so that they brown evenly. Cook about 2 minutes in all and drain in a sieve. Return the oil to the skillet and, when it is hot, add the remaining liver. Cook the same way and drain.

5. Add the butter to the skillet. Add the liver and toss. Add the onions and blend well. Add the vinegar and blend. Serve piping hot, garnished with chopped parsley. Serve with boiled potatoes.

Yield: Four servings.

Boiled Potatoes with Parsley

8 to 12 small, new, waxy
potatoes, or use 3 or 4
medium-size Idaho or Maine
potatoes

Salt
2 tablespoons melted butter
2 tablespoons finely chopped
parsley

1. Peel the potatoes. If the potatoes are small and new, leave them whole. If they are large, cut them into thirds or quarter them.

2. Place the potatoes in a saucepan and add water to cover and salt to taste. Bring to the boil and simmer until the potatoes are tender, about 10 to 15 minutes, depending on size.

3. Drain and pour the melted butter over them. Sprinkle with parsley and toss. Serve hot.

Yield: Four servings.

Beef

THE ULTIMATE MAIN COURSE IN THE WORLD OF hasty cooking is doubtlessly a slice of beef. If the meat is of first quality, it is culinary sacrilege to cook it for an extended period. There is an interesting misconception in the public mind about a filet mignon, which is generally considered the most luxurious cut of the animal. Actually, it is not the most expensive steak on the market, and, furthermore, it is all meat, no waste. The cost of a shell steak comes to considerably more.

Cost aside, the simplest adornment for a fillet of beef is, of course, melted butter with, perhaps, a sprinkling of parsley. There are times, however, when you might wish a sauce a bit more innovative, and one of the best is an easily made sauce bordelaise meaning, of course, a sauce in the style of Bordeaux and made with a red wine of the region. But any good, dry red wine will do, be it from Bordeaux, Burgundy, or California.

This sauce, in a professional kitchen, is made with a tediously prepared and long-simmered sauce known as an espagnole or demi-glace. Such a sauce is unreasonable except for the most dedicated amateur cooks; a substitute is essential. The solution—shocking though it will appear to purists—is tinned brown beef gravy. That's right, out of a can. Try it cooked with shallots and a reduction of dry red wine. You may be pleasantly surprised.

I prepared this dish recently and served it with braised Belgian endives, which require a far longer cooking time than the meat.

The two dishes complement each other, but any other green vegetable, such as broccoli or zucchini, would also be suitable with the beef.

Should you decide to prepare the endives with the beef, by all means put it on about 30 to 45 minutes before the dinner hour. The cooking period will depend on the size of the endives. As they cook there is more than ample time to prepare the meat and any other accompaniments you plan to serve before or after the meat.

Filet Mignon Bordelaise
(Filet mignon in a Bordeaux wine sauce)

1¼ pounds filet mignon, cut into
    4 slices, each approximately
    1 inch thick
    Salt and freshly ground
    pepper to taste
1 tablespoon peanut,
    vegetable, or corn oil

2 tablespoons butter
1 tablespoon finely chopped
    shallots
½ cup dry red wine
½ cup brown sauce or canned
    brown beef gravy

1. Sprinkle the meat with salt and pepper to taste. Heat the oil in a heavy skillet, large enough to hold the slices in one layer. Brown the meat on both sides, about 1 to 2 minutes to a side. Or cook longer if you prefer meat well done.

2. Transfer the meat to a warm serving platter. Pour off the fat from the skillet. Add 1 tablespoon of the butter and, when it is hot, add the shallots. Cook briefly, stirring, and add the wine. Cook until almost reduced by half. Add the brown sauce and cook about 2 minutes. Put through a fine strainer into a small saucepan. Add salt and pepper to taste. Swirl in the remaining tablespoon of butter. Serve piping hot spooned over the meat. Serve with braised endives, if desired.

Yield: Four servings.

Endives Braisées
(Braised endives)

4 heads Belgian endive
2 teaspoons butter
   Salt and freshly ground
   pepper to taste

½ teaspoon sugar
   Juice of ½ lemon
½ cup water

1. Trim around the stem ends of the endives to cut away any browned rims.

2. Place the endives in one layer, snugly, in a saucepan with a tight-fitting cover. Add the remaining ingredients and cover closely. Bring to the boil and cook about 30 to 45 minutes, or until tender and the liquid has evaporated. Toward the end of the cooking time, uncover and brown lightly on both sides, turning once.

Yield: Four servings.

THERE IS A DISH THAT ENJOYED AN OVER-whelming popularity back in the days when I first came to New York. To tell the truth, I never dined on the dish in its place of origin, but numerous customers who came to the Pavillon while I was chef there would request it.

It was called steak Diane and it was the specialty of the house—twenty years ago and more—at the old Drake Hotel. The person most closely associated with steak Diane was known in dining circles throughout the city as Nino of the Drake. His full name was Beniamino Schiavon, born in Padua, Italy; he died eleven years ago.

One of the key points in the preparation of the dish is the quick cooking of the steak itself. The total cooking time on both sides is about 2 minutes. This recipe calls for chives, but if chives are out of season, chopped shallots can serve the purpose, or even, for that matter, chopped scallions.

Almost any very tender cut of meat will do for this dish. The maître d'hôtel for whom the dish was celebrated generally used boneless sirloin, which was pounded to about ¼ inch thick. Filet mignon also works well. The pounding of the meat with a mallet is important, for it breaks down the fibers and hastens cooking.

Because of the haste with which the steak is cooked, an accompanying vegetable dish may be a bit more time-consuming and elaborate.

Steak Diane
(Steak in chive sauce)

4 filet mignon steaks, about 6 ounces each, or use 4 boneless sirloin steaks
Salt and freshly ground pepper to taste
2 tablespoons olive oil
3 tablespoons butter
3 tablespoons chopped chives or shallots

2 tablespoons Cognac
3 tablespoons chopped parsley
1 teaspoon imported mustard
½ teaspoon Worcestershire sauce
2 teaspoons meat broth, preferably beef, although chicken can be used

1. Place the slices of filet mignon or the sirloin steaks on a flat surface and pound with a flat mallet to about ¼-inch thickness.

2. Sprinkle the meat on both sides with salt and pepper.

3. Heat 2 tablespoons of oil and 2 tablespoons of the butter in a large skillet and, when it is very hot, add two of the steaks. Cook about 1½ minutes on one side and turn. Cook 30 seconds on the other side. Do not cook much longer or they will be overcooked and dry. Transfer the steaks to a hot serving dish.

4. Add the other steaks to the skillet and cook them identically in the fat that remains in the pan. Transfer the steaks to the serving dish.

5. Remove the skillet from the heat and add the chives. Return the skillet to the stove and cook about 10 seconds. Add the Cognac and stir. Add the parsley, mustard, and Worcestershire sauce. Add the broth and stir. Swirl in the remaining tablespoon of butter. Sprinkle the steaks with pepper and pour the sauce over them. Serve at once.

Yield: Four servings.

Mélange des Légumes
(Mixed buttered vegetables)

3 Idaho potatoes, about 1½
  pounds
½ pound string beans
  Salt to taste

3 tablespoons butter
1 clove garlic, barely crushed
  Freshly ground pepper to
  taste

1. Peel the potatoes and cut them into ½-inch slices. Stack the slices and cut them into ½-inch strips. Cut the strips into ½-inch cubes. Drop the cubes into cold water. Set aside.

2. Trim off the ends of the string beans and cut the beans into 1-inch lengths. Set aside.

3. Drain the potatoes and put them in a casserole or saucepan. Cover with water and add salt to taste. Bring to the boil.

4. In another saucepan, bring enough water to the boil to cover the beans when added. Add the beans and salt to taste. Bring to the boil.

5. Cook the potatoes about 3 minutes and drain.

6. As the beans continue to cook, melt the butter in a large skillet and add the potatoes. Add the crushed garlic clove and toss over high heat. Stir as necessary. When the potatoes start to brown, reduce the heat to moderate. Add salt and pepper to taste. Continue cooking, tossing and stirring, about 8 minutes.

7. When the beans have cooked for a total of 8 minutes, drain them.

8. Add the beans to the potatoes, toss and stir to blend. Cook 2 or 3 minutes to blend the flavors. Remove the garlic clove and serve.

Yield: Four servings.

I HAVE NOTED THAT THERE IS A GREAT DEAL OF mystique in the public mind about the complexity of widely ordered dishes in French restaurants. There are numerous dishes, excellent creations, which, made at home or in a professional kitchen, do not demand long-simmered sauces, a complicated series of steps, and legerdemain on the part of a chef.

There is steak au poivre, for example, which delights many American palates. It has a lot going for it—the piquant flavor of freshly crushed peppercorns and a light sauce made of butter, shallots, white wine, and cream. The steak should be of first quality, and a boneless shell steak is my choice. The peppercorns should—must—be freshly cracked and although a flat, heavy metal mallet works well for this, you can improvise by using the bottom of a clean heavy saucepan.

There are endless combinations of foods that go well with steak au poivre, two of which are outlined here.

One of these is Vichy carrots. To prepare them, the carrots are cut into thin rounds and cooked briefly with butter and only a couple of tablespoons of water. They are ready for the table in about 5 minutes total cooking time. The other is duchesse potatoes, which take longer but may also be prepared in advance if they are brushed with melted butter to keep a crust from forming.

Because of the quick-cooking nature of the carrots and steaks, it would be best to approach them by first preparing all the ingredients that go into them. Set them aside until ready to cook.

Start the cooking process with the potatoes. Before cooking the steak, start the carrots.

Follow the main course with salad and cheese, if you wish, and a simple purchased dessert.

Steaks au Poivre

(Steaks with crushed peppercorns)

4 boneless shell steaks, about 10 ounces each
Salt to taste
1 tablespoon peppercorns
3 tablespoons peanut, vegetable, or corn oil
5 teaspoons butter
2 tablespoons finely chopped shallots
½ cup dry white wine
½ cup heavy cream

1. Sprinkle the steaks with salt.

2. Using a mallet or the bottom of a heavy saucepan, crush the peppercorns but not too finely. Sprinkle the steaks with equal amounts of pepper on both sides. Press down with the hands to help the peppercorns adhere to the meat.

3. Heat the oil in a heavy skillet and, when it is hot and almost smoking, add the steaks. Cook about 3 minutes and turn. Cook about 2 minutes or longer, if you wish your steaks well-done, and remove to a warm platter.

4. Pour the fat from the skillet and add 2 teaspoons of the butter. Add the shallots and cook, stirring, until wilted. Add the wine and cook, stirring with a wooden spoon, until the wine has almost totally reduced. Add the cream and cook over high heat about 1 minute. Swirl in the remaining butter and pour the sauce over the steaks.

Yield: Four servings.

Pommes de Terre Duchesse
(Mashed potatoes with eggs)

6 medium-size potatoes
Boiling salted water
3 tablespoons butter
Salt and freshly ground
pepper to taste

¼ teaspoon freshly grated
nutmeg
2 whole eggs
2 egg yolks

1. Peel the potatoes and boil in salted water to cover until soft but still firm.
2. Put through a food mill and then beat with a wooden spoon until smooth.
3. Add the butter, salt and pepper, nutmeg, and eggs, which have been lightly beaten with the egg yolks. Whip until fluffy.

Yield: Four servings.

Carottes Vichy
(Steamed carrots)

5 to 6 carrots, about ¾ pound
3 tablespoons butter
Salt to taste

¼ teaspoon sugar
2 tablespoons water

1. Trim off and discard the ends of the carrots. Scrape the carrots. Cut the carrots into rounds about ⅛ inch thick.
2. Put the butter in a heavy saucepan and add the carrots, salt, sugar, and water. Cover closely and cook over high heat about 5 minutes. Serve hot.

Yield: Four servings.

THERE WAS A TIME NOT MANY YEARS AGO when mustard was generally regarded in this country as a condiment for hot dogs, assorted sausages, salamis, and ham sandwiches. More and more it has crossed my notice that mustard is being used to a far vaster extent these days as an ingredient to give a piquancy to sauces—and not only the likes of mayonnaise and hollandaise—but a variety of hot sauces as well.

It is also true that mustard flavors have increased in France under the banner of la nouvelle cuisine—a dab of mustard in cream sauces for mussels, for veal, and for chicken. One of the best "new" dishes I have sampled in some time was that of Jean Troisgros, who visited East Hampton recently. The dish consisted of thin slices of veal smeared with mustard, sprinkled with mustard seed, and cooked quickly on both sides. That dish can be served with a variety of sauces including one of fresh tomatoes.

Mustard also gives a fine and welcome lift to a tasty and well-textured steak and the preparation of such a dish literally takes minutes. Perhaps the best cut of meat for the dish is sirloin steak—and I recommend that you cut away the bone (it is then called in this country New York sirloin) which not only facilitates cooking, but adds, perhaps, a touch of elegance.

Basically, the dish consists of cooking the steaks 4 or 5 minutes to a side in very little, very hot oil. The steaks are transferred to a hot serving dish and the oil poured off. Chopped shallots, Cognac, and heavy cream are added in quick succession and, at the very last, a tablespoon or more of imported mustard is added to the sauce. Once mustard is added to a hot cream sauce, the sauce should not be allowed to boil; if it does, the flavor of the sauce is altered and not favorably.

Many dishes would go well with this steak—pan-fried potatoes, rice, or simply a vegetable. I recommend here a combination of vegetables cooked briefly in very little water and butter.

The vegetable preparation, in fact, should be done first—it requires considerably more time than the steak itself.

Steak à la Moutarde
(Steak with mustard cream sauce)

---

4 sirloin steaks, about ¾ to 1 pound each	2 tablespoons finely chopped shallots
Salt and freshly ground pepper to taste	¼ cup Cognac
	1½ cups heavy cream
2 tablespoons peanut, vegetable, or corn oil	1 tablespoon prepared imported mustard, such as
2 tablespoons butter	Dijon or Düsseldorf

1. Carefully trim around the bones of the steak. This will facilitate and hasten cooking. The trimmed steaks are known as New York sirloin. Sprinkle the steaks on both sides with salt and pepper.

2. Heat the oil in a large, very heavy skillet. A heavy copper or black iron skillet would be good for this. When the oil is hot and almost smoking, add the steaks. Cook about 4 or 5 minutes and turn. Continue cooking 4 or 5 minutes or to the desired degree of doneness.

3. Remove the steaks to a serving platter and keep warm. Pour off the fat from the pan. Add the butter and, when it is melted, add the shallots. Add the Cognac and ignite it.

4. Add the cream and bring to the boil. Cook over high heat, stirring often, about 5 minutes. Remove from the heat and stir in the mustard. Do not boil. Add salt and pepper to taste. Add any drippings that may have accumulated around the steaks. Strain the sauce over the steaks. Serve with rice or assorted vegetables.

Yield: Four servings.

Mélange des Légumes
(Blended vegetables)

1 or 2 carrots, trimmed,
    scraped, and quartered
1 medium-size zucchini
1 to 3 small turnips
⅓ pound fresh string beans

1 rib celery
2 tablespoons butter
2 tablespoons finely chopped
    onion
2 tablespoons water

1. Cut the quartered carrots into batons about 1 inch long. There should be about 1 cup.

2. Trim off the ends of the zucchini. Cut the zucchini into pieces the same size as the carrots. There should be about 1 cup.

3. Peel the turnips and cut them into pieces the same size as the carrots and zucchini.

4. Trim off the ends of the beans. Cut them into 1-inch lengths. There should be about 1 cup.

5. Cut the celery rib into 1-inch lengths. Cut each length into ½-inch strips. There should be about ½ cup.

6. In a very heavy saucepan melt the butter and add the onion and celery. Cook briefly and add the carrots, string beans, turnips, and zucchini. Add salt and pepper to taste.

7. Add the water and cover closely. If the saucepan is heavy enough and the cover fits snugly, this should be sufficient water. Take care the saucepan does not become dry or the vegetables will burn.

8. Cook over gentle to moderate heat, stirring and shaking the saucepan to redistribute the vegetables so that they cook evenly, about 8 minutes.

Yield: Four servings.

THERE ARE, GENERALLY SPEAKING, TWO STANdard and accepted methods of broiling foods in or on a home stove. The most obvious is the use of a kitchen broiler. This method of cookery can be exceedingly complicated for amateur cooks because of the variables involved—the intensity of the heat, the distance of the food from the source of heat and so on.

The other method, and frankly I prefer it, is what is known as "pan broiling." Purists may point out that this is not broiling at all but skillet cookery, but the results are admirable and the name simply implies that any foods destined to be broiled can also be cooked in a skillet or pan.

There is much less guesswork in pan broiling. The meat, or whatever, must be seared over high heat so that the juices are sealed within. The meat then continues to cook at a leisurely pace to the desired degree of doneness. This works particularly well with thick cuts of meat and is eminently suited to porterhouse steaks. For what it's worth by the way, I find that a prime porterhouse steak costs less than sirloin with bone in or club steaks.

A marchand de vin sauce is excellent for this and other steaks. Its preparation, if you will resort to half a cup of canned brown beef gravy, is simplicity itself. When the steak is done, it is removed and the skillet wiped out. A bit of butter and shallots are added, then half a cup of dry red wine is added and reduced. The "brown sauce" is swirled in and heated with another touch of butter and the sauce is ready to serve.

In restaurants, of course, they use a classic brown sauce rather than the canned gravy, but the latter is an acceptable substitute— as long as it is improved upon.

It is recommended that this menu include the usual salad with cheese as a second course and, if desired, a final course of fresh fruit or a purchased or previously made dessert.

Porterhouse Marchand de Vin
(Porterhouse with red wine sauce)

1 3-pound porterhouse steak,
about 2½ inches thick
Salt and freshly ground
pepper to taste

2 tablespoons peanut,
vegetable, or corn oil

3 tablespoons butter

1 tablespoon finely chopped
shallots

½ cup dry red wine

½ cup brown sauce or canned
brown beef gravy

1. Select a very heavy skillet for this. A heavy, traditional black iron skillet is excellent. Sprinkle the steak all over with salt and pepper. Use a fairly generous amount of black pepper. Pat it with the fingers to make the seasonings adhere.

2. Heat the oil in the skillet and, when quite hot, add the steak. The primary goal is to sear the steak well on both sides over moderately high heat. Cook the steak on the first side about 5 to 7 minutes until it is quite dark without burning.

3. Turn the steak and cook about 10 minutes on the second side until it is quite dark without burning. Remember that these cooking times are more or less arbitrary, but they were the times used when this recipe was tested.

4. After the steak has been seared on both sides (5 minutes on one side, 10 on the other), reduce the heat only slightly and turn it again. Cook about 10 minutes longer and turn again. Continue cooking, turning as necessary. The total recommended cooking time for the steak, start to finish, is about 45 minutes.

5. Remove the steak and cover loosely with aluminum foil. It is best for the steak to "rest" after cooking so that the interior juices are redistributed.

6. The moment the steak is removed from the skillet, pour off the fat from the skillet. Wipe lightly with absorbent paper toweling. Immediately add 1 tablespoon of the butter to the skillet and

stir to dissolve the browned particles that cling to the bottom of the skillet. Add the shallots and cook briefly. Add the wine and reduce about 30 seconds. Add the brown sauce and reduce to two-thirds. When boiling, remove from the heat and swirl in the remaining butter.

7. To serve, spoon a few tablespoons of the pan sauce onto each of four hot plates. Slice the steak and place the slices on the sauce.

Yield: Four servings.

Pommes de Terre Maître d'Hôtel
(Potatoes in cream sauce)

4 Idaho potatoes, about 1¾ pounds
  Salt to taste
1 cup heavy cream
⅓ teaspoon freshly grated nutmeg

Pinch of cayenne pepper
½ cup finely chopped scallions
  Freshly ground pepper to taste

1. Peel the potatoes and drop them into cold water.
2. Drain and cut them lengthwise into quarters. Cut each quarter into 1-inch lengths.
3. Add the pieces to a small skillet and add water to cover. Add salt to taste and bring to the boil. Simmer about 5 minutes. Drain.
4. Add the cream, nutmeg, cayenne, and onions. Add salt and pepper to taste. Bring to the boil and cover. Cook about 4 minutes, or until almost tender.
5. Uncover and cook about 1 minute longer, or until the potatoes are tender and the cream sauce is slightly thickened.

Yield: Four servings.

AS IN ANY OTHER MÉTIER, IF THE KITCHEN IS your domain (both professionally and as a hobby), food associations occur as naturally as thought. We were wondering about the possible origins of the dish known as London broil, which English sources assure us is of American inspiration, and then the speculation began. Perhaps there was a resturant called London in some town or city; perhaps it was an English chef or cook who first threw a flank steak on the grill and served it with mushroom sauce.

In any event, it was generally agreed that a London broil made with a flank steak of impeccable quality, seared and broiled quickly on both sides, and served with a conscientiously made mushroom sauce can, without qualification, be a memorable dish. And both the steak and the sauce are child's play to prepare.

The sauce, of course, is just as important as the steak, and when I recently made the dish, I decided on the mushroom sauce known in French as a sauce chasseur. It is not one of those thick, mucilaginous sauces made throughout the United States with canned mushrooms. This one is made with fresh butter, shallots, tomatoes, fresh mushrooms, and a dry white wine. It also uses beef broth. In the interest of texture, a touch of arrowroot or cornstarch is added to the sauce.

There is one important thing to remember: After the flank steak is grilled or broiled (the total broiling time is 10 minutes or less), it should be left to stand briefly to redistribute the inner juices. The steak should always be sliced on the bias or diagonally, in the interest of texture. The procedure: Heat the broiler or grill, prepare the meat and the green vegetable, string beans with lemon and parsley, simultaneously.

Bavette de Boeuf Sauce Chasseur
(London broil with sauce chasseur)

1 2-pound flank steak
2 tablespoons peanut, vegetable, or corn oil
Salt and freshly ground pepper to taste

3 tablespoons butter
3 tablespoons finely chopped parsley
Sauce chasseur (see recipe)

1. Preheat a broiler rack with the broiler set on high. Or use a charcoal grill, although the warm-up takes a while.

2. Rub the flank steak on both sides with oil and sprinkle with salt and pepper. Use a generous amount of pepper.

3. Place the meat on the broiler rack or on the hot grill and let it cook about 4 or 5 inches from the source of heat. Broil about 3 to 5 minutes and turn the meat. Broil on the other side 3 to 5 minutes. Cooking time will depend on the desired degree of doneness.

4. Transfer the steak to a hot platter and dot with butter. Let the steak stand in a warm place about 5 minutes to redistribute the internal juices of the meat.

5. Juices will accumulate as the steak stands. Add these to the sauce chasseur. Sprinkle the meat with chopped parsley and carve it on the diagonal. Serve with the sauce.

Yield: Four servings.

Sauce Chasseur
(Hunter's sauce)

⅓ pound mushrooms, sliced, about 2 cups
½ cup peeled and chopped fresh or canned tomatoes
1 tablespoon butter
1 tablespoon finely chopped shallots
Salt and freshly ground pepper to taste

⅓ cup dry white wine
½ cup beef broth
½ teaspoon chopped fresh tarragon, or ¼ teaspoon dried tarragon
1 teaspoon arrowroot or cornstarch
2 teaspoons water

1. Set the mushrooms and tomatoes aside in separate bowls.

2. Melt the butter in a saucepan and add the mushrooms, shallots, and salt and pepper to taste. Cook about 10 minutes.

3. Add the wine and simmer briefly over high heat. Add the tomatoes and beef broth and tarragon. Cook about 5 minutes, stirring occasionally.

4. Blend the arrowroot and water. Stir into the sauce. Cook briefly and serve.

Yield: One-and-a-half to two cups.

Haricots Verts au Citron
(String beans with lemon)

1 pound string beans, trimmed and cut into 2-inch cubes
Salt to taste
2 tablespoons butter at room temperature
Juice of ½ lemon
2 tablespoons finely chopped parsley
Freshly ground pepper to taste

1. Rinse the beans and drain them. Put them into a saucepan with water to cover and salt to taste.

2. Bring to the boil and simmer 10 minutes, or until tender. The beans must remain a trifle firm or al dente.

3. Drain the beans and return them to a hot saucepan. Add the butter and sprinkle with lemon juice, parsley, and pepper. Toss and serve hot.

Yield: Four servings.

THE IDEA HAS BEEN EXPLORED THAT THE COM-mon hamburger might have had Russian origins. The Russian name usually given for ground meat patties that are cooked and served with or without sauce, is *bitok* and sometimes *bitock* or *bitoke*. Many people have tried to associate the name with a distortion in pronunciation of the words "beef steak."

Bitoks are absolutely ideal for quick cookery. Although the raw meat is frequently blended with chopped onion before cooking, I personally dislike this technique. You get a more refined product if the meat is handled as little as possible without kneading. Simply press the unseasoned meat between the palms to make it adhere neatly as it is shaped into rounds like hamburgers.

I've never admired that old saying in French kitchens that goes, "C'est la sauce qui fait la poisson," or, "It is the sauce that makes the fish." In my own mind it smacks of the necessity of using a sauce to disguise the flavor of a fish that is none too fresh.

On the other hand, a well-made sauce can be an admirable addition to foods like plain, unadorned hamburgers, or, if you wish, bitoks. The sauce may be a simply made one of butter, chopped parsley, lemon juice, and a touch of Tabasco or perhaps Worcestershire. But a slightly more complicated sauce involving sour cream and, if you wish, a splash of Cognac, is a nice complement.

Fresh asparagus makes a fine accompaniment for this dish. So does plain rice cooked according to your favorite recipe.

The obvious way to go about such a meal is to prepare the rice and start it cooking. Scrape the asparagus and have them ready to cook. Shape the meat into patties and have all the ingredients measured and at hand. Use your own judgment as to when to start cooking the bitoks. Put the asparagus on to simmer and cook the meat and vegetable simultaneously.

Bitoks à la Russe
(Hamburgers with sour cream)

1½ pounds ground sirloin
   Salt and freshly ground
   pepper to taste
2 tablespoons plus 1 teaspoon
   butter

1 tablespoon finely chopped
   shallot
2 tablespoons Cognac
1 cup sour cream

1. Shape the meat into 4 compact patties. Do not knead the meat when working with it. Simply divide it into 4 portions and shape it, pressing between the hands, into 4 patties. Sprinkle the patties with salt and pepper.

2. Melt 1 tablespoon of the butter and, when hot, add the meat. Cook about 3 minutes to a side or longer if you prefer your meat well-done. Remove the patties to a warm platter. Pour off the fat from the skillet.

3. To the skillet, add 1 teaspoon of the butter and the chopped shallot. Cook briefly and add the Cognac. Cook briefly and add the sour cream and salt and pepper to taste. Heat thoroughly. Strain through a fine sieve into a saucepan. Reheat and swirl in the remaining tablespoon of butter. Serve with the bitoks.

Yield: Four servings.

Asperges au Beurre
(Buttered asparagus)

12 to 16 fresh asparagus spears
    Salt to taste

2 tablespoons butter, melted

1. Cut off the ends of the asparagus, about 1 inch from the bottom. Place the asparagus in a skillet and add water to cover and salt to taste. Bring to the boil and simmer until barely tender, about 2 to 5 minutes, depending on the size of the spears.

2. Drain quickly and add the melted butter. Serve hot.

Yield: Four servings.

THERE IS AN INTERESTING IF CURIOUS NOTION that French chefs live on the likes of foie gras and sturgeon, cocks' combs and caviar. That they turn up their nose at the thought of such down-to-earth fare as American hot dogs and corn on the cob and barbecued spareribs. Nothing could be further from the truth. I, personally, have a great liking for liverwurst sandwiches, pastrami on rye, and a well-made hamburger. On occasion, however, when I serve typically American—and un-French—foods in my home, there may be a temptation at times to give these dishes a French touch.

Take hamburgers. Now there's nothing wrong with the standard burger-on-a-bun, tomato ketchup, and sliced onion included. But a hamburger cooked to resemble a steak au poivre can be an elegant and tasty dish that nobody could criticize. It isn't a question of putting on airs; it's a question of taste.

Hamburgers au poivre, if one wishes to call them that, are easy to make. You simply coat them on both sides with crushed peppercorns; cook them for a reasonable time on both sides; and, finally, add a judicious amount of butter, shallots, red wine, and Cognac. A bit of beef broth and parsley and the dish is done. The entire preparation and cooking time should require considerably less than half an hour.

This preparation goes very well, I discovered recently, with another American invention, potatoes O'Brien, a dish I learned to make soon after my arrival in this country, nearly forty years ago.

Don't ask me who O'Brien was. No one ever bothered to say. But the combination of cubed potatoes plus sweet peppers and pimientos, properly cooked, has a lot going for it by way of flavor. There are those who say that potatoes O'Brien should be made with cream, but that's another recipe.

If you should make this combination of dishes—to be prepared and cooked in less than an hour—get all the ingredients ready, peeled and chopped and cubed as necessary, before starting to cook. The two can then be cooked—within reason—simultaneously.

Steak Haché au Poivre
(Hamburgers with peppercorn sauce)

1½ pounds ground chuck
    Salt to taste
1½ to 2 tablespoons crushed
    peppercorns
  2 tablespoons butter
  1 tablespoon finely chopped
    shallot

¼ cup dry red wine
1 tablespoon Cognac
¼ cup beef broth
2 tablespoons finely chopped
  parsley

1. Shape the meat into 4 patties of equal size. Sprinkle with salt and sprinkle all over with crushed peppercorns. Press down on the meat to help the peppercorns adhere.

2. Heat a heavy iron skillet and do not add fat of any kind. When the skillet is quite hot (if oil were used, it would almost smoke), add the patties. Cook about 5 minutes on one side.

3. Using a spatula or pancake turner, quickly scoop up the patties and turn them over. Cook about 5 minutes longer (if you want them well-done, cook about 10 minutes longer).

4. Remove the patties to a warm platter and add 1 tablespoon of the butter and the shallots to the skillet. Cook, stirring with a wooden spoon, until the shallots are wilted. Add the wine and cook about 1 minute. Add the Cognac and let it reduce to about half. Add the broth and cook until reduced to about 3 tablespoons. Swirl in the remaining butter. Return the patties to the skillet, turning once off the heat. Serve garnished with chopped parsley.

Yield: Four servings.

Pommes de Terre "O'Brien"
(Potatoes with peppers and pimientos)

6 to 8 potatoes, about 1½ pounds
Salt to taste
3 tablespoons peanut, vegetable, or corn oil
⅓ cup finely chopped onion
Freshly ground pepper to taste
1 cup cubed sweet green pepper
1 tablespoon butter
⅓ cup cubed pimiento

1. Peel the potatoes and cut them into ½-inch cubes. There should be about 3 cups. As they are cubed drop them into cold water.

2. Drain the potatoes and add them to a saucepan or small skillet. Add water to cover and salt to taste. Bring to the boil and simmer about 1 or 2 minutes. Drain well.

3. Heat the oil in a skillet and add the potatoes. Cook, stirring and shaking the skillet as necessary, until the potatoes become golden, about 8 to 10 minutes.

4. Add the onion, salt, and pepper and cook briefly. Add the green pepper and cook, stirring gently, about 3 minutes.

5. Add the butter and cook about 2 minutes. Add the pimiento and stir gently. Cook until heated through.

Yield: Four servings.

DURING A RECENT DISCUSSION ABOUT BEEF Stroganoff—one of the long-time, classic dishes in quick cookery—I had to admit I had never heard of the dish's origin. Someone recalled one of the rare books on Russian food to have been printed in this country, *The Best of Russian Cookery*, by Princess Alexandra Kropotkin (Charles Scribner's Sons, 1964).

According to that source, the dish was named for a member of Russian nobility, Count Paul Stroganoff. He was a member of the Court of Czar Alexander II and a member of the St. Petersburg Imperial Academy of Arts. The count was known as a *fin bec* during the latter part of the eighteenth century, but at what particular time beef Stroganoff was created and named for him is not divulged in the princess' notes.

There are many variations of beef Stroganoff. Some use sliced onions, others chopped. Some include mustard, others paprika. Some add a touch of tomato purée, others don't. Only beef and sour cream seem to be the invariable ingredients.

Quite honestly, I can't recall the origin of my version of the dish. In any event, it is one that I prepared hundreds, if not thousands, of times while I was chef at Le Pavillon. It has one touch that I have never seen elsewhere and that is cornichons, or small, imported sour pickles. The pickles are cut into fine julienne strips and added at the end of the cooking time.

Perhaps the most ordinary accompaniment for beef Stroganoff is rice. An alternative is noodles. I happen to enjoy it with sautéed potatoes, but it is a question of personal taste. Take your choice.

The beef Stroganoff cooks in less than 10 minutes. Should you decide on potatoes, get them started, then proceed to the ingredients for the beef.

Beef Stroganoff

1 pound beef fillet, cut into
  julienne strips
1 tablespoon sweet or hot
  paprika
  Salt and freshly ground
  pepper to taste

2 tablespoons butter
⅓ cup finely chopped onion
½ cup dry white wine
1 cup sour cream
½ cup cornichons (sour
  pickles) cut into thin strips

1. Sprinkle the meat with paprika, salt, and pepper and blend well.

2. Melt the butter in a very hot skillet and add the meat, stirring to separate the pieces so that they cook evenly, about 2 or 3 minutes. Remove the meat with a slotted spoon.

3. Add the onion to the skillet and cook, stirring, about 1 minute. Add the wine and cook down to reduce by about half. Lower the heat and add the sour cream, stirring. Do not allow the sauce to boil or the sour cream will curdle.

4. Return the meat to the skillet and stir to blend. Add the sour pickles and blend. Serve with noodles, rice, or sautéed potatoes.

Yield: Four servings.

Pommes Lyonnaise
(Potatoes sautéed with onions)

1½ pounds small potatoes
  Salt
¼ cup peanut oil
½ cup thinly sliced onion

Freshly ground pepper to
taste
1 tablespoon butter

1. Do not peel the potatoes. Place them in a kettle with water to cover and salt to taste.

2. Cook until tender, about 20 minutes. Drain and let cool. When cool enough to handle, peel them.

3. Cut the potatoes into ¼-inch-thick slices or slightly larger.

4. Heat the oil in a skillet and, when it is quite hot, add the potatoes. Cook, shaking the skillet and stirring gently. Turn the potatoes with a spatula. Take care to keep the slices whole. Cook about 6 to 8 minutes.

5. Add the sliced onion and salt and pepper. Continue cooking, turning the potatoes gently until nicely browned on all sides, about 5 minutes. Dot with the butter and heat through.

Yield: Four servings.

IF YOU WERE TO PLAY A GAME OF WORD ASSOCI-
ations with cooks and chefs who are much involved in
food, the name Provence would conjure up in the cook's
mind tomatoes and garlic, and assorted herbs; Greece would
summon thoughts of lamb, tomatoes, and feta cheese; China
would bring to mind images of garlic and ginger, soy sauce, and
fermented black beans. Similarly, the name Hungary or dishes
labeled hongroise, as they are called in French, brings up
thoughts of paprika, onions, sweet peppers, and cream, either
sweet or sour.

A good many dishes bearing the name hongroise are ideally
suited to hasty cooking, foods that can be made ready for the
table in less than 60 minutes. The basic procedure for the preparation of these dishes is as follows: Butter or oil is heated in
a skillet and onions and sweet peppers are added. These are
cooked quickly. In another skillet a bit more butter is heated,
small pieces of beef coated lightly with paprika are added, and
this too is quickly cooked. If the meat is overcooked it will become dry. The two elements are combined, tossed together, and
cream is added as a final ingredient. The cream is cooked until it
thickens slightly, only 4 to 5 minutes. Then the dish is ready.

A simple platter of buttered noodles would be infinitely appropriate as an accompaniment. But if you want to be just a touch
more creative, you might consider a hastily made skillet of sautéed potatoes.

Sauté de Boeuf Hongroise
(Beef strips with paprika cream sauce)

1¼ pounds lean, tender, boneless beef, preferably from shell steak
Salt and freshly ground pepper to taste
2 teaspoons paprika
2 tablespoons butter
1 cup finely minced onions
2 cups thinly sliced sweet green or red peppers, preferably a combination of both
½ cup dry white wine
1 cup heavy cream

1. Cut the meat into strips about ½ inch thick and 2 inches long. Sprinkle with salt and pepper and paprika. Blend well with the fingers to coat the meat.

2. Melt half the butter in a heavy skillet and add the onions and green peppers. Sprinkle with salt and pepper. Cook, stirring, about 5 minutes.

3. Meanwhile, melt the remaining butter in a skillet and add the beef pieces, stirring and turning over high heat about 2 minutes. Remove the pieces of meat and set aside. Do not wash or wipe out the skillet.

4. Add the green pepper mixture to the skillet in which the meat cooked. Add the wine and cook about 1 minute, stirring.

5. Add the cream. Bring to the boil and cook over high heat about 4 or 5 minutes. Add the meat and drippings and serve.

Yield: Four servings.

Pommes Sautées
(Sautéed potatoes)

5 new, thin-skinned, red or white potatoes, about 1¼ pounds
Salt and freshly ground pepper to taste
⅓ cup peanut, vegetable, or corn oil

1 tablespoon butter
1 small clove garlic, finely minced
2 tablespoons finely chopped parsley

1. Put the potatoes in a saucepan or kettle and add water to cover and salt to taste. Simmer about 20 minutes, or until tender.

2. Drain the potatoes and when cool enough to handle, peel them. Cut each potato into ¼-inch-thick slices.

3. Heat the oil in a well-cured, black iron skillet, preferably with curved sides. Add the potatoes. Add salt and pepper to taste.

4. Cook, stirring and tossing gently, about 5 to 8 minutes, or until nicely crisped and brown. Try not to break up the potato slices as they cook.

5. Drain the oil from the potatoes. Add the butter and let it melt. Sprinkle with garlic and parsley. Stir and toss gently and serve.

Yield: Four servings.

AS ANYONE CONVERSANT WITH CHINESE COOK-ing can testify, there is one broad and far-reaching category of food preparation known in English as the "stir-fry" technique. This involves adding small pieces or thin slices of food to a wok containing oil and cooking over very high heat and as hurriedly as possible before serving.

I mention this because a vast majority of the beef dishes used in stir-fry cookery are made with flank steak cut on the bias into very thin strips. There is, of course, a very good reason for this. It is the quality of flank steak—its tenderness and juiciness—that adapts itself admirably to quick cooking. It is no exaggeration to say that where French cooking is concerned, flank steak could be used in any hasty cooking that calls for thinly sliced (and far more expensive) filet mignon or club steak.

One such recipe is beef à la Deutsch, which is a quick sauté (one could say that a quick sauté is to a French chef what stir-frying is to a Chinese) of beef with mushrooms, green peppers, shallots, and cream. I have no earthly idea why this dish is known as à la Deutsch or German style. It is an excellent bit of cookery, and for all I know it was created by a good German chef. In any event, the name is a convenient coinage to express a basic style of preparing one particular dish.

Because the dish embraces both meat and vegetables, and because it is lightly sauced (the sauce is lightly laced with sherry wine), buttered noodles are a hastily made and ideal accompaniment. The noodles may be served simply tossed with butter. Or you may add a few poppy or caraway seeds. Crushed or chopped green peppercorns, which have become somewhat voguish within recent years, may also be used as a neat and flavorful addition. By all means, however, use the peppercorns packed in a plain nonacid brine rather than those that are freeze-dried or packed in vinegar.

Boeuf à la Deutsch
(A quick sauté of beef)

1½ pounds flank steak
  Salt and freshly ground
  pepper to taste
3 tablespoons peanut,
  vegetable, or corn oil
1 tablespoon butter
1 cup diced sweet green
  peppers
¼ pound mushrooms, thinly
  sliced, about 2 cups

2 tablespoons finely chopped
  shallots
¼ cup plus 2 teaspoons dry
  sherry wine
½ cup beef broth
¾ cup heavy cream
1 tablespoon arrowroot

1. Put the flank steak on a flat surface. Trim it of all surface fat. Cut the beef lengthwise into strips 2 inches wide. Cut the strips crosswise into ½-inch lengths. Sprinkle with salt and pepper and toss.

2. Use a large heavy skillet. Heat the oil and, when it is very hot and almost smoking, add half the meat. Cook, shaking the skillet and stirring to redistribute the pieces, about 1 or 2 minutes. Spoon the meat from the skillet. Quickly add the remaining meat and cook, shaking the skillet and stirring about 1 or 2 minutes.

3. Add the meat to the first batch.

4. To the skillet add the butter. When the butter is melted, add the green pepper and mushrooms. Cook until the mushrooms wilt. Add the chopped shallots and cook, stirring, about 1 minute.

5. Add ¼ cup of the sherry. At the boil, add the beef broth. Cook about 1 minute and add the cream.

6. Blend the arrowroot with the 2 teaspoons of sherry. Blend. Stir this into the sauce. Cook, stirring, and add the meat. Stir to

coat and heat through. Add salt and pepper to taste and serve piping hot.

Yield: Four to six servings.

Nouilles au Beurre de Poivre Vert
(Noodles with green peppercorn butter)

½ pound thin or medium
   noodles
Salt to taste

1 teaspoon green peppercorns
   packed in liquid
3 tablespoons butter

1. Cook the noodles in boiling salted water to cover to the desired degree of doneness.

2. Chop the peppercorns and add them to a skillet large enough for tossing the noodles when added.

3. Add the butter to the peppercorns and blend.

4. Drain the noodles and add them to the peppercorn butter. Toss.

Yield: Four servings.

Pork and Ham

T O COOK WITH HASTE AND PRECISION IMPLIES cooking efficiently. And to cook efficiently implies familiarization with the basic techniques of cookery. One of the most useful formulas is the one used for breading foods, which we speak of in French kitchens as à l'anglaise (English style) or foods *panés* or *panées* (breaded).

The breading technique is simple. There are three steps. First, the food is dipped or dredged in flour. Any excess flour should be shaken off to leave a light coating.

Second, the food is dipped in raw egg that has been beaten, more often than not with salt, pepper, and a little water. Third, the food is dipped in crumbs, coating the food all over. When the food is removed from the crumbs, it is best to tap it lightly with the flat side of a heavy knife to help the crumbs adhere.

Finally, the food is cooked in heated butter or oil or a combination of both. When it is golden brown on one side, the food is turned and browned on the other. If you are dealing with food that cooks rapidly—such as fish—by the time the food is browned on both sides it is generally ready to serve. Some foods require much longer cooking and that would include pork chops. On the other hand, the chops recommended in this recipe are not only thin, they are pounded lightly to hasten cooking. Total time is about 10 minutes.

Ideally, all the ingredients for this meal should be made ready before you start to cook. The accompanying dish proposed for the pork chops is a purée of carrots and potatoes. After the carrots and potatoes are put on to cook (total time about 20 minutes), start breading and cooking the chops. The vegetables, incidentally, can—within reason—be reheated to advantage.

Côtes de Porc Panées
(Breaded pork chops)

8 thin (about ½-inch thick) loin pork chops, about 1¼ pounds
Salt and freshly ground pepper to taste
1 cup flour
1 egg, lightly beaten
2 tablespoons water
2 cups bread crumbs
⅓ cup peanut, vegetable, or corn oil
1 tablespoon butter

1. Sprinkle the chops with salt and pepper. Place between two sheets of plastic wrap and pound lightly with a flat mallet.

2. Dip the chops lightly in flour.

3. Beat the egg lightly with water and salt and pepper to taste. Dip the chops in this, smearing it over with the fingers so that it adheres.

4. Dip the chops in the bread crumbs so that they are coated all over. Pat lightly with the flat side of a heavy knife to help the crumbs adhere.

5. Heat the oil and butter in a large heavy skillet and cook the chops until they are golden brown on one side, about 3 to 4 minutes. Turn and cook on the other side about 3 or 4 minutes. It may be necessary to do this in two steps if all the chops will not fit in the skillet.

Yield: Four servings.

Purée de Légumes
(Puréed carrots and potatoes)

4 carrots, about ¾ pound
3 potatoes, about 1¼ pounds
  Salt to taste
2 tablespoons butter

Freshly ground pepper to taste
¼ teaspoon freshly grated nutmeg
½ cup hot milk

1. Trim off the ends of the carrots and scrape them with a swivel-bladed vegetable scraper. Cut them into 1-inch lengths. There should be about 2 cups.

2. Peel the potatoes and cut them into eighths. Place the carrots and potatoes in a saucepan and add cold water to cover and salt to taste. Bring to the boil and simmer about 20 minutes, or until the vegetables are tender. Do not overcook or they will be watery and mushy.

3. Put the vegetables through a food mill, potato ricer, or process in a food processor. Return them to a clean saucepan.

4. Add salt, butter, pepper, and nutmeg and blend. Place over the heat and add the hot milk, beating rapidly with a wooden spoon. Serve immediately.

Yield: Four servings.

MUCH HAS BEEN MADE OF VARIOUS MANIFES-
tations involved in the *nouvelle cuisine* of French
cookery. One of the dishes that has captured the public
fancy is poulet au vinaigre, actually a sauté of chicken with a
trace of vinegar and, generally, tomato among the ingredients.

The use of vinegar as an important ingredient in serious cookery is not a new invention. The mildly acid taste of the liquid
has long been part of the sauces used with certain foods, principally pork and such sauces as Robert and charcuterie.

Vinegar, as a matter of fact, complements foods that have
somewhat high fat contents, including pork chops.

There is here a version of sautéed pork chops with sauce Robert. The components include not only vinegar but a touch of tomato, dry white wine, and a dab of mustard for added piquancy.

Pork chops are best cooked either in a short span of time, to
prevent them from drying out, or over a long period of time, to
make them more tender.

In the dish here, the pork chops should be cooked rapidly,
preferably 5 to 6 minutes to a side. The thickness of the chops is
a factor. The thinner the chops, the faster they will be in and out
of the skillet.

The total cooking time for this dish is approximately 20 minutes. To my mind an ideal side dish for such chops is puréed
potatoes, which should be cooked during the same period as the
chops. They may be finished with butter and milk at the last
moment.

Côtes de Porc Sautées
(Sautéed pork chops)

8 pork chops, each about ½ inch thick
Salt and freshly ground pepper to taste
2 tablespoons peanut, vegetable, or corn oil
½ cup finely chopped onion
6 tablespoons plus 1 teaspoon dry white wine

2 tablespoons red wine vinegar
1 cup chicken broth
1 tablespoon tomato paste
1 teaspoon cornstarch
1 tablespoon imported mustard, such as Dijon or Düsseldorf

1. Sprinkle the chops with salt and pepper.

2. Heat the oil in a heavy skillet in which the chops will fit in one layer. Add the chops and cook about 5 minutes, or until well browned on one side.

3. Turn the chops on the other side and cook 5 to 6 minutes. The chops must be cooked rapidly over very high heat or they will toughen. Total cooking time should be from about 10 to 12 minutes.

4. Remove the chops to a warm serving platter and pour off most of the fat from the skillet. Add the onions and cook briefly, stirring. Add 6 tablespoons of the wine and the vinegar and stir with a wire whisk to dissolve the brown particles that cling to the bottom and sides of the pan.

5. Add the chicken broth and tomato paste and stir to blend. Cook about 5 minutes. Blend the cornstarch and remaining 1 teaspoon of wine and stir it into the sauce.

6. Spoon and scrape the sauce into a saucepan and add the mustard. Add any juices that have accumulated around the chops, salt, and a generous amount of black pepper. Heat

the sauce without boiling and serve with the chops. Serve with puréed potatoes.

Yield: Four servings.

Purée de Pommes
(Puréed potatoes)

1½ pounds potatoes
  Salt to taste
¾ cup milk

3 tablespoons butter at room temperature
⅛ teaspoon freshly grated nutmeg, or to taste

1. Peel the potatoes and quarter or cut them into 2-inch cubes.
2. Put the potatoes in a saucepan and add cold water to cover and salt to taste. Bring to the boil and simmer 20 minutes, or until the potatoes are tender.
3. Drain the potatoes and put them through a food mill or potato ricer. Return them to the saucepan.
4. Meanwhile, bring the milk to the boil.
5. While the milk is being heated, use a wooden spoon and add the butter to the potatoes while beating. Add salt and nutmeg to taste and beat in the hot milk.

Yield: Four servings.

SOMEWHERE, YEARS AGO, I READ AN ESSAY ON pork that quoted Auguste Escoffier: "However deservedly pork may be praised, it could never have been included among the preparations of first-class cookery (except subsidiarily) had it not been for the culinary value of ham." I have never known the source of that quote but it fascinates me that he spoke of ham exclusively and not of the entire range of charcuterie. I consider the sausages and salamis, the pork-based pâtés and terrines of my homeland to be among the great contributions to civilization.

It is true that pork is generally regarded as something to feast on more in the home than at grand banquets. And yet, there is a great deal to be said for the infinite preparations of the meat.

A loin of pork, studded discreetly with garlic and seasoned with thyme and roasted to a golden brown, is a great creation—particularly if it is served with a mound of mashed potatoes. But, of course, that requires a lengthy time to cook.

A tender loin pork chop makes for fine dining on a winter's day and, although pork must be cooked longer than most meats, a savory platter of chops can be cooked in much less than 60 minutes.

The recipe here—pork chops sautéed with apples—is not tedious to prepare and it is certainly tempting fare with its light sauce made of white wine and a little chicken broth.

As a vegetable accompaniment, Brussels sprouts are excellent. Like pork, sprouts may not achieve poetic heights, but in season they can be delectable. Both the pork and the sprouts require about the same cooking time.

Filets de Porc aux Pommes
(Loin pork chops with apples)

4 loin pork chops, each about
   1 inch thick, about 2½
   pounds
   Salt and freshly ground
   pepper to taste
1 tablespoon peanut,
   vegetable, or corn oil

2 apples, peeled, cored, and
   quartered
1 clove garlic, unpeeled
¼ cup dry white wine
⅓ cup chicken broth

1. Sprinkle the chops with salt and pepper.

2. Heat the oil in a heavy skillet large enough to hold both chops and quartered apples—when they are added—in one layer.

3. Add the chops and garlic to the skillet and brown well on one side, about 5 minutes. Turn and brown on the other side, about 10 minutes.

4. Push the chops aside and add the apples in one layer. Continue cooking 15 minutes, turning the apples so that they brown and cook evenly.

5. Remove the chops and apples to a serving dish. Pour off the fat from the skillet. Add the wine, stirring to dissolve the brown particles that cling to the bottom and sides of the pan. Add the broth and simmer down to a saucelike consistency. Discard the garlic. Pour the sauce over the chops and apples and serve.

Yield: Four servings.

Choux de Bruxelles
(Brussels sprouts)

1 pint [10 to 12 ounces]
   Brussels sprouts
Salt to taste

2 tablespoons butter
¼ cup finely chopped onion

1. Trim off the ends of the sprouts and make a small gash in the bottom of each. Add to a saucepan with water to cover and salt to taste.

2. Bring to the boil and simmer to the desired degree of doneness, 10 minutes or longer. Drain.

3. Melt the butter in the saucepan. Add the onion and cook until wilted. Add the sprouts and cover. Cook 5 minutes, shaking the pan occasionally.

Yield: Four servings.

IF THE MAIN DISH OF THE MEAL IS TO BE PORK chops, there are two ways to cook them—fast and slow. If they are to be braised—that is, browned and cooked slowly—the time element is not critical.

The pork chops here—they are called hongroise because they contain paprika and, to a French mind, paprika is associated with Hungary—fall into the "cooked quickly" category. The total cooking time is about 25 minutes for the chops, 5 minutes more for the sauce. Thus the chops should be cooked about half an hour before they are to be served. If they stand, they are more than apt to become tough and chewy.

The accompaniments for the chops include baked acorn squash, which requires 45 minutes of cooking and should, therefore, be placed in the oven early. And then there's a sauté of Brussels sprouts. The cooking time for this varies—about 25 minutes—but the sprouts can be cooked, drained, and set aside and then sautéed quickly in butter before serving.

A Boston lettuce salad, with cheese, followed by sweetened orange sections, would be appropriate.

Côtes de Porc Hongroise

(Pork chops with paprika in cream sauce)

4 loin pork chops, about 2 pounds
   Salt and freshly ground pepper to taste
1 teaspoon paprika
2 teaspoons peanut, vegetable, or corn oil

¾ cup finely chopped onion
½ cup dry white wine
½ cup heavy cream
1 tablespoon imported mustard, such as Dijon or Düsseldorf

1. Sprinkle the chops on both sides with salt, pepper, and the paprika.

2. Heat the oil in a heavy skillet and add the chops. Cook about 10 minutes, or until nicely browned on one side. Turn and cook 15 minutes longer. Pour off the fat.

3. Sprinkle the onion between the chops and cook briefly. Remove the chops to a warm platter. Add the wine to the skillet and cook, stirring, until the liquid is almost totally reduced. Add the cream and cook over high heat about 5 minutes. Remove from the heat and stir in the mustard. Serve the chops with the sauce spooned over.

Yield: Four servings.

Courges au Four
(Baked acorn squash)

---

2 acorn squash
2 tablespoons butter
2 tablespoons brown sugar

Salt and freshly ground
pepper to taste

1. Preheat the oven to 400 degrees.
2. Split the squash in half. Using a spoon, scrape out and discard the seeds and fibers from the cavity. Cut off and discard a thin slice from the bottom of each squash half, so the squash will rest flat during baking.
3. Rub the cavity of each squash half with one-quarter of the butter, and sprinkle the cavities with equal amounts of brown sugar. Sprinkle with salt and pepper. Place in a baking dish and bake 40 to 45 minutes, or until the flesh is tender.

Yield: Four servings.

Choux de Bruxelles Sautés au Beurre
(Sautéed Brussels sprouts)

1 pint, about ¾ pound
Brussels sprouts

Salt and freshly ground
pepper to taste
1 tablespoon butter

1. Pull off and discard any tough outer leaves from the Brussels sprouts.

2. Trim the bottoms neatly. Cut a cross in the bottom of each.

3. Put the sprouts in enough boiling salted water to cover them. Let the water return to the boil, and simmer the vegetable about 20 to 25 minutes, or until tender.

4. Melt the butter in a heavy skillet and add the sprouts. Sprinkle with salt and pepper to taste and cook quickly, shaking the skillet until the sprouts are golden brown all over. Serve.

Yield: Four servings.

SOME OF THE BEST AND MOST QUICKLY MADE dishes of the Italian kitchen, particularly those kitchens that specialize in cooking in the style of Naples, are those with pizzaiola. These sauces have a tomato base, which has been reduced considerably, and olive oil and a touch of garlic. Plus one indispensable ingredient, oregano. Beef quickly cooked—grilled, pan-fried—adapts itself well to a pizzaiola sauce, but I prefer pork chops. The recipe here includes a variation on the basic sauce—the use of mushrooms and green peppers. On the day the recipe was tested, both ingredients happened to be lying in the refrigerator with no other immediate destination.

Now an agreeable accompaniment for pork chops pizzaiola would be a simple dish of buttered noodles, but the refrigerator that day also yielded a spare eggplant. There was time to cook this, too, and yet remain well within the scope of an hour in the kitchen, so another simple but appetizing recipe happened—slices of eggplant brushed with a blend of butter and Parmesan cheese, salt, and pepper, and baked until tender. This dish goes well with the tomato sauce in which the pork chops are served and remains within the scope of Neapolitan cookery.

The total cooking time for the pork chops is approximately 15 minutes, which offers ample time to prepare both the noodles and, if desired, the eggplant. If I were to choose wine for this meal, it would be along the lines of a Valpolicella or a Bardolino. A salad made with crisp leaves of romaine lettuce and a nice ripe slice of Gorgonzola cheese, which is available in abundance in the best shops, would be nice accompaniments.

Côtes de Porc "Pizzaiola"
(Pork chops in tomato sauce with oregano)

2 cups imported canned
  tomatoes
  Salt and freshly ground
  pepper to taste
4 loin pork chops, about ½
  pound each
2 tablespoons olive oil

2 teaspoons chopped garlic
1½ cups thinly sliced fresh
  mushrooms
1½ cups green pepper cut into
  1-inch pieces
½ cup dry white wine
1 teaspoon dried oregano

1. Put the tomatoes in a saucepan and bring to the boil. Cook, stirring occasionally, until reduced to about 1½ cups. Add salt and pepper to taste.

2. Sprinkle the chops with salt and pepper.

3. Heat the oil in a skillet and brown the chops on all sides, about 5 minutes to a side. Add the garlic, mushrooms, and green peppers. Cover closely and cook about 5 minutes. Add the wine, tomatoes, oregano, and salt and pepper to taste.

4. Cover closely and cook about 35 to 40 minutes. Serve with buttered noodles sprinkled with Parmesan cheese.

Yield: Four servings.

Aubergines au Four "Parmigiana"
(Baked eggplant parmigiana)

1 1½- to 2-pound eggplant
4 to 5 tablespoons butter at
  room temperature
3 tablespoons grated
  Parmesan cheese

Salt and freshly ground
pepper to taste
Chopped parsley for garnish

1. Preheat the oven to 400 degrees.

2. Peel the eggplant and trim off the ends. Cut the eggplant into 6 to 8 slices, each about ½ inch thick.

3. Blend the butter and cheese and spread the eggplant slices on both sides with the mixture. Sprinkle with salt and pepper.

4. Arrange the slices on a baking sheet in one layer. Bake 15 to 20 minutes, or until the eggplant is tender throughout. Serve sprinkled with chopped parsley.

Yield: Four servings.

DURING A BRIEF VISIT TO BELGIUM WE chanced to stop in a little-known restaurant outside Brussels. It was a small place and generally undistinguished, but we were tempted by one dish that the owner, a gentleman from Liège, told us was his own creation and a specialty of the house. I don't recall his name, but the dish I remember well. Perhaps all the more so because it is reminiscent of a dish I've eaten in France called pork chops avesnoise.

Basically it consists of pork chops that have been browned on both sides and cooked until done. They are then smeared with a mixture of cheese, mustard, egg yolk, and cream and glazed under a broiler until done. Very simple. Very quick. And very, very good. My version of this dish I call liègeoise—in the style of Liège.

The chef from Liège had embellished on these ingredients a bit and added garlic, chives, and a touch of white wine, which gives the dish a bit more character. The total cooking time for that dish is scarcely half an hour, and the preparation time negligible.

More and more one can find small baby carrots of good flavor in plastic bags, and those need only to be scraped before cooking. Carrots go well with the pork dish, particularly if they have the added fillip of fresh mint.

To prepare these dishes in less than an hour, it is best to assemble and prepare all the ingredients for the chops. As the chops are browned on both sides there is ample time to scrape the carrots and get the ingredients for that dish ready.

Côtes de Porc Liègeoise
(Pork chops glazed with cheese)

4 loin pork chops, about 1½ pounds total weight
Salt and freshly ground pepper to taste
1 tablespoon peanut, vegetable, or corn oil
¼ pound grated Gruyère or Swiss cheese, about 1 cup
1 tablespoon imported mustard, such as Dijon or Düsseldorf

1 tablespoon heavy cream
½ teaspoon finely chopped garlic
1 tablespoon finely chopped chives
1 egg yolk
2 tablespoons dry white wine
2 tablespoons water

1. Sprinkle the chops with salt and pepper.

2. Heat the oil in a heavy skillet and add the chops. Cook until nicely browned on one side, about 10 minutes. Turn and continue cooking until browned and cooked through.

3. Preheat the broiler.

4. As the chops cook, blend the cheese, mustard, cream, garlic, chives, and egg yolk. When the chops are cooked, smear one side with equal portions of the cheese mixture, smoothing it over.

5. Run the chops under the broiler until the topping is browned and nicely glazed.

6. Meanwhile, pour off the fat from the skillet in which the chops cooked. Add the wine to the skillet, stirring, and add the water. Bring to the boil. Stir to dissolve the brown particles that cling to the bottom and sides of the skillet. Pour the hot sauce over the chops and serve.

Yield: Four servings.

Carottes à la Menthe
(Carrots with mint)

¾ pound carrots, preferably small baby carrots
Salt to taste
3 tablespoons heavy cream

Freshly ground pepper to taste
1 or 2 teaspoons chopped fresh mint

1. Trim and scrape the carrots. If small, leave them whole. Otherwise, quarter or slice them. Add them to a saucepan with water to cover and salt to taste. Bring to the boil and simmer until tender, 15 minutes or less.

2. Drain the carrots and add the cream. Add salt and pepper and simmer about 3 minutes. Serve sprinkled with fresh mint.

Yield: Four servings.

THE WORLD OF FOOD HAS SUCH BROAD HORI-zons that it is as amusing as it is astonishing how deeply exercised "food enthusiasts" can become over one recipe or another. That is not to say that I will abide transgressions against classic French cooking and will not make my protests about misnomers in the name of Escoffier as loud as possible.

What I have in mind arc the supposed "purists" who are opposed to variances from what their palates are accustomed to. For example, the purist who is vehemently opposed to putting any kind of sauce on fresh bay scallops because they suffer from any but the simplest preparations, namely broiling or sautéing. My defense is that while I admire the simple preparations of the delicacy, cooking is an adventure and a well-made wine or cream sauce can be an admirable change.

In the same vein, whenever I print a recipe for almost any food—poultry, fish, or meat—to be combined in a recipe with berries or fruit, there is the inevitable response of those who deplore such liaisons. No need to point out the time-honored links of duck with orange (à l'orange); sole with grapes (véronique); or game dishes with currant jelly among the ingredients.

One day I "created" a dish of pork chops with orange that was to my taste—and to the taste of those who dined at my table—a worthwhile experiment. It came about because I had pork chops (about three-fourths of a pound each) and a large seedless orange that had been placed, accidentally perhaps, in a monthly shipment of grapefruit.

This is not a complicated recipe by any means. It requires little of the tedium, for example, of duck à l'orange or duck with cassis. The pork chops are cooked thoroughly for about half an hour (they will remain juicy). The chops are removed and onions plus various liquids are added (broth, lemon juice, and tomatoes). Orange slices are added and the chops are served with the sauce. Rice with parsley is the obvious accompaniment for the dish.

Côtes de Porc à l'Orange
(Pork chops with orange)

4 large pork chops, about ¾ pound each
Salt and freshly ground pepper to taste
3 tablespoons butter
1 large seedless navel orange
½ cup finely chopped onion
Juice of ½ lemon
1 cup chicken broth
1 tablespoon tomato paste
½ teaspoon sugar

1. Sprinkle the chops with salt and pepper.
2. Melt 2 tablespoons of the butter in a very hot skillet and add the chops.
3. Cook over moderately high heat about 10 minutes, or until nicely browned. Turn the chops and cook 10 minutes longer. Continue cooking, turning the chops often so that they cook evenly. Turn the pieces on their sides to brown and crisp the fat around the rim. Total cooking time should be about 30 minutes.
4. As the chops cook, trim off the ends of the orange. Cut the unpeeled orange into eight rounds.
5. Remove the chops to a serving platter and pour off the fat from the skillet.
6. To the skillet add the onion. Cook, stirring, until wilted. Add the lemon juice and stir. Add the broth and tomato paste and stir to blend, cooking gently. Add the sugar and salt and pepper to taste.
7. Add the orange slices. Add any juices that have accumulated around the chops. Cook, turning the orange slices, about 3 minutes.
8. Remove the orange slices from the skillet and arrange them around the chops. Swirl the remaining tablespoon of butter into the sauce and pour the sauce over all.

Yield: Four servings.

Riz Persillé
(Parsleyed rice)

3 tablespoons butter
2 tablespoons chopped onion
1 cup raw rice
1½ cups water
1 bay leaf

Salt and freshly ground
pepper to taste
Tabasco sauce to taste
2 tablespoons finely chopped
parsley

1. Melt 2 tablespoons of the butter in a saucepan and add the onion. Cook until wilted. Add the rice and stir briefly.

2. Add the water, bay leaf, salt and pepper, and Tabasco.

3. Bring to the boil. Cover and simmer 20 minutes.

4. Add the remaining tablespoon of butter and parsley. Stir to blend.

Yield: Four servings.

IF I WERE ASKED TO SPECIFY THE EASIEST DISH to prepare for entertaining from one to fifty or more people, it most likely would be choucroute garnie, or sauerkraut with the appropriate garnishes. It is a dish that even a beginner in the kitchen can master with an absolute guarantee of success, provided, of course, that the cook can follow the most basic instructions. A sauerkraut dinner may be as simple or as elaborate as you may want it. The garnie can range from frankfurters to the best assortment of sausages, ham, salamis, and so on that the charcuterie can supply.

The best-known sauerkraut preparation in French kitchens is choucroute à l'alsacienne, or sauerkraut Alsatian style, for Alsace is thought of as the sauerkraut capital of the nation. The dish is also known as choucroute à la strasbourgeoise, and the two are essentially the same—garnishes for them vary and include an assortment of sausages plus, at times, smoked pork, or smoked goose.

The basic preparation of the sauerkraut simply involves cooking the pickled cabbage on a bed of onion and garlic that have been cooked in rendered bacon fat. Various seasonings are added (juniper berries are a traditional seasoning for the dish but they are not always easily obtainable in America; thus they are optional), then the meats. The dish is covered and cooked until done. Depending on the cook or chef, the sauerkraut is cooked for from one to four hours and many people consider it better when reheated the following day. Some cooks, particularly those of Swiss persuasion, add grated potato blended with milk to the cooking.

Here is how to make an excellent and easily made choucroute garnie that cooks in exactly 60 minutes. The dish includes, incidentally, boulettes (okay, meatballs) of pork. They are optional.

[287]

Choucroute Garnie
(Sauerkraut with meats)

2 pounds sauerkraut
2 slices bacon, chopped
1 cup finely chopped onion
1 teaspoon chopped garlic
1 bay leaf
6 crushed juniper berries, optional
½ teaspoon caraway seeds
½ cup dry white wine
½ cup chicken broth

Salt and freshly ground pepper to taste
4 pork meatballs, optional (see recipe)
1 1-pound ham steak in a single slice
1 1-pound Polish sausage (kielbasi), pricked in several places with the tines of a fork

1. If you like sauerkraut that is relatively sour, do not rinse it, but simply squeeze it dry. If you like it less sour, however, run it under cold water and drain in a colander. Press to extract excess moisture.

2. Heat the bacon in a casserole or Dutch oven and cook until rendered of fat. Add the onion and garlic and cook until the onion is wilted.

3. Add the sauerkraut. Tie the bay leaf, juniper berries, and caraway seeds in a small cheesecloth bag and add it. Add the wine, chicken broth, and salt and pepper to taste and bring to the boil. Arrange the meatballs, ham steak, and sausage in or over the sauerkraut. Cover closely and cook 1 hour. Discard the cheesecloth bag. Serve with steamed potatoes and mustard on the side.

Yield: Four servings.

Boulettes de Porc
(Pork meatballs)

⅓ pound ground pork
2 tablespoons bread crumbs
2 tablespoons grated onion
½ teaspoon finely chopped garlic
1 tablespoon sour cream
1 teaspoon finely chopped parsley
Salt and freshly ground pepper to taste
⅛ teaspoon freshly grated nutmeg

1. Blend all the ingredients in a mixing bowl.
2. Shape into 4 balls. Use in cooking sauerkraut.

Yield: Four meatballs.

Pommes Vapeur
(Steamed potatoes)

1¼ pounds red, new, waxy potatoes, or 2 large Idaho potatoes
Salt to taste
1 tablespoon butter

1. Peel the potatoes. If they are new potatoes, there should be at least eight. Leave them whole. If they are large Idaho potatoes, quarter them, which is to say, cut each potato into four equal pieces.

2. Place the potatoes in a saucepan and add water to cover and salt to taste. Bring to the boil and simmer until tender, 15 or 20 minutes, depending on size. Do not overcook.

3. Drain and add the butter, shaking the saucepan until the pieces are coated.

Yield: Four servings.

SINCE COMING TO THIS COUNTRY IN 1939 TO work as a chef at the French Pavillon restaurant of the New York World's Fair, I have detected a certain snobbery in the public's mind when it comes to what are called "peasant dishes," on which I thrived as a child and which I still enjoy in maturity.

One such dish is a *potée,* a "country" dish that is popular in many areas of France. A *potée* is any kind of dish made in an earthenware casserole, but it usually consists of pork products, such as sausages or smoked meats, cooked with an assortment of winter vegetables, principally cabbage and potatoes.

I grew up in a very small town in Burgundy, not far from Chablis. One kind of *potée* that came out of my family kitchen consisted of smoked pork butt, cabbage, turnips, celery, and carrots, all of them cooked in a kettle suspended in the fireplace. I consider it an ideal dish for cold weather dining, and, happily, it takes slightly more than half an hour to cook.

Almost any supermarket or grocery store carries smoked pork butts (sometimes labeled porkettes). These are like small boneless hams and they are fully cooked.

A *potée,* with its various ingredients, is a main course unto itself.

I have named this dish, incidentally, after my home town of Tonnerre. Although no potatoes are included in the recipe, there is no reason why 4 medium-size potatoes, washed and peeled, could not be added to the stew along with the cabbage, turnips, and carrots. After the main course—a romaine lettuce salad, with cheese, and for dessert a mélange of fruits. The mélange should be made as the *potée* cooks.

Potée Tonnerreoise
(Boiled dinner with smoked pork butt)

1 1¼-pound cabbage
1½ pounds smoked pork shoulder butt (porkette)
4 ribs celery, trimmed and tied into a bundle
2 leeks, trimmed, partly split and well washed
1 small onion, peeled and stuck with 2 whole cloves
8 cups water
2 allspice
1 bay leaf
4 peppercorns
2 sprigs fresh thyme, or ½ teaspoon dried thyme
4 sprigs fresh parsley
Salt to taste
2 turnips, about ¾ pound total weight, peeled
4 small carrots, about ⅓ pound total weight, trimmed and scraped
Dijon or Düsseldorf mustard

1. Pull off and discard any tough outer leaves from the cabbage. Cut out the core. Quarter the cabbage and set aside.

2. Combine in a kettle the pork butt, celery bunch, leeks, onion, water, allspice, bay leaf, peppercorns, thyme, parsley, and salt. Cover and bring to the boil. Simmer 10 minutes.

3. Add the cabbage, turnips, and carrots. Cover and simmer about 25 minutes longer, or until the pork is fork-tender. Serve the vegetables with the sliced pork butt. Serve with mustard on the side.

Yield: Four servings.

Mélange des Fruits
(Fruits and berries with spirits)

2 cups fresh strawberries or an equal amount of cubed fruits, such as pears and apples

1 seedless orange

2 tablespoons orange juice

3 tablespoons confectioners' sugar

2 tablespoons Grand Marnier

1 tablespoon kirschwasser

1 tablespoon Cognac

1 tablespoon framboise

1. Rinse the strawberries. Remove and discard the hulls. Rinse well and put them in a mixing bowl.

2. Peel the orange. Cut it into sections. Add this to the strawberries. Add the orange juice.

3. Sprinkle with the confectioners' sugar and refrigerate for 1 hour or longer.

4. When ready to serve, add the remaining ingredients. Toss well and serve.

Yield: Eight servings.

IN THE HIERARCHY OF FOOD THERE IS NO DOUBT that sausages in general are what could be called food for the masses or a peasant concept in food preparation. It is true that sausages are a far cry from foie gras and caviar, and yet I have yet to meet a connoisseur of cooking or eating who doesn't, on frequent occasions, feel a well-defined hunger for what are called, in my place of birth, saucisses de porc or pork sausages. There are country sausages and sausages Toulouse-style, sausages from Lyons and the notable garlic sausages or saucissons à l'ail which, when wrapped in pastry, have been, for several decades, in luxury restaurants and bistros in France as well as in America, a choice first course, more often than not served with a wine-flavored warm potato salad judiciously seasoned with herbs.

Sausages are, compared to many meats, relatively inexpensive because they can be made from the odds and ends, the scraps of pork (of course you can use other things, including veal and even goose). In my Burgundy childhood, we were often served sausages at the family meal. It never occurred to me then that one of the reasons for the frequency of sausages on our family table was not only the fact that the sausages tasted good; they were a budget item in that country hamlet where I lived.

One of my favorite preparations—because it was a considerable change from the usual grilled sausages with mashed potatoes or sausages cooked with sauerkraut and white wine (two dishes that remain to this day personal favorites)—was sausages cooked and served with a light tomato sauce (generally of fresh tomatoes) and rice.

This is a dish that can be prepared without strain within the space of one hour, although it does include three separate but easily made components. The sausages are simply put in the oven to grill; then a hasty tomato sauce and the rice are prepared. There is a plus in the fact that the dish is very much sufficient to serve as a complete meal. The logical way to prepare the dish is to put the sausages on to cook in the oven, proceed to the rice, which requires slightly in excess of 15 minutes, and then make the quick tomato sauce. The three can be assembled in 5 minutes or less.

Saucisses au Riz
(Baked sausages with rice)

---

2 pounds sweet or hot Italian sausages, or a combination of both
4 tablespoons butter
2 tablespoons finely chopped onion
1 clove garlic, finely minced

1 bay leaf
1 cup rice
1½ cups chicken broth
½ cup dry white wine
2 cups fresh tomato sauce (see recipe)

1. Preheat the oven to 400 degrees.
2. Prick the sausages with a two-pronged fork in several places. Place them in a skillet with about ¼ inch of water and bring to the boil on top of the stove. Put the skillet in the oven and bake about 25 to 30 minutes, or until the sausages are browned and cooked through. Check the sausages after about 10 minutes. If liquid has accumulated, pour it off. Continue baking.
3. Meanwhile, melt 2 tablespoons of the butter in a small casserole and add the onion. Stir until the onion is translucent, and add the garlic and bay leaf. Cook about 1 minute, stirring, and add the rice. Cook about 3 minutes, stirring. Add the broth and bring to the boil on top of the stove. Cover and place in the oven along with the sausages. Bake exactly 20 minutes. No longer. Uncover and stir with a fork to make the rice fluffy.
4. When the sausages are done, remove them. Pour off the fat from the skillet.

5. When ready to serve, add ½ cup of tomato sauce to the rice and stir to blend. Spoon equal portions of the rice in the center of four plates. Place one serving of sausage in the middle of the rice and serve the tomato sauce on the side.

Yield: Four to six servings.

Sauce Tomate
(Tomato sauce)

---

2 or 3 tomatoes, about 1¼ pounds or use 3 cups of canned tomatoes
2 tablespoons butter

½ cup finely minced onion
1 clove garlic, finely minced
Salt and freshly ground pepper to taste

1. Remove the core from the tomatoes. Cut the tomatoes into 1-inch cubes. There should be about 3 to 4 cups.
2. Melt half the butter in a saucepan and add the onion and garlic. Cook, stirring, about 1 minute and add the tomatoes and salt and pepper to taste.
3. Cook about 5 minutes. Pour the mixture into the container of a food processor or use an electric blender.
4. Blend to a fine sauce. Spoon into a saucepan. Add the remaining butter and heat.

Yield: About two cups.

THE TWO BASIC AND MOST DESIRABLE QUALI-ties in food are flavor and texture. One vegetable that yields a fascinating, different, and admirable combination of both is endive, that white, pointed member of the chicory family that is a specialty of Belgium.

Endive is most commonly thought of as an ingredient for the salad bowl (and its eminence and elegance in that uncooked state is not to be disputed).

When cooked, Belgian endive takes on a flavor that is slightly bittersweet, full-bodied, but not overpoweringly so.

One of the best-known family-style dishes in France is Belgian endive (asparagus is also similarly utilized) wrapped in thin slices of ham, covered with a mornay sauce, preferably made with genuine Gruyère cheese, and baked.

Some meals, if they are to be prepared within the course of an hour, must be plotted with special care. This one is a case in point.

The endive requires approximately 30 minutes to cook. As it cooks there will be ample time to prepare the cheese or mornay sauce for the ham, and, if desired, to prepare a salad such as cucumber with dill. The baking time for the dish is approximately 10 minutes.

Endives et Jambon au Gratin

(Endives and ham baked in cheese sauce)

8 thin slices cooked ham,
about ½ pound
8 whole braised endives,
drained (see recipe)
3 tablespoons plus 1 teaspoon
butter
¼ cup flour
2½ cups milk

Salt and freshly ground
pepper to taste
⅛ teaspoon freshly grated
nutmeg
Cayenne pepper or Tabasco
sauce to taste
¼ pound grated Gruyère
cheese, about 1½ cups
2 egg yolks

1. Preheat the oven to 425 degrees.

2. Place the ham slices on a flat surface. Place on each slice a braised endive crosswise in the center. Roll each ham slice to enclose the endive.

3. Melt the 3 tablespoons butter in a saucepan and add the flour, stirring with a wire whisk. When blended, add the milk, stirring rapidly with a whisk. Add salt, pepper, nutmeg, and cayenne. Cook, stirring often, about 5 minutes.

4. Add about 1 cup of the cheese and stir until melted. Add the yolks, stirring rapidly with the whisk. Bring just to the boil, stirring, but do not boil or the sauce will curdle.

5. Rub the bottom of a baking dish (a dish that measures 13 x 8 x 2 inches is suitable) with the remaining 1 teaspoon of butter.

6. Arrange the ham rolls in the baking dish. Spoon the sauce over all. Sprinkle with the remaining grated cheese.

7. Place in the oven and bake 10 minutes, or until piping hot and bubbling and browned. If the top is not uniformly brown, run the dish briefly under the broiler to brown.

Yield: Four servings.

Endives Braisées
(Braised endives)

8 large, unblemished endives,
   about 1½ pounds
2 tablespoons butter

Salt and freshly ground
   pepper to taste
Juice of ½ lemon
½ cup cold water

1. Wash the endives in cold water and drain.

2. Butter a heavy skillet in which the endives will fit in one layer. Sprinkle the pan with a little salt and arrange the endives over the pan. Sprinkle with salt and pepper.

3. Sprinkle with lemon juice and add the water. Cover closely and cook 30 minutes. Watch carefully that the cooking liquid does not boil away and the endives burn. If absolutely necessary, add a little more water to prevent sticking and burning.

Yield: Eight pieces.

Salade de Concombres à la Scandinave
(Cucumber and dill salad)

1 to 3 cucumbers, depending
   on size
1 tablespoon sugar
Salt to taste
¼ cup white vinegar

2 tablespoons chopped fresh
   dill
Freshly ground pepper,
   preferably white pepper, to
   taste

1. Peel the cucumbers and split them in half. Scoop out the seeds with a melon-ball cutter. If so-called "gourmet" cucumbers are used, it is not necessary to cut in half or to remove the seeds.

2. Slice the cucumbers crosswise. There should be about 4 cups. Put the slices in a mixing bowl. Add the remaining ingredients and toss to blend. Add more seasonings, such as vinegar, sugar, and so on to taste, if desired.

Yield: Four servings.

Pasta

THE COOKING OR CULINARY HABITS OF VARI-
ous countries have intrigued me since I first became a
chef a good many years ago. A friend of mine, an Italian, reminded me once again recently that tarragon is almost unknown and little used as a flavoring in Italy. In fact, there are
very few Italians who know that the name of the herb is *dragon-
celle*.

It isn't so curious, I thought, when I recalled that in my early
youth the sweet herb known as basil *(basilique* in French), so
much prized in Italian cooking, was practically unknown in the
kitchens of Burgundy where I was raised.

Similarly, I had never heard of dining on freshly cooked and
hot pasta tossed with a cold and well-seasoned fresh tomato
sauce. For my taste, the combination is as irresistible as it is intriguing. I have dined on that combination on many occasions
with numerous friends from Italy within recent years.

In preparing such dishes, my Italian friends remind me, they
must be made at the heart of the tomato season, when the tomatoes themselves have been sun- and vine-ripened, for that is
also the time when fresh basil flourishes best and is at its most
potent.

The essentials for these dishes (and various kinds of pasta can
be used, from the ubiquitously known spaghetti or spaghettini to
tubular pasta like penne) are, in addition to the red ripe tomatoes

and fresh basil, a good grade of olive oil, garlic, parsley, salt, and pepper. There are, I have discovered or surmised, numerous variables, including chopped chiles or dried hot pepper flakes.

I have heard lengthy discussions on whether cheeses are appropriate to include or serve with these cold-sauce dishes, and on this matter I take no sides. I have had it with and without cheese and am happily pleased with either version.

Two recipes for these dishes are outlined here. The first, and most basic, is hot spaghetti with cold tomato sauce. In this version, a couple of tablespoons of Gorgonzola cheese may be added. The second recipe is made with penne (tube-shaped, they resemble straight broken macaroni), and it contains Fontina cheese plus grated Pecorino or Parmesan cheese.

The cold sauces, incidentally, are far more quickly made, for obvious reasons, than a cooked spaghetti sauce.

Ed Giobbi's Hot Spaghetti with Cold Tomato Sauce

2 pounds ripe tomatoes at room temperature (see note)

2 cloves garlic, finely minced

⅓ cup loosely packed fresh basil leaves, coarsely chopped

¼ cup loosely packed parsley, coarsely chopped

⅓ cup olive oil, plus additional olive oil for the cooked spaghetti, optional

Salt and freshly ground pepper to taste

1 pound spaghetti or spaghettini

1. Combine the tomatoes, garlic, basil, parsley, ⅓ cup olive oil, and salt and pepper to taste in the container of an electric blender or food processor.

2. Blend thoroughly.

3. Drop the spaghetti into boiling water and cook, stirring as necessary, to the desired degree of doneness. Drain. Return the spaghetti to the kettle and add, if desired, a touch of olive oil. Immediately add the tomato sauce. Toss quickly and serve immediately. This dish is generally not served with grated cheese.

Yield: Four to six servings.

Note: It is imperative that the tomatoes be at room temperature. Two tablespoons of Gorgonzola cheese may be added to the tomato mixture before blending.

Sirio Maccioni's Pasta de l'Estate
(Pasta with fresh, uncooked tomato sauce)

3 large ripe tomatoes, about 2½ pounds
4 large whole cloves garlic, peeled but left whole
1 small hot red or green chili, chopped, or use about ½ teaspoon or less hot red pepper flakes
½ cup coarsely chopped fresh basil
Salt and freshly ground pepper to taste
½ cup olive oil
1 pound penne or other tubular pasta
¼ pound Fontina or Muenster cheese
½ cup grated Pecorino or Parmesan cheese

1. Wash and wipe the tomatoes. Remove the cores from the tomatoes. Chop the tomatoes. There should be about 6 cups. Put them in a large bowl.

2. Add the garlic, chopped chili, basil, salt and pepper, and olive oil. Let stand at room temperature for several hours, or chill overnight. But let return to room temperature before serving.

[302]

3. Cook the penne according to package directions.

4. Meanwhile, grate or shred the Fontina, using the coarse blade.

5. When the pasta is cooked, drain it. Spoon off about ¼ cup of the surface oil from the tomatoes and add it to the pasta. Add the Parmesan cheese and toss. Add half the tomato sauce and toss. Add half the remaining sauce and Fontina cheese and toss. Serve in soup bowls with the remaining sauce spooned on top.

Yield: Four servings.

TASTE IS ONE OF THE MOST SUBJECTIVE THINGS on earth. I have no quarrel with the man who despises caviar. At today's prices, I might even envy him. I have one very close friend, a professional in the field of food, who can't abide the smell or taste of cheese. Even cream cheese. Since my childhood, I have had drilled into my skull the philosophy of Lucretius who lived more than two thousand years ago: "What is food to one, is to others bitter poison."

All this is by way of introduction to the following recipe, which will be to some palates the most mundane of all dishes, spaghetti with meatballs. It may not be gourmet fare to some, it is not authentically Italian (and it certainly isn't French), but it is a dish that delighted my children (now grown) throughout their childhoods.

As a matter of fact, there was a gathering of my offspring one evening recently and one of them asked for the dish specifically. I turned to the family kitchen, and about 45 minutes later we sat down to dine on the dish, along with a loaf of homemade French bread and a salad.

In the course of the evening, one of them suggested that if it was good enough for their palates, it was good enough for this book, and, on reflection about the subjective nature of taste, I could not disagree.

In all honesty, I don't know when this "recipe" came about. It is simply a blending together of compatible flavors which seem logical, and perhaps, just a touch Neapolitan.

Over the years, I have been told by Italian cooks that most of their tomato sauces are long simmered, and I knew one old lady who told me that three days were required to make her family's ancestral salsa di pomodoro alla napoletana.

As far as this recipe is concerned, the most time-consuming thing is the preparation of the meatballs, a simple blend of meat with onions cooked until translucent, plus bread crumbs, egg, and parsley. It does take a moment or two to shape them. But once the meat is browned and the tomatoes added, that's all there is to it. While the sauce simmers, there's plenty of time to make ready a simple tossed salad.

Spaghetti with Meatballs

1¼ pounds ground chuck
1 teaspoon peanut, vegetable, or corn oil
½ cup finely chopped onion
½ cup finely chopped parsley
½ cup fresh bread crumbs
1 egg, lightly beaten
Salt and freshly ground pepper to taste
1 tablespoon olive oil
1 cup finely chopped onion
1 teaspoon finely minced garlic

1 1-pound 12-ounce can imported tomatoes with tomato paste
¼ to ½ teaspoon dried rosemary leaves
¼ teaspoon dried marjoram
¼ teaspoon dried oregano
1 dried hot red pepper, optional
1 pound spaghetti or spaghettini
2 tablespoons butter

1. Put the meat in a mixing bowl and set aside.
2. Heat the oil and cook the ½ cup onion until wilted. Let it cool slightly.
3. Add the onion to the meat. Add the parsley, bread crumbs, egg, and salt and pepper. Blend well with the hands.
4. Shape the mixture with the hands into approximately 16 balls.
5. Using a large skillet, heat the oil and add the meatballs. Cook, turning the balls as necessary, so that they brown evenly, about 5 minutes.
6. Holding the lid over the skillet, drain off the fat.
7. Scatter the 1 cup onion and garlic around and between the meatballs.
8. Crush the tomatoes and add them. Add the rosemary, mar-

joram, oregano, dried red pepper, and salt and pepper to taste. Bring to the boil. Cover and simmer 20 minutes.

9. Cook the spaghetti to desired doneness. Add the butter and salt and pepper to taste. Serve with the meatballs and sauce.

Yield: Four servings.

Salade de Cresson et Endives
(Watercress and endive salad)

---

1 large or 2 small bunches
  watercress
1 Belgian endive
½ to ¾ cup thinly sliced,
  loosely packed cucumber
  slices

1 tablespoon lemon juice
2 teaspoons imported mustard
  Salt and freshly ground
  pepper to taste
4 tablespoons oil, preferably
  walnut oil

1. Cut off the tough stems of the watercress and discard.
2. Cut off the end of the endive and cut the head into bite-size pieces.
3. Rinse the watercress and endive in cold water and drain or spin dry. Put in a salad bowl. Add the cucumber slices.
4. Put the lemon juice, mustard, and salt and pepper in another small bowl. Using a wire whisk, beat in the oil. Pour the dressing over the salad and toss.

Yield: Four servings.

ONE OF THE GREAT POSITIVE ASPECTS OF LIV-ing in New York is the ability to sample to one degree or another almost all the world's assorted cuisines—Chinese, Russian, Japanese, Greek, Italian, and many others.

One of the most appealing of the ''foreign'' dishes encountered during my stay here, which spans about thirty years, is the Italian (and I am told Neapolitan) creation, linguine with white clam sauce. Although I have eaten clams or *palourdes* of one sort or another (there are many different kinds of clams) all my life, I had never eaten a cooked clam dish until my arrival in America.

Years ago an old Italian chef taught me his ''secret'' of making linguine with clam sauce and his recipe is by far the best I've tasted. Most clam sauces are too liquid to coat the strands of pasta with which they are served. Thus, when you finish the dish you are left with a puddle of clam liquid. I am opposed to ''thickening'' the sauce with cornstarch, as a few cooks do; it sort of vulgarizes the concept.

My Italian friend told me that he always uses the clam juice plus water to cook the linguine in. This gives the clam flavor to the pasta. At the end, he makes a quick clam sauce with the chopped clams, garlic, oil, and parsley. The end result is a fine, harmonious blending of clams and linguine.

A white clam sauce is one of the most quickly prepared of all sauces, assuming, of course, that the cook can open clams quickly. If you live in a clam area (and clams are sold in most fish shops in coastal areas), you can have the clams opened by the fish merchant, but make certain that he saves both the clams and their natural juice.

A fine accompaniment (or first course) for linguine with white clam sauce would be roasted peppers sautéed with garlic and oil and vinegar. You could use canned pimientos with anchovies (plus chopped garlic, oil, and vinegar). But home-roasted peppers, cooked under the broiler and peeled before sautéing, are more special. The peppers can be made in advance and kept in the refrigerator. They are as good a few days later as they are when freshly cooked.

Linguine with Clam Sauce

36 littleneck clams
1 pound linguine
⅓ cup olive oil
1 tablespoon finely chopped garlic

¼ cup finely chopped parsley
Freshly ground pepper to taste
⅛ teaspoon hot red pepper flakes

1. Open the clams or have them opened. Save both the clams and their juice. There should be about 1½ cups of clam juice and 1 cup of clams. Chop the clams coarsely. Set aside.

2. Add 6 cups of water and the clam juice to a kettle for cooking the linguine. Bring to the boil and add the linguine. Cook until tender but al dente.

3. Heat the oil in a skillet and add the garlic. Cook briefly, stirring. Do not brown. Add the chopped clams and cook, stirring, briefly. Add the parsley and pepper flakes and cook briefly.

4. Add the drained linguine and toss to blend. Spoon out into hot soup bowls. Serve equal portions of the sauce that concentrates on the bottom of the skillet onto each serving. A brief sprinkle of more olive oil on the dishes before serving is not amiss.

Yield: Four servings.

Poivrons Sautés à l'Italienne
(Sweet peppers sautéed Italian-style)

5 to 6 sweet red or green bell peppers
¼ cup olive oil
4 cloves garlic, peeled, each cut in half
½ teaspoon dried oregano
Salt and freshly ground pepper to taste
2 tablespoons red wine vinegar

1. Preheat the broiler to high.

2. Line a baking tray with aluminum foil and arrange the peppers on it. Place about 4 or 5 inches from the source of heat and cook, turning occasionally, until the skin of the peppers is slightly burnt and charred all over.

3. Hold the peppers under cold running water and pull away the skin. Drain well. Cut away and discard the cores. Cut the peppers in half and scrape away the seeds.

4. Heat the oil in a skillet and add the garlic. Cook briefly until the garlic starts to brown. Do not brown. Add the pepper halves and stir over high heat, turning the pepper pieces. Add the oregano and salt and pepper to taste. Cook about 2 minutes altogether.

5. Add the vinegar and cook just to heat through, about 10 seconds. Remove from the heat.

6. Transfer the pepper halves to a serving dish and pour the sauce with garlic over them. Chill before serving. The peppers are better if left to stand overnight.

Yield: Four servings.

ONE OF THE MOST COMMON QUESTIONS PUT to anyone who gives serious thought to cooking—particularly if he works at it professionally—is what is a "gourmet" dish? It's a question I've given an appreciable amount of thought to and discussed at some length with my colleagues. And, to my mind, a "gourmet" dish is difficult if not impossible to pigeonhole or categorize, except to say that it is any food prepared with a mixture of conscience, care, and intelligence.

It might be a liverwurst sandwich on good bread with lettuce and mayonnaise. It might be a platter of long-simmered sauerkraut with well-chosen sausages—to name but two of the things that have given pleasure to my palate over the years.

Thus the recipe on this page. Who on earth, you might ask, would call the likes of spaghetti with meatballs a gourmet's delight? I would, provided the dish is made with "conscience, care, and intelligence."

The meat must be tender, succulent, and lean. But not too lean, otherwise it will taste dry. The tomato sauce must be simmered until well concentrated and tastefully seasoned. Incidentally, "gourmet" cooking does not imply blandness. A touch of piquance in certain foods is, at times, highly desirable. Think of diable sauces, sauce Robert, and sauce charintière.

Actually, spaghetti with meatballs (*boulettes de viande* sounds more rarefied) is not the quickest dish in the world to prepare. It can be made, however, in less than an hour, and, with a tasty green salad, a loaf of crusty bread, and a good bottle of red wine, it would happily meet my qualifications for a gourmet dish.

Boulettes de Viande "Marinara"
(Pork meatballs in marinara sauce)

1½ pounds ground pork, beef, or veal, or a combination of meats
¼ cup chopped parsley
1 clove garlic, finely chopped
¼ cup grated Parmesan cheese
½ cup bread crumbs
Salt and freshly ground pepper to taste

1 egg
1 tablespoon olive oil
2 cups marinara sauce (see recipe)
1 pound cooked spaghetti (see recipe)
Grated Parmesan cheese

1. In a mixing bowl, combine the pork, parsley, garlic, ¼ cup grated Parmesan cheese, bread crumbs, salt and pepper, and egg. Blend well and shape into 16 balls of equal size.

2. Heat the oil in a skillet large enough to hold the meatballs without touching. Cook until nicely browned all over, at least 10 minutes.

3. Combine the meatballs with the marinara sauce and simmer 15 to 20 minutes. Serve on pasta; sprinkle with grated Parmesan cheese.

Yield: Four to six servings.

Sauce "Marinara"
(Marinara sauce)

4 cups canned Italian plum
  tomatoes
1 tablespoon olive oil
1 teaspoon finely chopped
  garlic

2 teaspoons dried oregano
3 tablespoons chopped parsley
  Salt and freshly ground
  pepper to taste

1. Put the tomatoes in a saucepan and cook until reduced by half. Stir often to prevent sticking.

2. Heat the oil in another saucepan and add the garlic. Cook briefly, and add the tomatoes, oregano, parsley, and salt and pepper to taste and blend.

Yield: About two cups.

Spaghetti Cooked by a New Technique

Bring 5 quarts of water to a vigorous boil and add salt to taste. Add 1 pound of spaghetti. Stir well until the water returns to the boil. Cook 2 minutes.

Remove the pot from the heat and cover first with a clean cloth, then with a lid. Let stand 9 minutes without uncovering the pot. Drain and toss with 1 tablespoon butter or olive oil. Serve with a sauce.

Yield: Four to six servings.

Cold Dishes

WHEN I NOTED THAT CHICKEN, MORE THAN any other food, is the most ubiquitous "meat," employed by the rich and poor alike, I failed to add that this is not only true of Western cuisines; it is also true in Asian kitchens. Some of the greatest "foreign" dishes in the world are based on chicken cooked in one form or another. The Indonesian table is well known for its satays of chicken, the Japanese dine finely on *mizutake*, chicken cooked at table in a broth with noodles and vegetables (and in Japan there are also specialty restaurants serving nothing but chicken where the raw breasts are thinly sliced and eaten raw like *sashimi*). Java, Vienna, and the American South are noted for their fried chicken, although the techniques and flavors are disparate.

One of the most interesting and spiciest chicken dishes with which I am familiar, and for which I have a particular liking, is a cold chicken dish made with shredded cooked boneless breast and served on a bed of cold noodles with a sesame paste made biting hot with hot chili oil. Over the years I have spent many hours in the kitchen with Virginia Lee, and the recipe came to my attention while she was preparing recipes for her Chinese cookbook.

The dish, which looks fairly complicated, is as easy as the breeze to prepare. It is made with skinless, boneless chicken breast which is simmered briefly until cooked through. The breast is shredded and set aside. The fine noodles are cooked for a very few minutes in the broth and the sauce is nothing more than a quick blending of assorted ingredients, which include vinegar, sugar, and finely minced garlic. Although it is normally served as an appetizer at a several-course Chinese feast, it can be served as an admirable main course for warm-weather dining.

A bit less exotic for the warm season is another cold chicken dish that can be made similarly from briefly cooked breast, or it could be made with leftover boiled chicken from another meal. This is a salad known in France as a mayonnaise de volaille or "chicken mayonnaise." In the version printed here, which can also serve as a main course, the salad is garnished with anchovies, which offer a curiously compelling contrast in flavors.

Mayonnaise de Volaille aux Anchois
(Chicken salad with anchovy garnish)

4 cups cooked, skinless, boneless chicken cut into bite-size cubes
1 cup finely diced celery
¼ cup drained capers
1½ cups mayonnaise
¼ cup finely chopped onion
Boston lettuce leaves

4 to 8 anchovy fillets
2 giant-size or large stuffed olives
2 hard-cooked eggs, peeled and quartered
1 or 2 ripe tomatoes, quartered

1. Put the chicken cubes in a mixing bowl and add the celery, capers, 1 cup of the mayonnaise, and onion. Toss to blend well.
2. Arrange the Boston lettuce leaves with edges slightly overlapping to serve as a base for the salad.
3. Spoon the salad into the center and smooth it over like a mound. Spoon the remaining ½ cup of mayonnaise all over it.
4. Garnish the salad with the anchovy fillets, overlapping or in a pattern.

5. Cut the olives into thin crosswise slices and garnish between the anchovies. Arrange the eggs and tomatoes around the base and serve.

Yield: Four servings.

Poulet aux Nouilles Froides Façon de Virginia Lee
(Virginia Lee's chicken and cold noodles with spicy sauce)

1 large chicken breast	2 tablespoons red wine vinegar
6 ounces fine egg noodles	1 teaspoon plus 1 tablespoon sesame oil
¼ cup sesame paste	
3 tablespoons water	¼ cup peanut or corn oil
2 teaspoons hot chili oil, optional	2 tablespoons finely chopped garlic
3 tablespoons light soy sauce	

1. Bring about 6 cups of water to the boil and add the breast. Do not add salt. When the water returns to the boil, simmer about 10 or 15 minutes. Remove the breast but save the broth.

2. Bring the broth to the boil and add the noodles. Cook, stirring occasionally, about 5 to 7 minutes. Drain and run under cold water until chilled. Drain thoroughly and add to a mixing bowl. Add the teaspoon of sesame oil and toss.

3. Using a knife or the fingers, cut or pull the chicken into fine shreds.

4. Put the sesame paste in a bowl and add the water, stirring. Add the chili oil, soy sauce, wine vinegar, the tablespoon of sesame oil, peanut oil, and garlic.

5. Arrange the noodles on a serving dish. Cover with the chicken and spoon the sauce over.

Yield: Four servings.

IN SOME WAYS, AMERICA'S DINING HABITS ARE curious. There is a vegetable that I have known since my cradle days that is widely used all over Europe in salads, in soups, in marinades, and so on, which is, for no accountable reason, treated as a rare oddity in this country. The vegetable is known in France as céleri-rave, and in America and England as celery root, knob celery, or celeriac.

By far the best known use for the vegetable in this country is as an appetizer known as céleri rémoulade, in which the raw vegetable is cut into the finest julienne strips and blended with a well-seasoned mayonnaise. The vegetable is splendid when whipped and creamed and served like mashed potatoes, but that is another matter.

It is certainly true that céleri-rave, or celery root, is grown and can be purchased in America. It is a more or less round root, generally quite large and "knobby" in appearance. When it is in season it is a delight to dine on. In French restaurants in this country, where it enjoys its greatest popularity, it is generally served alone as a first course, or in combination with slices of pâtés or terrines or other cold meats or salads.

A salad of céleri rémoulade—with a few embellishments—can make an excellent luncheon dish with a loaf of French bread, followed by a fine imported cheese.

The embellishments I have in mind are either a fine julienne of salami or cold mussels. Mussels, incidentally, cook quickly and cool quickly. They could, of course, be cooked the previous night.

The rémoulade sauce is easy to prepare. Although it is preferably made with homemade mayonnaise, a good grade of the commercial variety is certainly acceptable. The only really time-consuming factor in preparing céleri rémoulade is actually the preparation of the celery root itself. It must be peeled and then cut into the thinnest possible slices. The slices are stacked and cut into the finest possible shreds.

[316]

Céleri Rémoulade avec Moules
(Celeriac in mayonnaise sauce with mussels)

1 quart mussels
2 tablespoons wine vinegar
1 knob celery (also called root celery and celeriac), about ¾ pound
1 cup mayonnaise, preferably homemade

1 tablespoon prepared mustard, such as Dijon or Düsseldorf
Salt and freshly ground pepper to taste

1. Place the mussels in a saucepan and add half the wine vinegar. Cover and bring to the boil. Cook about 5 minutes, or until the mussels open. Remove from the heat and let cool.

2. Remove the mussels from the shells. Discard the shells but save at least 2 tablespoons of liquid.

3. Peel the celery and cut it into thin slices ⅛ inch thick or less. Stack the slices, a few at a time, and cut them into the finest possible strips. If a food processor is available, the celery may be quartered and shredded, using the fine shredding blade. Put the celery in a mixing bowl.

4. Add the mussels to the celery. Blend the mayonnaise, remaining vinegar, and the reserved mussel liquid. Add this to the celery mixture. Add salt and pepper to taste, and toss well to blend. Serve.

Yield: Eight or more servings.

Céleri Rémoulade avec Salami
(Celeriac in mayonnaise sauce with salami)

1 knob celery (also called root celery and celeriac), about ¾ pound
¼ pound thinly sliced salami
1 tablespoon imported mustard, such as Dijon or Düsseldorf
1 cup mayonnaise, preferably homemade
1 tablespoon white vinegar
1 tablespoon water if the mayonnaise is very thick
Salt and freshly ground pepper to taste

1. Slice the celery and cut it into thin slices about ⅛ inch thick or less. Stack the slices, a few at a time, and cut them into the finest possible shreds. If a food processor is used, the celery may be quartered and shredded, using the fine shredding blade. Put the shredded celery in a mixing bowl.

2. Stack the salami and cut it into very thin strips. Add it to the celery. Add all the remaining ingredients and toss well to blend thoroughly. Serve.

Yield: Eight or more servings.

THERE ARE SOME "HASTY" FOODS IN THIS world that I consider culinary abominations. I would count among them instant rice and the frozen dinners that abound on the freezer shelves of supermarkets. There are some precooked foods, however, that are an absolute boon to anyone who has menu planning and cooking by the kitchen clock in mind, and one of them is sliced boiled or baked ham. For the most part, the quality of store-bought hams is uniform and they have—generally speaking—been cooked in the simplest manner possible. Plain, sliced boiled ham can be transformed in a hundred different ways into main dishes—baked in cheese sauce, gratinéed with potatoes, and tossed in cold salads for summer.

One of the most interesting salads we've contrived combines a basic bowl of cubed boiled ham with cut-up endive, two foods which, cold or hot, complement each other. The crispness and slightly sweet-bitter taste of raw endive make a fine foil for the texture and flavor of the ham.

The tie that binds the two is a ravigote sauce in the classic French tradition. It consists basically of a vinaigrette sauce (vinegar and oil) plus capers, parsley, chopped onion, chives, and tarragon. In preparing the dish, fresh herbs are worth searching for, although dried herbs may be used, or the herbs may even be omitted. Ravigote, if you care about etymology, has to do with "re-invigorating" or making fresh.

A boiled ham and endive ravigote salad makes an excellent warm-weather dish and could be served as a light repast—at lunch, for example—with hot French bread. Or it could be served with one or more salads, such as sliced tomato or cucumber.

One of my personal favorite salads for summer or winter is a salade pommes vin blanc, which is to say, a potato salad with a white wine dressing. This salad is traditionally served lukewarm and contains, in addition to the potatoes and a light sprinkling of white wine, oil, salt, and pepper.

Both the salads could easily be made within the space of an hour.

Salade de Jambon et Endives Ravigote
(Ham and endive salad)

The ham and endives:
1¼ pounds thinly sliced boiled ham
2 large Belgian endives

The sauce ravigote:
2 teaspoons imported mustard
1 tablespoon red wine vinegar
Salt and freshly ground pepper to taste

½ cup peanut, vegetable, or corn oil
1 tablespoon drained capers
2 tablespoons finely chopped fresh parsley
2 tablespoons finely chopped onions
1 tablespoon finely chopped fresh chives
1 tablespoon finely chopped fresh tarragon

1. Stack the ham slices on a flat surface and cut them into ½-inch cubes. There should be almost 4 cups. Put the ham in a bowl.

2. Trim off the base of each endive. Pull off and reserve about 12 of the best outside endive leaves to be used as garnish. Coarsely chop the remaining endives. There should be about 2½ cups. Add this to the ham.

3. Put the mustard, vinegar, and salt and pepper in a small mixing bowl. Add the oil gradually, stirring vigorously with a wire whisk. Add the capers, parsley, onions, chives, and tarragon. Blend well.

4. Pour the sauce over the ham mixture and stir to blend.

Yield: Four to six servings.

Salade de Pommes Vin Blanc
(Potato salad with white wine)

2½ pounds potatoes
Salt and freshly ground
pepper to taste
⅓ cup dry white wine

½ cup peanut, vegetable, or
corn oil (or use olive oil if
you prefer)

1. Rinse the potatoes and put them in a large saucepan with cold water to cover. Bring to the boil and simmer until tender, 20 minutes or longer, depending on size. Do not cook until mushy.

2. Preheat the oven to 200 degrees.

3. Drain the potatoes and when they are cool enough to handle, peel them. Cut them into ¼-inch-thick slices and put them into a heatproof mixing bowl. Sprinkle with salt, pepper, wine, and oil. Toss while warm. Cover the bowl with foil and put in the oven briefly to warm through. Turn into a serving dish and serve while warm.

Yield: About eight cups. To prepare half that amount, simply divide all ingredient amounts in half.

I HAVE BEEN ASKED A FEW THOUSAND TIMES over the years if I ever eat and savor foods that come in cans, and the answer, of course, is yes. There are times when my appetite craves sardines; on occasion I will dine on canned tuna with a good deal of relish; and if there is absolutely no fresh salmon to be had, I can willingly feast on the canned variety.

Although I hope destiny will forbid the day when I have to exist on foods from the pantry shelf, my larder is well stocked with a variety of items which can and have come in handy in certain "emergency" situations: a return home after a long weekend; a lazy Saturday lunch between fishing forays in Gardiner's Bay; an impromptu lunch for unexpected guests (and no time for shopping in town).

The fact is that there are numerous dishes that can be made from pantry items that are highly palatable.

One year, on a trip through Italy, we were twice served tuna (I will vouch that in both cases the tuna had come from tins) that had been blended with the cooked white kidney beans that are known as cannellini. In an "emergency" situation I have reproduced this dish using canned cannellini, which are quite commonly found in supermarkets in this country. Mind you, I do not contend that canned beans are the equal of those cooked from a dried state. I do say that the tinned version makes a highly acceptable substitute, even if the beans *en boîte,* to use the French phrase, are a trifle overcooked and somewhat less than firm to the bite. Suffice it to say that this particular salad (it can serve as an appetizer or a main course) consists of simply opening two cans and blending the contents with various seasonings, plus oil and vinegar.

There is also another "pantry salad" listed here. It is similarly made with tinned chick-peas, drained and blended with canned salmon. If you have the time, cook the beans or peas from the dried state. And by all means, use cooked, fresh salmon if it is available. These recipes are for "emergency" occasions—but good.

Haricots Secs avec Thon
(Cannellini beans with tuna)

---

1 20-ounce can cannellini (white kidney beans) drained, about 2 cups
¼ cup finely chopped scallions or onion
½ teaspoon finely minced garlic
½ teaspoon crumbled dried oregano
2 tablespoons finely chopped parsley

1 tablespoon red wine vinegar
Juice of ½ lemon
¼ cup olive oil
Salt and freshly ground pepper to taste
2 7-ounce cans tuna packed in oil
Tomato slices for garnish

1. Put the drained beans in a mixing bowl and add the scallions, garlic, oregano, parsley, vinegar, lemon juice, olive oil, and salt and pepper to taste.

2. Drain the tuna and flake it (not too finely). Add it to the bean mixture and toss gently. Serve garnished with sliced tomatoes.

Yield: Four servings.

Salade de Saumon et Pois Chiche
(Salmon and chick-pea salad)

3 cups freshly cooked or canned chick-peas, drained
½ cup finely chopped onion
½ cup finely chopped celery
1 teaspoon garlic
4 tablespoons finely chopped parsley
4 tablespoons finely chopped dill
3 tablespoons red wine vinegar
½ cup olive oil
Salt and freshly ground pepper to taste
2 cups freshly cooked or canned salmon, drained
1½ cups peeled and seeded ripe tomatoes cut into cubes, optional
Cucumber slices for garnish

1. In a mixing bowl combine the drained chick-peas, onion, celery, garlic, parsley, and dill.

2. Add the vinegar, oil, and salt and pepper and toss to blend.

3. Drain the salmon and pick over to remove the bones and soft skin. Add the salmon and, if desired, cubed tomato to the peas and toss to blend. Serve chilled, garnished with cucumber slices.

Yield: Four servings.

ONE OF THE GREAT, UNQUESTIONABLE CULInary blessings of the summer season, particularly, perhaps, for those who are concerned about cooking times, are lobsters. A 1½- to 2-pound lobster, which is sufficient for one (and oftentimes two) servings, steams in about 12 minutes. One says "steams." Actually, the lobsters are cooked in a quantity of water with such seasonings as bay leaf, thyme, and, if desired, a dried hot pepper. It may be neither here nor there to the reader, but many home cooks tend to overcook lobsters, just as they do shrimp, by half an hour or longer.

Lobster is superb, of course, hot from the kettle. Or at room temperature. Or cold. This is another of those foods which might be cooked in quantities larger than what are needed for one feast. Leftover lobster meat is a gustatory delight in salads, recipes for which number in the thousands.

Three recipes for summer feasting are outlined here. One is for basic steamed lobsters. Another is for a sauce verte or green mayonnaise to be served with them (if you're not up to making the mayonnaise, go ahead and use your melted butter and lemon halves). And a third is for a memorable lobster salad.

There are many variations of sauce verte in this world (it is salsa verde in Italian). Some recipes for making the green mayonnaise call for an assortment of greens and herbs, such as spinach, sorrel, tarragon, and so on. The version here simply calls for mayonnaise with the addition of a quick purèe of watercress, parsley, and dill. The flavor is as fresh as spring water.

The lobster salad is a quick version of a salad we dined on when exploring restaurants for that much publicized and costly meal we dined on at Chez Denis, in Paris, some years ago. The salad, lightly flavored with tarragon, is "bound," as we say in French, with fresh mayonnaise and tossed with finely shredded— a chiffonade—of romaine or other lettuce. It should be eaten the moment it is prepared; otherwise the lettuce will lose its crisp texture.

Homard à la Sauce Verte
(Steamed lobster with green mayonnaise)

4 1½-pound lobsters
16 cups water
   Salt to taste
16 peppercorns

2 bay leaves
2 sprigs fresh thyme, or ½ teaspoon dried thyme
1 dried hot red pepper

1. Select a kettle large enough to hold the lobsters when they are added.

2. Add the water, salt, peppercorns, bay leaf, thyme, and hot red pepper. Bring the water to a full rolling boil. Add the lobsters and cover. When the water returns to the boil, let cook for 12 minutes.

3. Remove the lobsters and hang them by the tail to drain.

4. Split two of the cooked lobsters lengthwise. Discard the tough sac near the eyes. Arrange the halves on two or four platters and garnish with parsley. Serve with green mayonnaise (see recipe).

Yield: Two to four servings.

Sauce Verte
(Green mayonnaise)

1 egg yolk
1 tablespoon vinegar
1 tablespoon prepared mustard
   Salt and freshly ground pepper to taste

1 cup plus 1 tablespoon peanut, vegetable, or corn oil
½ bunch watercress, rinsed, patted, or spun dry
1 tablespoon chopped parsley
1 tablespoon finely chopped dill

1. Put the egg yolk in a mixing bowl and add the vinegar, mustard, and salt and pepper to taste.

2. Start beating with a wire whisk and gradually add the oil, beating vigorously. When thickened and smooth, set aside.

3. Put the watercress, parsley, dill, and 1 tablespoon of oil in the container of a food processor or blender. Blend to a fine purée. Add this to the mayonnaise.

Yield: About one-and-one-quarter cups.

Chiffonade de Homard
(Lobster in tarragon sauce with lettuce)

---

4 1½-pound lobsters, steamed (see recipe), or use 3 cups lobster meat
1 egg yolk
2 teaspoons tomato ketchup
1 teaspoon imported mustard
1 tablespoon tarragon vinegar
½ teaspoon Worcestershire sauce

Salt and freshly ground pepper to taste
1 cup peanut or olive oil
2 teaspoons finely chopped fresh tarragon, or ½ teaspoon dried tarragon
1 teaspoon Cognac
10 or 12 romaine lettuce leaves, rinsed and patted dry

1. Remove the meat from the lobster, cut into bite-size slices, and set aside.

2. Add the egg yolk, ketchup, mustard, vinegar, Worcestershire, and salt and pepper to a bowl. Start beating with a wire whisk, gradually adding the oil. When thickened and smooth, add the tarragon and Cognac.

3. Stack the lettuce leaves and shred them. Add the lobster and sauce to the lettuce and toss. Serve before the lettuce wilts.

Yield: Four servings.

[327]

ALTHOUGH AVOCADOS ARE NO NOVELTY TO-day in the metropolitan areas of France, they were a total rarity in the days of my youth there. The first time I recall ever seeing an avocado—they are known in French as *avocats*—was after my arrival in America during the New York World's Fair in 1939, and to me they seemed wholly exotic.

I greatly enjoy avocados today, but to my taste they are, in one sense, a bit like snails or spaghetti. It is what you put on them that gives them their deserved stature in the world of food. It may be a simple dressing with lemon and a fine olive oil. Or avocado halves may be stuffed with a seafood or other salad, to describe but a few of their multitude of uses.

It is a commonplace that the specialties of any region are made with the ingredients that are native to that region. Thus the crayfish of Louisiana, the Dungeness crabs of the West Coast, the snails of Burgundy, and the corn-based specialties of the American South.

I am convinced that had avocados been native to Provence they would have been an inevitable ingredient in the celebrated salad of that region, the salade niçoise. Cubed avocado in a traditional niçoise is a "natural," as you will discover if you try the quickly made avocado and tuna salad given below.

One of the most natural "teamings" in the world of food is the West Coast specialty, crab Louis in avocado halves.

There are many versions of the Louis dressing, and no one apparently knows the origin of the name. The dressing itself is sometimes attributed to an early chef of the St. Francis Hotel in San Francisco. There is a recipe for the sauce in an early edition of the *Hotel St. Francis Cook Book* which I have in my library. That version calls for mayonnaise blended with French dressing, chili sauce, and Worcestershire sauce.

The recipe below for crab Louis with avocado halves is my own version of several Louis dressings that I have sampled. Either of these dishes would serve as a complete lunch for a summer menu.

Salade Niçoise aux Poires d'Avocat

(Tuna and avocado salad)

½ pound fresh mushrooms
2 tablespoons lemon juice
  Salt and freshly ground
  pepper to taste
1 large or 2 small avocados
2 7-ounce cans tuna fish
  packed in oil
1 2-ounce can flat anchovy
  fillets
1 ripe tomato, about ½ pound
1 small red onion, peeled

  Rind of one lemon, cut into
  very fine strips
8 black olives
8 stuffed green olives
6 tablespoons olive oil
2 tablespoons red wine vinegar
1 teaspoon finely chopped
  garlic
2 tablespoons finely chopped
  parsley
2 hard-cooked eggs, peeled
  and quartered

1. Thinly slice the mushrooms. There should be about 3 cups. Put the mushrooms in a mixing bowl and add the lemon juice and salt and pepper. Toss to blend.

2. Peel the avocados and cut them in half. Discard the pits. Cut each half into 4 lengthwise slices. Cut the slices into large cubes. Add this to the mushrooms and toss to coat.

3. Drain the tuna and break it into bite-size lumps. Add this to the bowl.

4. Drain the anchovy fillets and cut them into small pieces. Add them to the bowl.

5. Core the tomato and cut it into 1-inch cubes. Add this to the bowl.

6. Cut the onion into thin slices. Break the slices into rings and add them to the bowl.

7. Add the lemon rind and olives.

8. Combine the oil, vinegar, and garlic with salt and pepper to taste. Beat well to blend and pour this over the salad. Sprinkle with the parsley. Toss well before serving. Garnish with hard-cooked egg quarters.

Yield: Six or more servings.

Poires d'Avocat avec Mayonnaise de Crabe
(Avocados with crab Louis)

1 egg yolk
2 teaspoons imported prepared mustard
½ teaspoon Worcestershire sauce
2 teaspoons red wine vinegar
Salt and freshly ground pepper to taste
½ cup peanut, vegetable, or corn oil
1 tablespoon chili sauce

¼ cup finely chopped scallions, green part and all
4 large stuffed green olives, chopped, about ¼ cup
1 pound lump crabmeat, picked over to remove all trace of shell and cartilage
4 ripe avocados
Lettuce leaves
2 hard-cooked eggs, sliced, optional

1. Put the yolk in a mixing bowl and add the mustard, Worcestershire sauce, and vinegar. Beat with a wire whisk. Add the oil gradually, beating rapidly with the whisk.

2. When thickened and smooth, add the chili sauce, scallions, and olives. Blend.

3. Put the crab in a mixing bowl and add half the sauce. Blend gently so as not to break up the crab lumps more than necessary.

4. Split the avocados in half and discard the pits. Pile equal portions of the crab into the avocado halves. Spoon the remaining sauce over. Serve on a bed of lettuce leaves. If desired, garnish the crab filling with egg slices.

Yield: Four servings.

Metric Conversion Tables

TEMPERATURES

Fahrenheit°/ Celsius°	(Actual Celsius°)	Fahrenheit°/ Celsius°	(Actual Celsius°)
−5°F/ −20°C	(−20.6°C)	180°F/82°C	(82.2°C)
32°F/0°C	(0°C)	190°F/88°C	(87.8°C)
37°F/3°C	(2.8°C)	200°F/95°C	(93.3°C)
50°F/10°C	(10°C)	205°F/96°C	(96.1°C)
60°F/16°C	(15.6°C)	212°F/100°C	(100°C)
70°F/21°C	(21.1°C)	225°F/107°C	(107.2°C
75°F/24°C	(23.9°C)	228°F/109°C	(108.9°C)
80°F/27°C	(26.7°C)	238°F/115°C	(114.4°C)
85°F/29°C	(29.4°C)	250°F/120°C	(121.1°C)
100°F/38°C	(37.8°C)	275°F/135°C	(135°C)
105°F/41°C	(40.6°C)	285°F/140°C	(140.6°C)
110°F/43°C	(43.3°C)	300°F/150°C	(148.9°C)
115°F/46°C	(46.1°C)	325°F/165°C	(162.8°C)
120°F/49°C	(48.9°C)	350°F/180°C	(176.7°C)
125°F/52°C	(51.7°C)	375°F/190°C	(190.6°C)
130°F/54°C	(54.4°C)	400°F/205°C	(204.4°C)
135°F/57°C	(57.2°C)	425°F/220°C	(218.3°C)
140°F/60°C	(60°C)	450°F/230°C	(232.2°C)
150°F/66°C	(65.6°C)	475°F/245°C	(246.1°C)
160°F/71°C	(71.1°C)	500°F/260°C	(260°C)
165°F/74°C	(73.9°C)	525°F/275°C	(273.9°C)
170°F/77°C	(76.7°C)	550°F/290°C	(287.8°C)

POUNDS TO GRAMS AND KILOGRAMS

Pounds	Convenient Equivalent	Actual Weight
¼ lb	115 g	(113.4 g)
½ lb	225 g	(226.8 g)
¾ lb	340 g	(340.2 g)
1 lb	450 g	(453.6 g)
1¼ lb	565 g	(566.99 g)
1½ lb	675 g	(680.4 g)
1¾ lb	800 g	(794 g)
2 lb	900 g	(908 g)
2½ lb	1125 g; 1¼ kg	(1134 g)
3 lb	1350 g	(1360 g)
3½ lb	1500 g; 1½ kg	(1588 g)
4 lb	1800 g	(1814 g)
4½ lb	2 kg	(2041 g)
5 lb	2¼ kg	(2268 g)
5½ lb	2½ kg	(2495 g)
6 lb	2¾ kg	(2727 g)
7 lb	3¼ kg	(3175 g)
8 lb	3½ kg	(3629 g)
9 lb	4 kg	(4028 g)
10 lb	4½ kg	(4536 g)
12 lb	5½ kg	(5443 g)
14 lb	6¼ kg	(6350 g)
15 lb	6¾ kg	(6804 g)
16 lb	7¼ kg	(7258 g)
18 lb	8 kg	(8165 g)
20 lb	9 kg	(9072 g)
25 lb	11¼ kg	(11,340 g)

OUNCES TO GRAMS

Ounces	Convenient Equivalent	Actual Weight
1 oz	30 g	(28.35 g)
2 oz	60 g	(56.7 g)
3 oz	85 g	(85.05 g)
4 oz	115 g	(113.4 g)
5 oz	140 g	(141.8 g)
6 oz	180 g	(170.1 g)
8 oz	225 g	(226.8 g)
9 oz	250 g	(255.2 g)
10 oz	285 g	(283.5 g)
12 oz	340 g	(340.2 g)
14 oz	400 g	(396.9 g)
16 oz	450 g	(453.6 g)
20 oz	560 g	(566.99 g)
24 oz	675 g	(680.4 g)

LIQUID MEASURE CONVERSIONS

Cups and Spoons	Liquid Ounces	Approximate Metric Term	Approximate Centiliters	Actual Milliliters
1 tsp	⅙ oz	1 tsp	½ cL	5 mL
1 Tb	½ oz	1 Tb	1½ cL	15 mL
¼ c; 4 Tb	2 oz	½ dL; 4 Tb	6 cL	59 mL
⅓ c; 5 Tb	2⅔ oz	¾ dL; 5 Tb	8 cL	79 mL
½ c	4 oz	1 dL	12 cL	119 mL
⅔ c	5⅓ oz	1½ dL	15 cL	157 mL
¾ c	6 oz	1¾ dL	18 cL	178 mL
1 c	8 oz	¼ L	24 cL	237 mL
1¼ c	10 oz	3 dL	30 cL	296 mL

Cups and Spoons	Liquid Ounces	Approximate Metric Term	Approximate Centiliters	Actual Milliliters
1⅓ c	10⅔ oz	3¼ dL	33 cL	325 mL
1½ c	12 oz	3½ dL	35 cL	355 mL
1⅔ c	13⅓ oz	3¾ dL	39 cL	385 mL
1¾ c	14 oz	4 dL	41 cL	414 mL
2 c; 1 pt	16 oz	½ L	47 cL	473 mL
2½ c	20 oz	6 dL	60 cL	592 mL
3 c	24 oz	¾ L	70 cL	710 mL
3½ c	28 oz	⅘ L; 8 dL	83 cL	829 mL
4 c; 1 qt	32 oz	1 L	95 cL	946 mL
5 c	40 oz	1¼ L	113 cL	1134 mL
6 c; 1½ qt	48 oz	1½ L	142 cL	1420 mL
8 c; 2 qt	64 oz	2 L	190 cL	1893 mL
10 c; 2½ qt	80 oz	2½ L	235 cL	2366 mL
12 c; 3 qt	96 oz	2¾ L	284 cL	2839 mL
4 qt	128 oz	3¾ L	375 cL	3785 mL
5 qt		4¾ L		
6 qt		5½ L (or 6 L)		
8 qt		7½ L (or 8 L)		

INCHES TO CENTIMETERS

Inches ("in")	Centimeters ("cm") (Nearest equivalent)
1/16 in	¼ cm
⅛ in	½ cm
3/16 in	"less than ¼ in/¾ cm"
¼ in	¾ cm
⅜ in	1 cm
½ in	1¼ cm

Inches (''in'')	Centimeters (''cm'') (Nearest equivalent)
⅝ in	1½ cm
¾ in	2 cm
1 in	2½ cm
1½ in	4 cm
2 in	5 cm
2½ in	6½ cm
3 in	8 cm
3½ in	9 cm
4 in	10 cm
5 in	13 cm
6 in	15 cm
7 in	18 cm
8 in	20 cm
9 in	23 cm
10 in	25 cm
12 in	30 cm
14 in	35 cm
15 in	38½ cm
16 in	40 cm
18 in	45 cm
20 in	50 cm
24 in	60 cm
30 in	75 cm

Index

Brochettes d'agneau à l'indienne, 196
Brocoli
    au citron, 21
    salade de, et poires d'avocat, 74
Brocoli di râpé, steamed, 42
Brussels sprouts, 274
    sautéed, 277
Butter
    anchovy, broiled fish fillets with, 103
    green peppercorn
        corn on the cob with, 151
        noodles with, 265
    lemon, 159
    nutmeg, asparagus with, 85

C
Calf's liver
    and onions, 230
    sautéed with herbs, 227
Canned products, 11-12, 322
Cannellini beans with tuna, 323
Caper(s)
    and lemon garnish, veal with, 208
    sautéed sole with, and lemon, 129
Caraway seeds, noodles with, 216
Carême, Antonin, 140
Carré d'agneau persillé, 183
Carrotes
    et courgettes à la menthe, 33
    à la menthe, 283
    Vichy, 133, 240
Carrots
    chicken breasts with, and asparagus,
        29
    with mint, 283
    and potatoes, puréed, 268
    steamed, 133, 240
    and zucchini with fresh mint, 33
Céleri rémoulade
    avec moules, 317
    avec salami, 318
Celeriac in mayonnaise sauce
    with mussels, 317
    with salami, 318
Cheese
    noodles with, 39
    pork chops glazed with, 282
    sauce, endives and ham baked in, 297
    soufflé, 94
    See also Mozzarella, Parmesan cheese

Cherry tomatoes
    with garlic, 145
        and parsley, 130
    sautéed with shallots, 175
Chicken
    with applejack sauce, 47
    breasts
        with asparagus and carrots, 29
        breaded, 32
    and cold noodles with spicy sauce, 315
        with spinach, 26
    fricassée, with tarragon, 64
    grilled with mustard, 58
    with mixed grill, 55
    omelet
        poached, 83
        with tomato and cheese, 87
    with parsley sauce, 20
    parsleyed, with vegetables, 35
    poached, 84
        in cream sauce, 44
    in the pot, 50
    in red wine sauce, 38
    salad with anchovy garnish, 314
    sautéed, 17
        with rosemary, 18
        with tomatoes, 23
        with wine and herbs, 52
    with tarragon, 61
    in white wine, 41
Chicken liver(s)
    and mushrooms in Madeira wine
        sauce, 80
    pilaf with tomato and mushroom
        sauce, 72
    rice with, 24
        and mushrooms, 71
    with sage, 77
Chick-pea and salmon salad, 324
Chiffonade de homard, 327
Chive sauce, steak in, 236
Chopping boards, 5-6
Choucroute garnie, 288
Choux de Bruxelles, 274
    sautéed au beurre, 277
Clam(s)
    hot, with green sauce, 156
    sauce, linguine with, 308
Cold dishes, 313-330
Concombres
    salade de, à la scandinave, 298

[341]

Recipes and Notes

Recipes and Notes

Recipes and Notes

Recipes and Notes

Recipes and Notes

Recipes and Notes